Animated Documentary

Animated Documentary

Annabelle Honess Roe

© Annabelle Honess Roe 2013
Corrected Printing 2013
Softcover reprint of the hardcover 1st edition 2013 978-1-137-01745-1
All rights reserved. No reproduction, copy or transmission of this publication may be made without written permission.

No portion of this publication may be reproduced, copied or transmitted save with written permission or in accordance with the provisions of the Copyright, Designs and Patents Act 1988, or under the terms of any licence permitting limited copying issued by the Copyright Licensing Agency, Saffron House, 6–10 Kirby Street, London EC1N 8TS.

Any person who does any unauthorized act in relation to this publication may be liable to criminal prosecution and civil claims for damages.

The author has asserted her right to be identified as the author of this work in accordance with the Copyright, Designs and Patents Act 1988.

First published 2013 by
PALGRAVE MACMILLAN

Palgrave Macmillan in the UK is an imprint of Macmillan Publishers Limited, registered in England, company number 785998, of Houndmills, Basingstoke, Hampshire RG21 6XS.

Palgrave Macmillan in the US is a division of St Martin's Press LLC, 175 Fifth Avenue, New York, NY 10010.

Palgrave Macmillan is the global academic imprint of the above companies and has companies and representatives throughout the world.

Palgrave® and Macmillan® are registered trademarks in the United States, the United Kingdom, Europe and other countries

ISBN 978-1-349-43709-2   ISBN 978-1-137-01746-8 (eBook)
DOI 10.1057/9781137017468

This book is printed on paper suitable for recycling and made from fully managed and sustained forest sources. Logging, pulping and manufacturing processes are expected to conform to the environmental regulations of the country of origin.

A catalogue record for this book is available from the British Library.

A catalog record for this book is available from the Library of Congress.

Contents

List of Figures	vi
Acknowledgements	vii
Introduction	**1**
Animation and documentary's shared history	5
Scope and organisation	13
1 Representational Strategies	**17**
How animation is used in animated documentary	22
The ontology of animated documentary	27
2 Digital Realities	**41**
Dino-docs and strategies of visual and aural authentication	45
Tracing the sights and sounds of reality in Rotoshop and *Chicago 10*	55
Paratextual authentication	65
The excess of animated realism	67
3 Animated Interviews	**74**
Uncanny bodies	80
Absence as representational strategy	87
The expressive power of the disembodied voice	97
4 The World in Here	**106**
More than the interview seen: Sheila Sofian's illustrated interviews	112
Inside out: animating subjective experience	117
Hybrids of reality	124
Animated awareness	135
5 Animated Memories	**139**
(Dis)continuities: the self in history	146
The unspoken and the forgotten: the trauma in/of history in *Silence* and *Waltz with Bashir*	155
Afterword	**170**
Notes	174
Bibliography	180
Index	189

List of Figures

I.1	*The Sinking of the Lusitania* (dir. Winsor McCay, 1918)	7
1.1	*American Homes* (dir. Bernard Friedman, 2011)	35
2.1	*Planet Dinosaur* (dir. Nigel Paterson, 2011)	50
2.2	*Chicago 10* (dir. Brett Morgen, 2007)	57
2.3	*Grasshopper* (dir. Bob Sabison, 2003)	62
3.1	*Roadhead* (dir. Bob Sabiston, 1998)	86
3.2	*It's Like That* (dir. Southern Ladies Animation Group, 2003)	91
3.3	*His Mother's Voice* (dir. Dennis Tupicoff, 1997)	98
4.1	*Survivors* (dir. Sheila Sofian, 1997)	114
4.2	*Animated Minds: The Light Bulb Thing* (dir. Andy Glynne, 2003)	120
4.3	*A Is for Autism* (dir. Tim Webb, 1992)	127
4.4	*Ryan* (dir. Chris Landreth, 2004)	130
5.1	*Irinka and Sandrinka* (dir. Sandrine Stoïanov, 2007)	153
5.2	*Silence* (dir. Sylvie Bringas & Orly Yadin, 1998)	159
5.3	*Waltz with Bashir* (dir. Ari Folman, 2008)	164

Acknowledgements

I could not have conceived of or completed this book without the help and support of a number of people. I first started working on this topic as a doctoral student in the Critical Studies programme of the School of Cinematic Arts at the University of Southern California. I have my advisor, Michael Renov, to thank for introducing me to animated documentary and subsequently encouraging me to explore the boundaries of the documentary canon and for his continued support of my work. I continue to be grateful to Akira Lippit, George Wilson, Sheila Sofian, David James, Rick Jewell and Vanessa Schwartz for their support and guidance during my time at USC. Members of my student cohort have remained wonderful friends and sources of intellectual and moral support and Kristen Fuhs, Christopher Hanson and Jorie Lagerwey have generously given up their time to read and comment on parts of the manuscript.

Colleagues within the School of Arts at the University of Surrey have provided an environment in which my scholarship on animated documentary could develop. Helen Hughes' capacity for astute clarity has been much appreciated, and she, along with Hing Tsang and Lois Davis, has offered many stimulating conversations on documentary. I am grateful to Sherril Dodds and Rachel Fensham for their mentorship that has proved so valuable in the realisation of this book. The students to whom I teach documentary and animation studies offer a fresh perspective and insight, and continually reinvigorate my passion for the subject.

The communities of scholars that make up the Society for Animation Studies and attend the annual Visible Evidence documentary conference have provided vibrant and thought-provoking discussion and debate that has nurtured my work. In particular Paul Ward, Paul Wells, Caroline Ruddell, Nichola Dobson, Brian Winston, Patrick Sjöberg and Joshua Malitsky have been sources of great encouragement over the years. I am very grateful to the filmmakers and animators who have so willingly and generously shared their work and their thoughts with me both when I was working on my PhD and whilst writing this book, especially Liz Blazer, David Sproxton, Jonathan Hodgson, Marjut Rimminen, Bob Sabiston, Dennis Tupicoff, Orly Yadin, Samantha Moore, Ellie Land, Ruth Lingford and Shira Avni.

Thank you to my family and friends for continuing to be my greatest supporters and cheerleaders. Most importantly, to my husband, best friend and all-round favourite person Nick Roe, who never lets me give up and always believes I can do it, this one's for you.

Sections of this work have been published in different versions in the following: Uncanny Indexes: Rotoshopped Interview as Documentary. *Animation: An Interdisciplinary Journal* 7 (1) (March 2012), Sage; Absence, Excess and Epistemological Expansion: Towards a Framework for the Study of Animated Documentary. *Animation: An Interdisciplinary Journal* 6 (3) (November 2011), Sage.

Introduction

Animation and documentary make an odd couple. Theirs is a marriage of opposites, made complicated by different ways of seeing the world. The former conjures up thoughts of comedy, children's entertainment and folkloric fantasies; the latter carries with it the assumptions of seriousness, rhetoric and evidence. The long history of the hybridisation of animation and documentary, one that stretches back to the earliest days of the moving image, belies the incongruity of their pairing and suggests that, as in many things in life, opposites can attract in a meaningful way. Animation has long been used in non-fictional contexts to illustrate, clarify and emphasise, and animated segments have featured in non-fiction films ranging from Frank Capra's *Why We Fight* series (1942–5) to Michael Moore's *Bowling for Columbine* (2002). It is since the 1990s, however, that we have seen an increase in the production of what has become known as the 'animated documentary'. As well as appearing in the line-up of animation and documentary festivals worldwide with increasing frequency and prominence, feature-length animated documentaries have received mainstream theatrical releases – for example, *Chicago 10* (Brett Morgen, 2007) and *Waltz with Bashir* (Ari Folman, 2008) – and digital animation has been a staple of primetime television documentary series since prehistory was brought back to life by the BBC in *Walking with Dinosaurs* (Tim Haines and Jasper James, 1999).

In *Animated Documentary*, I explore a wide array of examples of animated documentary and question the implications of the use of animation as a representational strategy in documentary. In order to address this question, I look at the ways animation is used in animated documentary: what and how is the animation representing; how and why is animation being used instead of the conventional alternative?[1] This further implies an interrogation of the ontological differences between animation and live action, in terms of their relationship with reality. For while the indexical relationship between film and reality, something upon which documentary's claims to truth and evidence so heavily rest, is absent, animation is very much present, both lacking and exceeding the visual indexical bond between image and reality. This non-conventional relationship between image and reality in animated documentary also places greater emphasis on the soundtrack. The pairing of typical documentary sound, such as didactic voice-of-God narration or recordings of interviews, and animated images makes for an interesting combination that questions the way meaning is conveyed in animated documentary.

While animation might at first seem to threaten the documentary project by destabilising its claim to represent reality, I suggest that the opposite is the case. Animation, in part through its material differences from live-action film, shifts and broadens the limits of what and how we can show about reality by offering new or alternative ways of seeing the world. It can present the conventional subject matter of documentary (the 'world out there' of observable events) in non-conventional ways. It also has the potential to convey visually the 'world in here' of subjective, conscious experience – subject matters traditionally beyond the documentary purview. By releasing documentary from the strictures of a causal connection between filmic and profilmic, animation has the potential to bring things that are temporally, spatially and psychologically distant from the viewer into closer proximity. It can conflate history, transcend geography and give insight into the mental states of other people.

Despite the long shared history of animation and documentary, which is explored in more detail later, their cross-pollination has been relatively neglected by documentary studies. This neglect is rooted in several possible causes, one of which is that animated documentaries are most often made by those who are animators first and documentary makers second, that is, by filmmakers trained in the craft and art of animation, who have chosen to turn their attention to non-fiction subject matter. This means that animated documentaries might be argued to fit more easily into the animation canon (of both films and scholarly literature). However, more often than not it is less a case of argument, and more a case of awareness, in that animators and animation scholars are more attuned to new work being done in the field of animation than documentary scholars would be, something that reflects Paul Ward's claim that the 'relationship between practice and theory is especially acute in the field of Animation Studies,' which he attributes to the diversity of animation production methods and techniques (Ward, 2006: 229). There is also little question that animated documentaries are animated films, whereas there is potential debate as to whether animation is an acceptable mode of representation for documentary.

Bill Nichols comments in *Blurred Boundaries* (1994: 29) that the documentary is 'dependent on the specificity of its images for authenticity'. The authenticity of a documentary, and the strength of its claim to be such a type of film, are deeply linked to notions of realism and the idea that documentary images bear evidence of events that actually happened, by virtue of the indexical relationship between image and reality. Animation presents problems for this documentary ontology and this means that animated documentaries do not fit easily into the received wisdom of what a documentary is. Anecdotally, this is something I can attest to. A frequent response to mention of animated documentaries – 'does such a thing exist?' – is couched in the widely held assumptions regarding what a documentary should look like and what sorts of images it should contain. The presumption goes that documentaries should be observational, unobtrusive, truthful, bear witness to actual events, contain interviews and, even, be objective.[2]

In fact, it can easily be argued that documentary does not, and never has, fully upheld these characteristics. John Grierson's (1933: 8) definition of documentary as 'the creative treatment of actuality' has demonstrated longevity over 70 years of flux and change in the boundaries of documentary. The attraction lies, in part, in the broadness of this definition. It is easy to mould it to the user's requirements and it lends itself to such a large range of approaches and styles that it has proved resilient to aesthetic, ideological and technological developments in documentary making. It is, for example, equally as applicable to the non-interventional films of 1960s Direct Cinema, as to Errol Morris' interviews and stylised re-enactments and, indeed, to animated documentary. There is a promise in this Griersonian definition, however, as well as in the colloquial understanding of documentary, that these sorts of films should be about the events, experiences and people that exist in the actual world. As Nichols (2001: xi) suggests, documentaries 'address *the* world in which we live rather than *a* world imagined by the filmmaker' (emphasis in original). Nichols and Grierson help us think of animation as a viable means of documentary expression. After all, if Grierson's definition allows re-enactment (a staple of the British Documentary Movement), why not also animation as a way of creatively treating actuality? And thinking of a distinction between *the* and *a* world helps us differentiate between animation that is non-fictional and that which is based on make-believe.

Animation is no less complex a term to define than documentary. Norman McLaren's definition of animation as 'not the art of drawings that move but the art of movements that are drawn' is as attractive in its broadness as his one-time mentor Grierson's definition of documentary (quoted in Furniss, 1998: 5). For the purposes of this book, however, we might take our lead from Charles Solomon, who identifies two key factors inherent to animation. That is, that 'the imagery is recorded frame-by-frame' and 'the illusion of motion is created, rather than recorded' (quoted in Furniss, 1998: 5). These ideas, of frame-by-frame manipulation and the construction of an illusion of motion, are ones that apply to both handmade and digitally produced animation. They also encompass the broad range of techniques and styles that can be considered animation, including cel animation, puppet animation, Claymation, three-dimensional computer-generated animation and so on.

Mindful of this, I would suggest that an audiovisual work (produced digitally, filmed, or scratched directly on celluloid)[3] could be considered an animated documentary if it: (i) has been recorded or created frame by frame; (ii) is about *the* world rather than *a* world wholly imagined by its creator; and (iii) has been presented as a documentary by its producers and/or received as a documentary by audiences, festivals or critics. This last criterion is significant as it helps differentiate two aesthetically similar films that may be motivated by different intentions by their respective producers, or received in different ways by audiences. It also helps to narrow the field; advertising, scientific, educational and public service films, arenas in which animation is frequently utilised, fall beyond what I would consider an animated documentary (and thus, the scope of this book) because they are neither intended, nor received as documentaries.

The first criterion does not preclude films that combine animation and live action or the photographic, as in fact many animated documentaries do. It is impossible to put a quantitative requirement on the amount of animation that a film should contain in order for it to be classed an animated documentary. Instead, it is more useful to think about how documentaries that use animation and live action or other photographic material integrate their various media. For a film to be an animated documentary in such a case, the animation must be integrated to the extent that the meaning of the film would become incoherent were it to somehow be removed. An excellent example of this is *Abuelas* (Afarin Eghbal, 2011), an animated documentary about the 'Grandmothers of May Square' in Argentina and their quest to discover what happened to their children and grandchildren who were 'disappeared' during Videla's military dictatorship in the late 1970s and early 1980s. The film was shot on a digital stills camera and created using pixilation, an animation technique that manipulates the profilmic objects and bodies frame by frame. This creates a subtle jerkiness in imagery that otherwise appears as live action and this style of animation reflects the film's story of generations cleaved by external forces. The animated and the photographic are interwoven to such an extent that they cannot be parsed out from each other, meaning that one would be hard pressed to determine what percentage of *Abuelas* is animated and what percentage is photographic media and, even if one could, this would not necessarily enhance our reception or understanding of the film. This type of integration and cohesion, much like two chemical elements that have reacted to form a new substance from which neither original element could then be extracted, distinguishes an animated documentary that combines photographic media with animation from, for example, the documentaries discussed later that use animation for moments of interjection and intersection.

Animation and documentary's shared history

It is not my intention here to re-hash a history of animated documentary, much of which is covered in the existing literature (See: DelGaudio, 1997; Patrick, 2004; Strøm, 2003; Wells, 1997). Instead, this section aims to point out some significant tendencies in the early intersections between animation and documentary, as well as to suggest a turning point towards the development of the animated documentary as a form in its own right. It would be tempting to trace a neat linear history that takes us teleologically from these early intersections of animation and documentary to the more recent examples. However, the genesis of the animated documentary reveals a less direct, more convoluted trajectory. In *Remediation*, Jay Bolter and Richard Grusin (2000: 21, n.1), cite Foucault's conception of genealogy in making a connection between new and old media technologies and practices. They seek out 'historical affiliations or resonances and not origins', adapting genealogy to relationships of power to 'formal relations with and among media'. Thomas Elsaesser (2006: 18), on the other hand, rejects the concept of genealogy altogether in favour of the notion of archaeology, in his examination of the relationship between new media and early cinema. He tells us:

> An archaeology is the opposite of genealogy: the latter tries to trace back a continuous line of descent from the present to the past, the former knows only the presumption of discontinuity and the synecdoche of the fragment can hope to give a present access to its past.

Elsaesser maps film history as a network, rather than 'discrete units' and in doing this he draws attention to Foucault's claim that history is not continuous, but is rather a process of breaks, mutations and transformations (Elsaesser, 2006: 17; Foucault, 2008 [1969]: 6).

Just as Bolter and Grusin and Elsaesser point to the folly of examining new media as discrete from the history of cinema and visual arts, so too would one fall foul of an attempt to mark out contemporary animated documentary as separate, yet linearly descended, from the history of these two forms. Instead, the precedent for contemporary animated documentaries must be mapped as a network of both interweaving and independent threads. This is a history of mutual enrichment through a wide variety of different types of hybridisation of animation and documentary. Importantly, this intertwined history is not a teleological progression towards the current trend of animated documentaries. Just as Foucault's archaeology of the history of ideas 'does not seek to rediscover the continuous, insensible transition that relates discourses, on a gentle slope, to what precedes them, surrounds them, or follows them' (Foucault, 2008 [1969]: 115), the history of the overlaps between animation and documentary is not one of easy continuities. There is no single beginning, but rather many concurrent, international examples that demonstrate the instinct that documentary can be strengthened via animation, and vice versa. Similarly, there is no terminal point towards which this history progresses. What is important to take from this history, however, is that from early on animation was seen to have a unique representational function for the non-fiction moving image, one that could not be fulfilled by the conventional live-action, photographic-based alternative.

In 1918, pioneer American animator Winsor McCay made what is widely dubbed the 'first animated documentary,' *The Sinking of the Lusitania* (Patrick, 2004: 36; Wells, 1997: 42, 1998: 16). McCay, who was better known for his weekly comic strips, *Little Nemo* and *Dreams of a Rarebit Fiend*, and later his flamboyant vaudeville lightening sketch performances and animated high jinx with *Gertie the Dinosaur* (1914), turned to non-fiction upon the sinking of the British passenger liner *Lusitania* by a German submarine in 1915. Shocked at the death of innocent civilians, many of them American, but stymied by the absence of filmed footage or photographs of the sinking, McCay recreated the events, as retold by survivors, using animation.[4] His aesthetic approach to the material was modified from his usual animation style to suit the subject matter, and the look of the 12-minute long film resembles non-fiction media of the time, such as newspaper editorial illustrations and newsreels.[5]

Significantly, *The Sinking of the Lusitania* contains several textual implications of the suitability of animation to the representation of real life, a sentiment that is echoed in extra-textual material surrounding the film. An early intertitle tells the audience: 'you are looking at the first *record* of the sinking of the Lusitania' (emphasis added) and, in general, the images' perspective resembles those of an imaginary eyewitness, viewing the events from a distance (see Figure I.1). The *Lusitania* is mostly seen in 'long shots' that allow us, for example, to watch its slow but inevitable disappearance after the torpedo strike. Even the live-action prologue, in which we see McCay and his colleagues setting to work on drawing the film's images, suggests an unproblematic application of

Figure I.1   The point of view of an imaginary eyewitness in *The Sinking of the Lusitania* (dir. Winsor McCay, 1918)

animation as a medium for an actuality subject. McCay makes no distinction between live action and animation in terms of their ability to show us reality, and reviewers seemed equally content to accept that the film offered audiences a chance to '*witness* the whole tragedy, from the moment of the first attack to the heartrending ending' (Bioscope, 1919: 74, emphasis added). This critical response echoed the film's marketing by its production company as 'the World's Only *Record* of the Crime that Shocked Humanity!' (Quoted in Canemaker, 1987: 154, emphasis added).[6] *The Sinking of the Lusitania* demonstrates the early use of animation as a substitute for missing live-action material.

While McCay's film was the first commercially released 'animated documentary',[7] it is preceded by examples of animation being used in a non-fiction context. Animation has historically been used as a tool of illustration and clarification in factual films. British filmmaker Percy Smith made a series of films, including *Fight for the Dardanelles* (1915), which used animation to depict battles of the First World War. In the United States, Max Fleischer made animated films for the military as early as 1917 that were used to train soldiers heading to the battle zones of Europe. The realisation that animation could clarify and explain more effectively and efficiently than live action led to an even greater uptake of the medium by the US government in the Second World War. Perhaps inspired by the shorts already made for the National Film Board of Canada by the Walt Disney Studios to promote the Canadian war effort (See: Honess Roe, 2011),[8] the US Government commissioned Disney to make numerous educational and training films during the war and the studio also provided the animated sections for Frank Capra's *Why We Fight* series of seven propaganda films (1942–5). In these types of films we see animated maps, moving illustrations of military equipment and diagrams that explain military strategy.

This use of animation demonstrates that envisioned information is easier to understand and retain, and that much factual information is communicated more efficiently via animation than the spoken word. Many of these films also conveyed more than facts through their animation by using it for emphasis and visual association. Simple symbolism prevails throughout the *Why We Fight* series, such as pitting dark hues for enemy nations against paler colours for the Allies. This type of symbolism is established in the series' first animated sequence, in *Prelude to War* (1942), when a dark, black inky stain spreads across Japan, Italy and Germany as the narrator notes the cultural differences between those countries and the US. As James Elkins (1999: 224) has pointed out, 'the real subjects of maps usually [...] serve territorial, religious, or nationalist agendas'. The animated maps in the *Why We Fight* films serve a purpose beyond merely marking out geographical boundaries, they are also helping deliver the nationalist, propagandistic message of the series.

Outside of wartime, there is a long history of putting animation to educational use. While still working in the Midwest before moving to California, Walt Disney was commissioned to make two films on dental hygiene and with these early pedagogic endeavours he was following many of the pioneers of animation and cinema.[9] As early as 1910, Thomas Edison made instructional films that included animated sequences and, according to Richard Fleischer (2005: 27), Randolph Bray made partially animated educational films for the US Government prior to 1916. Subsequently, animators from the Soviet Union to the United States would use animation to explore the physical world. From the Fleischer Brother's *Einstein's Theory of Relativity* (1923) to Vsevolod Pudovkin's *The Mechanics of the Human Brain* (1926), animation was used as a prescient tool to explain, clarify and visualise.

Even earlier than this, Percy Smith became interested in the use of animation while working at the Board of Education at the turn of the Twentieth Century (Low, 1949: 157). While Smith mostly focused on cinematography and the use of such devices as time-lapse photography and microcinematography, he also made animated scientific films. *How Spiders Fly* (1909) used stop-motion animation to bring a model spider to life and was intended to help cure arachnophobia. For Smith, animation was a way of revealing aspects of the natural world that were previously unseen by the human eye and animation was another technique to access the 'new way of seeing' offered by the technologies developed from the Eighteenth Century onwards that expanded the realm of human vision (See: Beattie, 2008: 129–50). There are plenty of contemporary examples of animation being used in documentary for a specific purpose and animated segments are still used in a non-fictional context to clarify, explain, illustrate and emphasise. The uses of animated maps, charts, graphs and diagrams in mainstream formats ranging from television news to theatrical documentary are too numerous to mention. This illustrative function of animation has become commonplace to the point of being inconspicuous. Similarly, natural history, science and history programming now use digital animation as a matter of course to bring to life objects and events that are impossible to capture with the live-action camera.[10] For example, the BBC's recent *Wonders of the Solar System* (2010) displays CGI close-up images of far-off planets that would be impossible to film or photograph.

A frequent, and perhaps relatively recent, use of animation in live-action documentaries is to create moments of, often ironic, interjection or intersection. Here a segment of animation is inserted in a primarily live-action film to in some way enhance its meaning. In films such as *Bowling for Columbine* (Michael Moore, 2002), *Blue Vinyl* (Judith Hefland and Daniel B. Gold, 2002), *She's a Boy I Knew* (Gwen Haworth, 2007) and *The Age of Stupid* (Franny Armstrong, 2009), animation is rendered in a humorous and cartoon-like style as a way of contrasting with the seriousness of the documentaries' subject matter. Emily Hubley's simple line-drawing style of animation in *Blue Vinyl* punctuates Hefland's argument regarding our self-destructive reliance on PVC. The animated segments in *Bowling for Columbine* evoke the anarchic humour of the *South Park* (Trey Parker and Matt Stone, 1997-ongoing) television show and highlight the absurdity, as perceived by Moore, of America's relationship with firearms. Animation is put to a similar use in *The Age of Stupid*, where Jonathan Hodgson's three animated sequences reiterate and consolidate some of the film's key points regarding the environment, climate change and sustainability. The 'war on resources' segment concisely and ingeniously makes links between colonialism, capitalism and the depletion of natural resources by condensing the global history of human and natural exploitation, from prehistory to the Iraq War, into less than two minutes. In *She's a Boy I Knew*, Gwen Haworth interjects animated sections into her autobiographical account of her gender transition. Retro adverts and magazine extracts are brought into motion in a segment entitled 'how to be a girl...by Mom' that accents, in a light-hearted way, the issues Gwen's mother has with her take on being female. Haworth has commented that she included animation to 'lighten the mood' and add humour to her film, as she was concerned it might otherwise become too intense and serious. Animated interjections switch the mood and the contrast between live action and animation as modes of address creates moments of thematic and tonal punctuation in a documentary.

With the exception of *The Sinking of the Lusitania*, none of the historical examples, or the more recent documentaries that use animated interjections, would be described as animated documentaries, either by their makers or their audiences. They lack the sense of animation and documentary cohering into a single form in which the animation works to enhance our knowledge of an aspect of *the* world and to the extent that the separation of the animation from the documentary is either impossible, or would render the inherent meaning of the film incomprehensible. *The Age of Stupid* would still work as a coherent film without

Hodgson's animated sequences, despite being the poorer without them, just as the propagandist message of the *Why We Fight* films would still be present, if perhaps not quite as loud, without Disney's animated maps and charts. Films that do warrant classification as animated documentaries, such as *Waltz with Bashir*, *Walking with Dinosaurs* and the *Animated Minds* series (Andy Glynne, 2003, 2009), are documentaries that have animation embedded into their very core. The first-person accounts of mental health issues in *Animated Minds* are more than just radio documentaries. The animation adds something very specific to the way we interpret and understand the experiences being recounted. *Walking with Dinosaurs* depends on its realistic animated reconstructions of prehistoric life, in a style that copies the familiar aesthetic of natural history programming, to deliver its scientific hypotheses about the way dinosaurs lived. Ari Folman's personal journey to unearth suppressed memories of his role in the Sabra and Shatila massacre during the 1982 Lebanon War in *Waltz with Bashir* resonates thematically via the style of animation and the film's refusal to make an aesthetic distinction between past and present.

The animated documentary is archaeologically linked to the earlier examples of the use of animation in non-fiction scenarios, just as it is related to contemporary examples of non-fiction media utilising animation for specific purposes and animated interjections into live-action documentary. The possibilities for the convergence of animation and documentary into a coherent form, however, was anticipated by filmmakers on opposite sides of the Atlantic, and whose work is not usually considered as documentary – John and Faith Hubley in the United States and, in the United Kingdom, Aardman Animations. John Hubley, a key figure in the left-leaning and aesthetically innovative United Productions of America (UPA) animation company, worked with his wife Faith to set up their independent company in 1953. In 1959 they made *Moonbird*, a fantastical flight of fancy that matches animated visuals to a soundtrack on which their two young sons can be heard playing. They followed this up with two further films, *Windy Day* (1967) and *Cockaboody* (1973), which similarly pair documentary tape recordings of their children at play with animated interpretations of their make-believe worlds. What is seen in these films is often directly connected to what we hear the children talk about as they play; thus, when they talk about finding a rabbit, one pops into the scene and, in *Windy Day*, the Hubleys' garden morphs into the magical kingdom imagined by their daughters, in which Georgia plays 'Princess Polly' and Emily takes on the role of 'Prince Joel'. The Hubleys' visualisation of their children's imagination is enhanced by the films' expressive aesthetic, with a hand-drawn quality that resembles children's drawings.[11]

Aardman began combining stop-motion animation of plasticine puppets with documentary soundtracks in the 1970s. David Sproxton and Peter Lord produced two short films for the BBC in 1978 under the collective title of *Animated Conversations*. Both films, *Confessions of a Foyer Girl* and *Down and Out*, use documentary sound as their basis and malleable puppets are stop-motion animated against an audio track of eavesdropped conversations. In 1983 a subsequent five shorts commissioned by Channel 4 under the *Conversations Pieces* banner continued in the same vein, using soundtracks that were recorded by 'openly eavesdropping' in locations such as workplaces and community centres. *Creature Comforts*, part of a series called *Lip Synch* made in 1989, similarly used claymation with a documentary soundtrack, but this time the puppets were zoo animals, animated to interviews of people talking about human and animal living conditions. By this stage, Sproxton and Lord began more formally interviewing and recording their subjects, often using a trained radio journalist to do the interviews, whose voice they later cut out of the final soundtrack (Sproxton, 2008). While *Creature Comforts*, and its subsequent sequels and spin-offs, may be read as making astute observations on the human condition, with its matching and mismatching of animal form and human voice, it is rarely presented or understood as a documentary. The film does, however, effectively integrate documentary and animation into a coherent whole – in this case a comedy short. The critical and commercial success of this piece of genre integration, and the garnering of Aardman's first of many Academy Awards, elevated the profile of the now very successful animation studio and signalled to a wide audience the creative possibilities for the convergence of animation and documentary.

This brief survey demonstrates a long-standing relationship between animation and documentary. This history is not a linear path from *The Sinking of the Lusitania* to contemporary animated documentary production; it is far more fragmented than that. It is more a history of tendencies and inclinations, of flirting rather than courtship. Historically, documentary makers have utilised animation to illustrate, clarify, visualise and emphasise, using animation to make up for the shortcomings of live-action material. Concurrently, animators have turned their attentions to events occurring in *the* world. This shared history suggests animation and documentary are more compatible than they might at first seem. This was confirmed by the Hubleys and Aardman, whose work shows the potential for the seamless integration of animation and documentary material to create short films that are far more than the sum of their parts.

Since the 1990s there has been something of a boom in animated documentaries. This boom started slowly, with a few films appearing in the 1980s that were labelled as such. In 1985 Dutch filmmaker and writer Harrie Geelen released *Drawn People*, a 20-minute film about the impact of drug abuse and addiction on 1980s Dutch society that uses interviews with a cross-section of people, including drug users, social workers and representatives of the justice department. The majority of the film is in a simple animation style that evokes pencil drawings, with some limited use of colour. *Blind Justice* (prod. Orly Yadin), a series of four short animated documentaries, was commissioned and released by the United Kingdom's Channel 4 in 1987. The films, *All Men Are Created Equal* (Monique Renault), *Someone Must Be Trusted* (Christine Roche), *Murders Most Foul* (Gillian Lacey), and *Some Protection* (Marjut Rimminen), cover different aspects of how the law treats women and display a variety of hand-drawn animation styles according to their individual animators. In the 1990s the animated documentary boom began to pick up steam with the release of films such as *A Is for Autism* (Tim Webb, 1992), Dennis Tupicoff's *His Mother's Voice* (1997), Sheila Sofian's *Survivors* (also 1997) and Bob Sabiston's *Snack and Drink* (1999). The animated documentary was firmly established by the end of the Twentieth Century, as indicated by the cluster of films made around this time and the launch, in 1997, of a dedicated animated documentary stream at the DOK Leipzig festival in Germany. The boom built into the new millennium, to the point that animated documentaries are now an increasingly commonplace sub-form of documentary, as a quick search on video sharing websites such as YouTube and Vimeo demonstrates, as does the fact that animated documentaries are now included in animation and documentary festivals as a matter of course.[12]

Scope and organisation

The proliferation of animated documentaries means that while I have tried to include films that demonstrate variety in terms of theme, style, production technique and geographical origin, there are many fascinating and worthy examples that fall beyond the scope of my discussion. It is hoped, however, that the questions asked in this book, and the claims made regarding animated documentary, can be applied to films that are not specifically discussed and that *Animated Documentary* provides a springboard for expanding the discourse surrounding all forms of animated documentary and the use of animation in documentary and non-fictional contexts more broadly. The questions animation asks of documentary are more numerous than could be discussed in one book, and as such I hope *Animated Documentary* contributes to the continued growth of scholarly work on this form.

Chapter 1 considers how animation differs from live action as a representational strategy for documentary. To do this, it first looks at how animated documentaries have been theorised and categorised before suggesting a typology organised according to what function animation plays in an animated documentary – that is, what the animation is doing that the live-action alternative could not. This book suggests that animation is a fruitful means of documentary representation in part because it creates a conflation of absence and excess. That is, the expected indexical imagery of documentary is absent, and in its place is animation, which can take multiple different forms, all with a materiality, aesthetics, and style that goes above and beyond merely 'transcribing' reality (a quality David Rodowick (2007) suggests is characteristic of the photographic). In order to establish this claim, Chapter 1 explores how the ontology of film has been theorised, and puts this in contrast with the ontology of animation.

The focus of Chapter 2 is the relationship between animated documentary, representation and style, in particular, realism. This is addressed through the lens of animated documentaries that use computer-generated, digital animation to reconstruct historic and contemporary events in a way that mimics the look of both reality and photoreality.[13] I question how this visual mimicry is used to reinforce the documentary claims of television programmes and films such as *Walking with Dinosaurs* and *Chicago 10*. This reaffirmation of authenticity and validity comes not just from the texts themselves, through for example adopting the tropes of natural history documentaries and through conventional and didactic voiceover narration, but also through the paratexts that surround these programmes and films. It is also the case that the digital realism in these animated documentaries has a spectacular quality, where the closer to photorealism the image gets, the more it demands attention and 'what appears to be an attempt at *immediacy* (that is, increased transparency and realism) results in *hypermediacy* (that is, increased opacity and noticeability of the medium itself)' (Ward, 2006: 243).

The discussion of the importance of sound in animated documentary, and documentary more generally, is woven throughout this book, but it is given special attention in Chapter 3, which looks at animated interview documentaries. Absenting the physical bodies of documentary interviewees, and instead representing them via animation, questions how, and what type of, knowledge is conveyed in interview documentaries. Animation becomes a means of accentuating aspects of an interviewee's personality and story and the absence of a physical body can metaphorically reflect their socio-political status, such as in *It's Like That* (Southern Ladies Animation Group, 2003) and *Hidden* (*Gömd*, Aronowitsch, Heilborn and Johansson, 2002), two films about the plight of juvenile immigrants. Animation is also a means of embodying interviewees as 'vocalic bodies', bodies that are 'formed and sustained by the autonomous operations of the voice' (Connor, 2000: 35). In films like Dennis Tupicoff's *His Mother's Voice* (1997) the absence of a body or face to convey the subjective, situated knowledge of a grieving mother reveals the voice as an important means of carrying such meaning to viewers.

Chapter 4 approaches animated documentaries that convey subjective, conscious experience via animation that is evocative rather than directly representational. Using devices such as metaphor and metamorphosis and through exploring the expressive potential of a variety of materials and animation techniques, these films encourage us to imagine what it is like to experience the world from someone else's perspective. These perspectives are often very different from what the majority of us experience in our daily lives and this type of animated documentary lends itself to films about mental health issues, for example the *Animated Minds* films (Andy Glynne, 2003 and 2009) and unique brain states, such as in *An Eyeful of Sound* (Samantha Moore, 2009). Animation is also used in this way to make films about experiences that are hard to express in words and, because they do not have a visual manifestation, impossible to show in live action, such as a commuter's train of thought as he walks to work in *Feeling My Way* (Jonathan Hodgson, 1997) or the experience of orgasm in *Little Deaths* (Ruth Lingford, 2010). The animation in these films is not simply symbolic, it is 'neither presentation nor representation' (Tyler, 1986: 123). Instead, it encourages us to imagine, from our own point of view, and empathise with the unfamiliar experiences of other people.

Animation's ability to reveal subjective points of view is further explored in Chapter 5's examination of animated documentaries that use animation as an archaeological tool for exploring one's own past. Unlike the films in Chapter 4, these works of personal memory are told, and almost entirely made, from a first-person perspective. Films such as *Waltz with Bashir* (Ari Folman, 2008), *Learned by Heart* (*Sydämeen* kätketty, Marjut Rimminen and Päivi Takala, 2007), *Irinka and Sandrinka* (Sandrine Stoïanov, 2007) and *Silence* (Sylvie Bringas and Orly Yadin, 1998) demonstrate that the formal and aesthetic excess of animation can be used as a means of accessing the now absent past, especially pasts from which the filmmakers have been ruptured due to trauma or other events that cause a disruption in the continuity of personal and collective memory. The photographic has been theorised as a visual 'umbilical cord' (Barthes, 1981: 81) that directly connects us to the past, but I suggest that animation is often a more suitable means of bringing the temporally distal into closer proximity by allowing filmmakers to aesthetically weave themselves into the past. The way the animation is realised, its style and materiality, can also offer insight into the processes of remembering and forgetting that are integral to the formation of personal identity.

1
Representational Strategies

Despite the proliferation of animated documentary production since the 1990s, and their increased exposure through festivals, conferences and public viewing outlets, there was until recently only a handful of published scholarly material on the form. A recent special edition of *Animation: An Interdisciplinary Journal* (November 2011) on animated documentary and an increase in articles and chapters in other publications hopefully signals the beginnings of a critical mass in this area, something this book means to contribute towards. The purpose of this first chapter is to theoretically situate this book in the scholarly context that already exists for animated documentary. Exploring how animated documentaries have been understood and interpreted in the existing literature enables me to position my own suggestion that a useful way to think about how animated documentaries work is via a consideration of the functionality of animation, or what the animation is doing better than the viable live-action alternative (if there is one). The second half of this chapter addresses animation as a representational strategy for documentary by unpicking how the ontology of film has been theorised. Many of documentary's claims to represent reality are rooted in the ontology of film, a foundation that questions what the ontological differences between live action and animation imply for the use of animation in a non-fiction context.

The scholarly landscape for animated documentaries began to take shape in the late 1990s. In 1997, two essays appeared on the subject of animated documentary: Sybil DelGaudio's 'If truth be told, can 'toons tell it? Documentary and animation' in the journal *Film/History* and Paul Wells' 'The Beautiful Village and the True Village: A Consideration of Animation and the Documentary Aesthetic' in a special edition of *Art & Design Magazine* guest edited by Wells. These first forays into examining the existence and nature of animated documentaries were followed several years later by two further essays: Gunnar Strøm's 'The Animated Documentary' in 2003, and Eric Patrick's 'Representing Reality: Structural/Conceptual Design in Non-Fiction Animation' (*Animac* Magazine, 2004). Then, in 2005, the March issue of the online animation magazine *FPS* (*Frames per Second Magazine*) made animated documentaries its cover story and included three articles on the topic by both animators and scholars. The same year saw the release of Paul Ward's short book *Documentary: The Margins of Reality*, which includes a chapter on animated documentary.

Much of this early scholarship on animated documentary takes as its foundation key ideas from documentary studies, in particular, the desire to fit animated documentary into the organisational structure of documentary 'modes' first suggested by Bill Nichols (1991) in *Representing Reality*.[1] Ward argues for certain types of animated documentaries, namely ones that include documentary voiceover and interviews with participants, as fitting into the 'interactive' mode. He casts these animated documentaries as interactive not just because of the nature and origin of their audio tracks, but also because their production involves the collaboration of the documentary subject(s). DelGaudio (1997: 192), on the other hand, prefers to class animated documentaries within the 'reflexive' mode because, she claims, 'animation itself acts as a form of "metacommentary" within a documentary'. She is suggesting here that by adopting animation as a medium of representation, animated documentaries are necessarily passing comment on live action's ability, or lack thereof, to represent reality. This is especially the case, she argues, in animated documentaries that document events and topics that were not, or could not have been, captured on camera.

Both Strøm and Patrick see animated documentaries as examples of Nichols' 'performative' mode. According to Nichols (2001: 131), the 'performative documentary underscores the complexity of our knowledge of the world by emphasizing its subjective and affective dimensions'. His conceptualisation appears to welcome animation as a mode of representation, not least because of the necessarily subjective nature of much of animation production. Patrick (2004: 38) identifies this appeal with his claim that 'the very nature of animation is to foreground its process and artifice'. Furthermore, when Nichols (2001: 131) tells us that 'the world as represented by performative documentaries becomes, however, suffused by evocative tones and expressive shadings that constantly remind us that the world is more than the sum of the visible evidence we derive from it', it is as if he could be speaking directly to animation. I would suggest, however, that to shoehorn the animated documentary into one of Nichols' modes threatens to limit our understanding of the form. Ward's ascription of animated documentaries to the interactive mode is, as he admits, only applicable to certain types of animated documentary; not all animated documentaries have a documentary voiceover and even fewer are produced through an interactive relationship between producer and subject. Similarly, DelGaudio's definition of animated documentaries as reflexive excludes those films that are not necessarily critiquing live action's capabilities to represent reality. Even if animation is doing something live action cannot, it does not necessarily follow that the resulting film is self-consciously passing comment on the representational abilities of either approach. The assignment of animated documentaries to the performative mode is, I contend, equally limiting. Nichols' explanation of the performative mode is, at times, nebulous. Although these types of documentary foreground subjectivity, they also 'demonstrate how embodied knowledge provides entry into an understanding of the more general processes at work in society' (2001: 131). This is a definition of the performative documentary that is far harder to reconcile with animation.

We might question, then, whether it is in fact useful to try to fit animated documentaries into Nichols' modes of documentary production. Both Wells and Patrick come up, instead, with different typologies that may be more fruitful for a discussion of this form. Wells re-figures the modes of documentary production outlined by Richard Barsam and examines how animated documentaries fit into, and expand, these modes. In so doing he reconstitutes Barsam's categories into four 'dominant areas within the field of animation' (Wells, 1997: 41). By tracing similarities in overall tone, subject matter, structure and style, Wells determines these four dominant areas as the imitative mode, the subjective mode, the fantastic mode, and the postmodern mode.

Films in the imitative mode 'directly echo the dominant generic conventions of live-action documentary' (Wells, 1997: 41). As such, Wells claims, these films are often intended to educate, inform and persuade. The subjective mode often challenges the notion of objectivity through creating tension between the visual and the aural by combining humorous animated representations with 'serious' documentary voiceovers or by connecting to broader social issues through the individual expression of the animator (Wells, 1997: 43). Ultimately, the subjective mode uses animation to 're-constitute "reality" on local and relative terms'

(Wells, 1997: 44). The fantastic mode extends the subjective mode's commentary on realism and objectivity to the extent of rejecting realism entirely as 'an ideologically charged (often politically corrupt) coercion of commonality' (Wells, 1997: 44). The fantastic mode further challenges accepted modes of documentary representation by presenting reality through the lens of surrealist animation that bears little or no resemblance to either the physical world or previous media styles. The postmodern mode adopts the general characteristics of postmodernism in 'prioritising pastiche, rejecting notions of objective authority, and asserting that "the social", and therefore "the real", is now fragmentary and incoherent' (Wells, 1997: 44). Wells claims that one of the fundamental pursuits of the documentary project is the attempt 'to engage in the annunciation of commonality and the social dimension of the real' (Wells, 1997: 45). This pursuit is undermined, Wells contends, by the postmodern mode's questioning of the possibility of knowledge in itself.

Patrick adopts the notion of 'structures' to categorise animated documentaries, suggesting 'in making any kind of film, structure tends to be the skeleton that the content lives on' (2004: 39). He proposes three primary structures – the illustrative, narrated, and sound-based – and a fourth, the 'extended structure,' which is an extension of Wells' fantastic mode (Patrick, 2004: 39). 'The four structures encompass the range of possible approaches to animated documentaries without initial regard to concept, techniques or aesthetics' (Patrick, 2004: 39). Patrick takes a conceptual approach different from Wells, looking through the lens of storytelling rather than the films' relationship to reality. 'Illustrative', Patrick contends, is a more apt term to describe the films discussed by Wells under the imitative mode. These films illustrate 'events based on historical or personal evidence' and use this to structure the storytelling (Patrick, 2004: 40). The narrated structure uses a script to tell the story and these animated documentaries often use 'voiceover that recounts and connects the elements of the story' (Patrick, 2004: 40). The sound-based structure, by contrast, 'uses sound that has either been found or recorded in an unmanipulated, uncontrived way as the primary structuring device' (Patrick, 2004: 41). Patrick notes that this aural link between film and reality gives these films all at once a 'naturalistic or improvised' and 'dramatic and cinema verite' feel (Patrick, 2004: 41). Patrick dubs Wells' fantastic mode as 'expanded structure' because it 'expands the possibilities of the documentary form by transmuting the traditional storytelling method' (Patrick, 2004: 42). Like Wells, Patrick notes the highly subjective nature of this approach and how films in this category eschew a direct relationship or commentary on reality preferring instead a more surreal, symbolic or metaphoric approach. Patrick then goes on to observe conceptual trends within each mode, by which he means 'the very essence of the film...the content of what the filmmaker is talking about' (Patrick, 2004: 43). So, for example, the sound-based and narrated structures tend to be memorials or portraits of individuals or groups, and films with an illustrative structure often have a historical basis.

This discussion of two different approaches to categorising animated documentaries begs the question of the purpose of such an exercise. Patrick suggests that his structures are 'a springboard for studying the nature of the form' (2004: 45). While Patrick's and Wells' work helped, in the early days of scholarship on animated documentaries, to make the case for its identification as a discrete form, it is questionable whether their modes and structures help us understand this type of film or fulfil much of a purpose beyond a self-serving one of being able to divide films up among their suggested categories. This question of usefulness and purpose is exacerbated if one queries the founding assumptions of their approaches. For example, it is unclear whether 'illustrative', 'narrated' and 'sound-based' are actually structures of storytelling rather than modes of delivery. Patrick's omission of a detailed explication of what he understands by the terms 'structure' and 'storytelling' further muddies these waters.

Wells' approach, which devises categories that speak to the relationship between representation and reality, can be seen as responding to the so-called crisis of postmodernism in documentary. The year before Wells published his essay, an article by Noël Carroll appeared in the collection co-edited with David Bordwell, *Post-Theory: Reconstructing Film Studies* entitled 'Nonfiction Film and Postmodernist Skepticism' (1996). In this chapter Carroll takes issue with several theorists' (including Michael Renov, Bill Nichols and Brian Winston) discussion of the fictional elements or stylistic tendencies in some non-fiction. Carroll extrapolates (and, one could argue, misinterprets) these discussions to be wholesale rejections of a connection between documentary and reality. He characterises this as a new trend in scepticism regarding the documentary project, one that is inflected by postmodernism more generally. Even earlier than this, in 1993, Linda Williams' essay 'Mirrors without Memories: Truth, History and *The Thin Blue Line*' uses the lens of postmodernism to examine that film and suggests truth is relative and contingent. While Wells does not cite either of these essays directly, the way he formulates his modes suggests that the use of animation in documentary inherently critiques conventional documentary's attempts to objectively represent reality. Furthermore, he implies a teleology developing towards the postmodern mode that ultimately questions the coherence of reality itself.

The existence of a postmodern crisis in documentary has, however, since been debunked. Michael Renov (2004: 137) points out that the targets of Carroll's censure 'rarely addressed postmodernism in any direct way in their writings on documentary film'. Renov counters that Carroll's critique is a 'documentary disavowal' that fails to recognise that the form has long since abandoned such rationalist goals as objective, disinterested knowledge (2004: 137). Instead, he suggests documentary is more often concerned with 'contingency, hybridity, knowledge as situated and particular, identity as ascribed and performed' (2004: 137). Renov's words remind us that contemporary documentary studies rarely questions the notion that the form conveys knowledge. Rather, the pertinent questions are *how* this knowledge is conveyed and *what type* of knowledge it is. Wells' modes of animated documentary made sense in the theoretical landscape of the 1990s, when postmodernist doubts regarding the viability of the documentary project and the very possibility of representing reality were still circulating. Now, while we accept that objective representation is a fantasy, we also acknowledge that this does not entail a wholesale rejection of attempts to represent and convey reality. It is no longer pertinent to question whether or not conventional documentary and animated documentary can represent reality. Instead, I believe it is more interesting to ask what aspects of reality are being conveyed, and how that is being done.

How animation is used in animated documentary

One of the key claims of this book is that animation, freed from the 'indexical bind' (Nichols, 1991: 149) of conventional documentary, has the capacity to represent temporally, geographically and psychologically distal aspects of life beyond the reach of live action. It remains true, however, that there are different types of animated documentaries that present their varied subject matter through a multiplicity of styles and techniques. Furthermore, animation is not used in the same way in all animated documentaries. One way to demarcate different types of animated documentaries is to consider how the animation functions. In other words, what is the animation doing that the conventional alternative could not? I suggest that animation functions in three key ways: mimetic substitution, non-mimetic substitution and evocation. I believe this is not just categorisation for the sake of it, but rather a way to help understand how animated documentaries work. In particular, sorting these films into categories of functionality can help us understand in what circumstances animation might be a more suitable representational strategy for documentary than live action, a representational strategy that broadens and deepens the range of what we can make documentaries about.

One way that animation functions in animated documentaries is in a mimetic, or substitutive way. In these instances, the animation illustrates something that would be very hard, or impossible, to show with the conventional live-action alternative and often it is directly standing in for live-action footage. The animation here is substituting for something else. This is, in fact, one of the first ways animation was used in non-fiction scenarios in Winsor McCay's *The Sinking of the Lusitania*. More recent examples of substitutive animation can be seen in the BBC's 1999 natural history series *Walking with Dinosaurs*, and its later re-boot *Planet Dinosaur* (2011), and Brett Morgen's *Chicago 10* (2007). In *Chicago 10*, motion capture and traditional animation are used to recreate the trial of Abbie Hoffman and the other members of the anti-war movement accused of inciting riot in the run up to 1968's Democratic National Convention in Chicago. No filmed record of the courtroom exists and these sequences are based on the transcripts of the legal proceedings, which often descended into a circus-like state of chaos as the defendants refused to adhere to the proceeding's rules and regulations. In *Walking with Dinosaurs*, prehistoric creatures are created using 3-D computer animation that are superimposed on backdrops that had previously been filmed at suitable looking locations. Twelve years later the BBC once again reconstructed prehistoric life, this time entirely using digital animation techniques.

In these examples, the animation is used to stand-in for live action. This is necessitated for similar reasons in both cases, as well as in older examples such as *The Sinking of the Lusitania*: that there exists no live-action footage of the events being portrayed. In these examples, animation functions as a kind of re-enactment of historical events and this kind of animated documentary works very much like a documentary that uses reconstruction or re-enactment. In that sense, it calls on the viewer to make certain assumptions and allowances and, similar to a reconstruction, says 'this is a reasonable likeness of what these events looked like the first time they happened and we have chosen to reconstruct them, or in this case animate them, because we don't have a filmed record of that first time they happened.' Substitutive animation often strives to closely resemble reality, or rather, the look of a live-action recording of reality. In most of the examples in this category the animation is created using digital computer techniques, which are achieving ever-increasing levels of verisimilitude and photorealism.

Other animated documentaries also substitute animation for live action; however, whereas the animation in *Chicago 10* and *Walking with Dinosaurs* attempts to mimic the look of reality, these other films are not so constrained. Animated interview documentaries often use this approach, where a documentary soundtrack is loosely interpreted through animated visuals. The 2002 Swedish film *Hidden* (*Gömd*, Heilborn, Aronowitsch and Johansson) animates a radio interview with a young illegal immigrant. Unlike *Chicago 10*, this film has less concern for making the characters resemble their real-life counterparts. Similarly, *It's Like That* (Southern Ladies Animation Group, 2004) animates young asylum seekers as knitted puppets of small birds. In these animated documentaries, the animation works as non-mimetic substitution. There is no sense of these examples trying to make a visual link with reality or to create an illusion of a filmed image. Instead, they work towards embracing and acknowledging animation as a medium in its own right, a medium that has the potential to express meaning through its aesthetic realisation.

In both mimetic and non-mimetic substitution, the animation could be considered a creative solution to a problem: the absence of filmed material. Animation functions in both cases to overcome limitations of a practical nature. In the case of several animated documentaries, the existence of original filmed material is impossible. The dinosaurs preceded the motion picture camera by several millennia; no cameras were allowed to film the trial of Abbie Hoffman and his co-defendants; there is no visual record of the interviews with the Swedish and Australian child immigrants. In these examples, animation is one of many choices available to the filmmaker who could, conceivably, have used another documentary device such as reconstruction or archival material. Often, too, there are ethical considerations at play. The filmmakers of *Hidden* had a responsibility to protect the anonymity of their child subject. In Liz Blazer's *Backseat Bingo* (2003), a short animated documentary about the sex lives of senior citizens, she gained consent to interview her subjects on the promise that they would not appear on camera (Blazer, 2009). In both cases animation becomes an alternative to the silhouetted figure familiar from television interview documentaries and current affairs programming.

Evocation is the third function of animation in animated documentaries that responds to a different kind of representational limitation. Certain concepts, emotions, feelings and states of mind are particularly difficult to represent through live-action imagery. Historically, filmmakers have used various optical devices such as wavy lines, blurring the edges of the image and alterations of colour palate and film stock to indicate the representation of subjective states of mind. Similarly, certain camera angles inform the audience that we are seeing the world from a particular character's point of view. Animation, however, is increasingly being used as a tool to evoke the experiential in the form of ideas, feelings and sensibilities. By visualising these invisible aspects of life, often in an abstract or symbolic style, animation that functions in this evocative way allows us to imagine the world from someone else's perspective. In *Feeling My Way* (1997) Jonathan Hodgson uses animation to communicate his train of thought on his daily walking commute to work. *Animated Minds* (Andy Glynne, 2003, 2009) combines animated visuals with a soundtrack on which interviewees speak of their experience of living with mental illness. The style of animation reflects the experiences being described on the soundtrack and gives us a visualisation that aids our understanding of these internal worlds.

This function of animation has been used particularly to evoke the reality experienced by the films' subjects, realities that are often quite different from those experienced by the majority of society. In these instances, animation is used as an aide imagination that can facilitate awareness, understanding and compassion from the audience for a subject position potentially far removed from its own. Samantha Moore's 2009 film *An Eyeful of Sound* is a collaboration with people who have synaesthesia, the neurological condition that combines normally separated sensations. This condition can manifest in many ways, such as seeing an image when you hear a sound, or having the sensation of taste in response to seeing something, but Moore focuses in her film on people who see sounds. This topic is particularly suitable for using animation in an evocative way, as Moore's often abstract animation reacts to the film's score in the way that a synaesthetic person's brain responds to sound. Moore uses an interplay of animation and music, along with recorded interviews with her collaborators, to evoke the experience of audio-visual synaesthesia for the audience.

These three functions – mimetic substitution, non-mimetic substitution and evocation – are the three key ways animation works in animated documentary. They are not mutually exclusive, and any one animated documentary could potentially demonstrate all three functions of animation. But, thinking about the way the animation functions will be useful in terms of thinking about what aspects of reality the animated documentary is hoping to reveal to an audience. In the case of mimetic substitution, in examples such as *Chicago 10* and *Walking with Dinosaurs*, the animation tends to be offering us knowledge of something that we could have all seen, had we been alive in prehistoric times or a spectator in Judge Julius Hoffman's courtroom. This is, perhaps, the kind of knowledge that the documentary is, traditionally, evidential of: knowledge that is out there, in the shared historical world, which we all could have accessed equally if we were eyewitness to it. In non-mimetic substitution, such as *It's Like That*, the animation begins to add something, to suggest things through its style and tone. *It's Like That* makes a point about the incarceration of children with the representation of the young asylum seekers as soft, knitted birds, a clear metaphor for the innocence of the film's subjects. This shift from the observable is furthered through the evocative use of animation. Films like *Feeling My Way, Animated Minds* and *An Eyeful of Sound* are, instead of pointing outwards, pointing inwards towards the internal. These films, through the use of animation, are proposing documentary's ability and suitability as a strategy to represent the world *in here* of personal experience as well as the world *out there* of observable events. As an extension of this, films that engage with the personal memories of the filmmakers, such as *Waltz with Bashir* (Folman, 2008) and *Silence* (Yadin and Bringas, 1998), use animation as a tool to explore and reveal hidden or forgotten pasts, further demonstrating the medium's capacity for documenting the world from a subjective point of view.

While all documentaries purport to teach us something about *the* world, the use of animation as a representational strategy broadens the potential of documentary by expanding the range of what can be shown and told. Through mimetic substitution, non-mimetic substitution and evocation, animation responds to the limitations of live-action material. Rather than questioning the viability of knowledge through documentary, animated documentaries offer us an enhanced perspective on reality by presenting the world in a breadth and depth that live action alone cannot. Life is rich and complicated in ways that are not always available to observation, something that is reflected in the diversity of styles and subject matter of contemporary animated documentaries.

The ontology of animated documentary

In the Introduction, I suggested a definition of animated documentary based on a film's method of production, its subject matter and its reception. Animated documentaries are produced frame by frame, they are about *the* world rather than *a* world, and they are presented or received as animated documentaries by producers, audiences and critics. While this helps us differentiate animated documentaries from, for example, animated advertising, infomercials and educational films, it does not answer the question of how animated documentaries are ontologically different from conventional, live-action documentary. That is, what is different in terms of the nature and materiality of animated documentary and its relationship with reality? I believe this is a significant question because it is these differences that are potential stumbling blocks for animation's acceptance as a viable visual representational strategy for documentary.

The three functions of animation in animated documentary point us towards this ontological difference. Animation *substitutes* or it *evokes*. Both terms imply an absence – an absence of original filmed material due to practical constraints or impossibilities. We cannot capture footage of living dinosaurs any more easily than we can film emotions, feelings and mental states. If we wish to make an audio-visual documentary about these subjects, then something must be used instead of live action and the choice for that something is increasingly animation. Animation is more than a simple one-for-one stand-in, however. It is, to state the obvious, different from live-action film. This is why it is able to make up for the representational limitations of what it replaces. On the one hand, filmed footage, and its attendant presumed direct relationship with reality is missing. While, on the other hand, animation, through its potential multiplicity of styles, techniques and means of production, becomes a visual excess that we need to factor in when interpreting the nature, and meaning, of animated documentaries.

At the same time, animated documentaries often retain the same oral/aural link with reality as conventional documentaries, by using audio recording of interviews with documentary subjects for example, and 'there is a "realism" or indexicality to the sound that does not reside in the image' (Ward, 2005a: 98). This pairing of animation and documentary audio recordings draws attention to the significance of a frequently neglected area in documentary studies – sound, and particularly the voice, as a bearer of truth and meaning in documentary. This shift in balance in the audio-visual landscape of non-fiction warrants further attention in our quest to understand and interpret animated documentary.

As Michael Renov (2002) has noted, 'documentary studies' prevailing notions of indexicality, biased as they are in favor of the visual regime, are woefully inadequate.' Animated documentaries question the 'assumption that documentary visuals should merely "illustrate" the sound (or conversely, that documentary sound should act as nothing more than a "back up" to the images)' (Ward, 2005a: 99). There are examples of animated documentaries that use sound to reinforce the visual realm, such as Kenneth Branagh's narration in *Walking with Dinosaurs* (see Chapter 2), but, as Ian Garwood (2012: 40) has noted, after Michel Chion, 'novel ways of altering bodies on-screen [...] can involve a reimagining of the relationship between those bodies and their accompanying voices.' Similarly, novel, or just non-conventional, means of visual inflection in documentary, such as animation, encourage us to rethink not only the significance of what we are hearing, but also the relationship between what we hear, what we see and reality. In *His Mother's Voice* (Dennis Tupicoff, 1997), for example (discussed in detail in Chapter 3), the monologue of a grieving mother is simultaneously disembodied and embodied via animation. The voice powerfully conveys her grief, which, combined with the animation, enhances our understanding of the speaker's loss. Animation here metaphorically echoes the absence of a son, while the visual excesses of style and materiality, which go beyond merely visualising what we hear on the soundtrack, reinforce the significance of this absence. To consider the significance of the absence of a direct visual connection with reality, and the ontological visual excess, in animated documentaries, first we must explore how the relationship between reality and photographic-based media has been theorised, and the implications of this relationship for documentary film.

Susan Sontag (1997: 5) tells us 'photographs furnish evidence' and reminds us of the camera's historic use for surveillance and control. Similar claims are made for film as a medium whose images were, before the advent of digital image technology, produced using the same type of photochemical process. This status as evidence is afforded to photographic media by virtue of its unique existential bond with the world, as Peter Wollen (1998 [1969]: 86) first described it, and has taken on a great significance for documentary studies, as it fuels the idea that documentary has a special claim to evidence reality. This claim is succinctly articulated by Jane Roscoe and Craig Hight (2001: 6) when they say that documentary:

> holds a privileged position within society, a position maintained by documentary's claim that it can present the most accurate and truthful portrayal of the socio-historical world. Inherent to such a claim is the assumption that there is a direct relationship between the documentary image and the referent (social world).

It is worth unpicking the basis for this claim, as it is one that is so frequently made and so seemingly essential to documentary; and, one that is undermined by the use of animation.

Peter Wollen was the first scholar, in 1969, to interpret Andre Bazin's ontology of photography via Charles Sanders Peirce's semiotics. In particular, Wollen conflated Bazin's assertion of the ontological uniqueness of photography with the indexical sign. Bazin did not use the term 'indexical' in his discussion of cinema, but Wollen (1998 [1969]: 86) observes, 'Bazin repeatedly stresses the existential bond between sign and object which, for Peirce, was the determining characteristic of the indexical sign.' Equally significant for documentary is the commonly held belief that 'a photograph shows us (or ought to show us) "what we would have seen if we had been there ourselves"'(Snyder & Allen, 1975: 149). This too can be traced back to Bazin, who says in his essay 'The Ontology of the Photographic Image', that the camera can 'create the illusion of three-dimensional space within which things appeared to exist as our eyes in reality see them.' (Bazin, 2005 [1967]: 11) David Rodowick (2007: 9) calls this photography's power of analogy. These two claims for photography often become entwined. That is, by virtue of the indexical relationship with reality, photographs are forced, through the process of light from an object refracting through the camera lens and hitting film, to correspond directly with what was in front of the camera and thus what the photographic image shows us is what we would have seen ourselves.

This mutually dependent relationship of causality and analogy has maintained dominance in the interpretation of moving images, especially documentary ones. Documentaries are special and can make truth claims about things that really happened because of the indexicality of their images. The indexical nature of live-action moving images means there is a causal requirement for whatever is being shown on screen to have actually taken place in front of the camera and the analogous quality means that what we see on screen is what we would have seen were we there in person. Therefore, we can take documentaries as evidence, as good as witnessing something for ourselves, with our own eyes. This argument works both ways, with the requirement that for a film to be documentary it must maintain this relationship between image and reality and show us things as they really happened. These requirements of causality and analogy are what make, for some, the use of re-enactment in documentary problematic. And it is these requirements that, surely, rule animation out as a viable means of documentary representation because of the lack of direct causal link and analogical relationship between animation and reality.

These founding myths of the ontology of photography and film, which have such significant implications for documentary, deserve further interrogation. In fact, film is far from so ontologically simple, and scholarship in this area, from theorists of film, photography, new media, and beyond, reveals the lack of consensus on the ontology of photographic media. More nuanced readings of Bazin along with interrogations into photographic media, many spurred by the advent of digital photography and image manipulation, query whether indexicality, and interpreting the photographic via semiotics, help us understand how and why photographic media comes to be taken as evidence of the profilmic. So too has the assumption been thrown into doubt that what makes the photographic unique is the spatial analogy between image and original.

Tom Gunning (2007) has observed that the understanding of indexicality perpetuated by film theory is usually based on a limited understanding of Peircian semiotics and I am sure that a number, if not the majority, of scholars and theorists, myself included, who fall back on indexicality to distinguish film from other forms of visual representation, have not made a close reading of Peirce's philosophy. This is implied by Brian Winston and Hing Tsang (2009: 457) when they chide on this matter that '[B]odies of complex work have been not untypically reduced to easy citations from secondary sources.' Gunning and Winston and Tsang point out that the index was, for Peirce, part of a complex philosophy that was more than a system of signs, but that also encompassed metaphysics, pragmatics and theories regarding how we experience the world. The second-hand, tunnel-vision interpretation of Peirce has led to an oversimplified parity between photographs as indexes or 'the impression or trace' of reality (Gunning, 2007: 30).

In fact, indexical signs are both more and less than traces of reality. For example, as Mary Ann Doane (2007a: 2) notes, a pointing finger and the pronoun 'this' are classed as indexes by Peirce. These are indexes by virtue of their deictic function of physically and linguistically pointing to something else. Empty of any meaning in their own right, these gestures and words only have substance when we know to which object, event or person they indicate. Furthermore, photographs are both more and less than indexical signs. Wollen emphasised the importance of the presence in the photographic of all three signs that made up Peirce's triadic system (index, icon and symbol). Yet, the index subsequently came to dominate in interpretations of the photographic's relationship with reality. In particular, Winston and Tsang seek to reclaim the significance of the icon, the sign of resemblance, to photography and film. They cite Piercian scholar Göran Sonneson, who claims that 'first and foremost, the photograph is an iconic sign' (Sonneson quoted in Winston & Tsang, 2009: 461). Sonneson takes things even further when he says that our interpretation of a photograph does not depend on us knowing its indexical status and 'it will continue to convey its significations to us, whether we are certain it is a photograph or not' (Sonneson quoted in Winston & Tsang, 2009: 461). Coming at the matter from a different angle, this is a characteristic of photography, and its reception, echoed by Tom Gunning (2004: 41) when he says 'our evaluation of a photograph as accurate [...] depends not simply on its indexical basis [...], but on our recognition of it as looking like its subject.' He later goes further by saying 'the indexical may have little relation to photography's iconic properties.' (44)

These observations somewhat destabilise the perpetuated assumption that we take documentaries as evidence because of the indexicality of their images. Is it really, as Bill Nichols (1991: 150) notes, that the 'indexical bond of photochemical and electronic images to that which they represent [...] provides [...] a seemingly irrefutable guarantee of authenticity'? Especially if, as some theorists suggest (see Rodowick, 2007; Rosen, 2001; and Doane, 2007b), digitally recorded images do not maintain the same relationship with reality as photographic ones, yet no one seems to be making an argument for digitally recorded documentaries (as most are at this point) being any less authentic than ones recorded on film. Or is it more to do with the fact that documentaries look like reality, as we might have witnessed it ourselves?

The mutual dependency of resemblance and causal connection to reality in the photographic is further complicated by observations of how easily photographs can be made to *not* look like what we see in front of the camera. Winston and Tsang (2009: 461) point out that photographs can 'be physically "forced" through framing, development, and printing, etc., *not* to correspond point-by-point to nature' (emphasis in original). Scholar of photography, Joel Snyder, is another dissenting voice in the dominant understanding of the ontology of the photographic. In a 1975 essay written with Neil Walsh Allen, he establishes the absurd level of qualification required to justify the claim that the photographic shows us what we would have seen with our own eyes. Such qualifications include spatial and temporal specificities along with acknowledging the qualities of different types of photographic film and the way it is developed (Snyder & Allen, 1975: 152). In a later essay, Snyder points out that it is not the objects in front of the camera that affect the photographic film, but light. Therefore, one could take two photographs of the same object, but make them look very different by varying the amount of light to which you expose the film. A completely over-exposed image (which would be a white blank) or a completely under-exposed image (which would be black) would both have the same causal relationship with the object in front of the camera, but they would resemble neither each other, nor the original object (Snyder, 1980: 508). Snyder even goes further than Winston and Tsang and claims that it is impossible for photographs to show things as we would have seen them due to fundamental differences between the way the human eye sees and a photographic image (Snyder, 1980: 507). So, if the technical creation of the filmed images, with its use of lenses, perspective, framing and so on, means that film does not really show us things as we would have seen them with our own eyes, does this mean animation, which most definitely does not show the world as we see it, is equally as acceptable as a representational strategy for documentary?

The reluctance to reduce physical causality and resemblance echoes some of the fundamental claims made by Bazin regarding the ontology of photography, claims that are reinforced in the writings of Roland Barthes on the same subject. In the same essay that Bazin tells us photographs allow us to see things as we do in reality, he also somewhat contradictorily says that 'no matter how fuzzy, distorted, or discoloured, no matter how lacking in documentary value the image may be, it shares, by virtue of the process of its becoming, the being of the model of which it is the reproduction; it is the model' (Bazin, 2005 [1967]: 14). Barthes (1981: 88) too claimed that the *noeme*, or nature, of photography is not to do with analogy and it is not photography's ability to create an accurate likeness that makes it unique among representational arts. Indeed, it is frequently observed that there are plenty of indexical signs that do not look like their referent. Philip Rosen (2001: 88) gives the example of weather vanes (which do not look like wind) and Peirce (1991: 239–40) himself acknowledges that a bullet hole remains an index of a bullet even if no one recognises it as such.

In an extremely thorough analysis of Bazin's writing, Daniel Morgan (2006) demonstrates quite how complicated Bazin's ontology of photography is. Photography was, for Bazin, not just about indexicality, or the physical link between image and reality, but something more, something that perhaps Bazin himself did not understand, demonstrated, Morgan suggests, by his use of multiple, incongruous, metaphors for the photographic. Tom Gunning (2004) does not deny that the photographic holds a special power for us, and that this power is to do with the relationship between the photograph and reality, but he prefers to understand this uniqueness phenomenologically, rather than semantically. That is, he differentiates ontology and indexicality and claims that it is photography's capacity to put 'us in the presence of something' (46) rather than refer to something that is unique. This takes us back to Bazin and Barthes, for both of whom this potential of co-presence of viewer of photograph and object of photograph was vitally important. Indeed, when Bazin (2005 [1967]: 15) denies that photographs are simply a substitute for 'the order of natural creation' he seems to be denying that photographs are signs. Barthes described photographs as an 'emanation of a *past reality*' (1981: 88, emphasis in original). It is this, almost spiritual quality, of past contact that leads us, Dudley Andrew (2005: xvi) claims, to 'venerate' objects such as shrouds. The psychospiritual and temporal aspects of photography are clearly significant to Bazin (2005 [1967]) who sees photography and film as the teleological culmination of our 'mummy complex' (9) and our desire to 'embalm time' (14) and to be in contact with something from the past.

Several theorists have posited that the photographic maintains a privileged position among forms of visual representation due to its complicated relationship to past and present, a relationship that animation seemingly cannot emulate. In fact, David Rodowick prefers to call photographs transcriptions, rather than representations, because they allow the 'present witnessing of past durations' (Rodowick, 2007: 136). It is not, for Rodowick, that photography offers a spatial resemblance, or equivalence, of the original scene. Rather, it is that they make 'past time spatially present' (56). This temporal relationship is one that is difficult to express in language, and Laura Mulvey (2006: 57) identifies it as a complexity of tense, as suggested by Barthes when 'he sums up photography's essence as "this was now."'

The importance for documentary of this filmic connection between present and past is emphasised by Thomas Austin (2008: 51), when he talks about how documentary can be seen to 'enact a search for, and testify to the continuing significance of, the "then" in the "now"'. This spiritual quality of film affords the photographic a privileged position that animation could seemingly never hold. Yet, as digital animation potentially becomes indistinguishable from the photographic (Manovich, 2002: 180) and if resemblance leads to the assumption of causality, then it is perhaps possible that animation could fake this feeling of co-presence. Tom Gunning (2004: 45) gives a redolent example in questioning whether knowing how photographs are made engenders our interest and investment in them as images and objects:

> If a friend shows me a pen and tells me it was the one Herman Melville used to write *Moby Dick* my fascination with the pen is dependent on this fact. If I find out my friend is joking and bought the pen at a dime store, my fascination vanishes. But when I am told a photograph has been digitalized I may cease to believe its truth claim, but I think I am still intrigued by it.

This leads one to question whether the important thing is to know that an image was created in a past moment of co-presence with the object, or whether it looks as if it did, something that animation is increasingly, incrementally, progressing towards.

One could argue that animation, precisely because it does not require the existence of the profilmic in the same way as live action, is at greater liberty to conflate the 'then' and the 'now'. The wonder and awe inspired by the *Walking with Dinosaurs* series comes from the images' ability to show us the 'then' 'now' in a realistic way, as if we were watching footage captured by a wildlife documentary crew. Animation can show past events that have, due to various reasons of practicality or possibility, eluded live action. In films such as *Waltz with Bashir* and *Silence*, it can engage with personal and collective memory in a performative and expressive way that circumvents the strictures of official, written history and that reflects on the nature of remembering. Animation can also play with time and space, contracting and expanding them to pass comment on the passage of time and the connections between events.

This concertinaing of time, as well as space, is what Jonathan Hodgson does so artfully in his 'War on Resources' animated segment in the mostly live-action climate change documentary *The Age of Stupid* (Franny Armstrong, 2009) when he compresses time (from prehistory to the Iraq War) and (global) space to make a pointed comment about the relationship between colonialism, capitalism and the depletion of natural resources, all in under two minutes. The delightful architecture animated documentary *American Homes* (Bernard Friedman, 2011) uses animation to tell the history of American architecture and covers two millennia and nearly an entire continent in twelve minutes. Dozens of buildings, from an earth lodge to a contemporary sustainable home, are consecutively built and dismantled in simple line-drawn animation, resembling architects' plans, on a white background (see Figure 1.1). A small map of the United States in the bottom righ corner of the screen orients the viewer geographically, while subtitles inform the period and style of housing. On the soundtrack twenty different architects, artists and cultural commentators reflect on the nature and purpose of architecture, as a reflection of us and of its historical context. The film is at once both meditative and instructive without being didactic, a visually condensed history of domestic dwellings in the United States accompanied by philosophical musings on the meaning of architecture.

Animation is equally, if not more, suited to exploring 'how time has left (and will leave) its traces, however intermittently, on diverse places and bodies' (Austin, 2008: 51). Something Austin suggests is an 'abiding quest in much documentary output'. Animation, because of its different ontological relationship with reality, and because it does not propose a direct link with the past, acknowledges more readily than live action

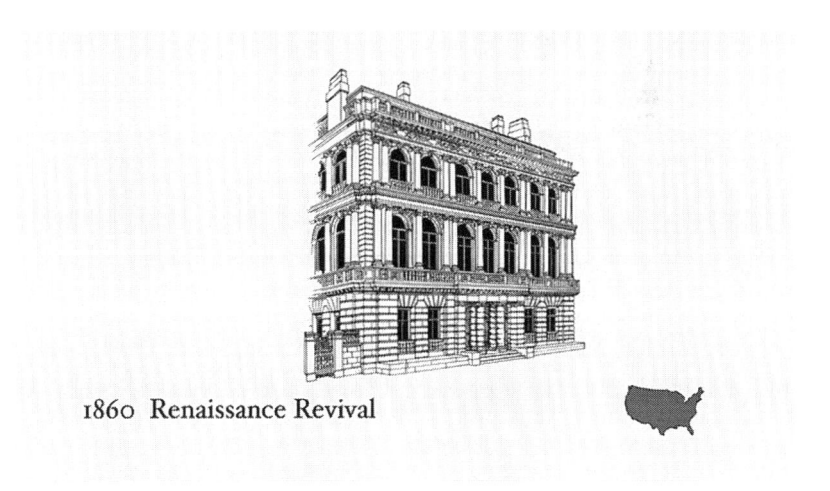

1860 Renaissance Revival

Figure 1.1 The built environment is de-/reconstructed in *American Homes* (dir. & prod. Bernard Friedman, 2011)

that such attempts at 'temporal recovery [are] in a sense doomed to be incomplete, imperfect, almost always less successful than intended'. It is often through such imperfections that animated documentary's endeavours to bring the temporally, spatially, and psychologically distal into closer proximity are enriched because it is in these gaps between animation and representation that we, as viewers, are prompted to make connections and conclusions that might not be overtly stated on screen.

What can we conclude from looking over the complex and convoluted landscape of film ontology? Rodowick (2007: 12–13) suggests that the reason new media presents such an apparent challenge for film theory is that we have never been certain of the ontological status of film. We could argue the same is true for the challenge of interpreting animated documentaries within the prevailing theoretical tropes of documentary studies. We have seen that the relationship between (documentary) film and reality is far from simple. Indexicality and resemblance, the mutually dependent qualities that enable us to claim documentary images as witnessing events as we might with our own eyes, can be thrown into question. Indexical signs do not always resemble and resemblance is no guarantee of indexicality. In any case, perhaps it is not semiotics that makes photographs special, but rather their ability to transcend spatial and temporal boundaries, by bringing something temporally distal into spatial proximity, in order to satisfy a deep-felt need to preserve and revisit the past.

Indexicality has become a shorthand way of claiming the validity of documentary film, a quick and easy way of defending a documentary's inherent claim to truthfully represent reality. Yet, the basis for this claim is far from clear. Is it that documentary images are a physical link to reality? Or, that they look like reality as we might have seen it ourselves? Perhaps it is a more abstract notion of documentary images pointing to a reality beyond themselves? Or, a quasi-magical quality of bringing something past into the present? Another alternative way of understanding documentary is via an 'innovative Deleuzian aesthetics', suggested by Ilona Hongisto, that thinks of film not as a means of representation, but as something that 'captures and expresses the real in its process of actualization' (Marks, 2011: 310). My object here is not a postmodern quest to undermine the strength of documentary's claim to evidence reality, but rather to observe this claim is far from a simple one. Indeed, as discussed in Chapter 2, perhaps the truth claim is based more on culturally determined aesthetics and style than anything inherent in the means of image production.

However we understand the nature of documentary's relationship with reality, this relationship is surely severed when animation is used instead of live-action film as the means of visual representation. There is no physical causal link between animated image and the reality it might depict, so animation cannot evidence or witness things as we might have done with our own eyes. What we see in an animated image did not exist in front of the camera in that form. Cels, static puppets, paint and brushes, grains of sand, could not be mistaken for the animated films that they create. In cameraless animation, such as the films of Len Lye and Norman McLaren, there exists no profilmic at all. Yet, animation can in some ways offer a direct connection to moments passed in time. It is possible to argue, as has Mary Anne Doane, that animation is indexical:

> certainly in the sense that it is deictic through its framing and use of simulated camera movement. But even in terms of the more common sense of index as trace, animation involves photography and a 'that has been' of the graphic image in front of the lens (Doane, 2007b: 148, n.3).

There is a causal process at play that results in the final animation. Drawn animation, for example, as Birgitta Hosea (2010: 363) observes, bears 'the trace of the presence of an artist's body'.

In a suggestion that is significant for animated documentary, Doane claims that 'animation is only nonindexical if the "real" associated with the index is yoked to a traditional notion of realism or to the filming of only objects/ places not constructed or generated by human beings' (149, n.3). This would be a concept of the real that documentary is indeed yoked to, even if we can make animation fit into our understanding of index (as trace, as deixis) as it applies to live-action film, so any attempt to over-emphasise the ontological similarities of animation and live action would only limit our understanding of animated documentary.

In addition to thinking about what animation is not, we must also think about what it is, be that in relation to the ontology of live-action film or as a multifarious means of representation in its own right, one that is of a different order to live-action film (be it digital or photographic). Animation production techniques range from computer-generated photorealism to painting on glass, from traditional hand-drawn cel animation to stop motion. The range is so large that it is almost impossible to talk of 'animation' in any cohesive way (see Ward, 2006b). Can we, for example, meaningfully compare the photorealism of motion captured feature films such as *The Polar Express* (Robert Zemeckis, 2004) with the artisanal style of stop motion with plasticine puppets used by Aardman Animations in *Wallace and Gromit in The Curse of the Were-Rabbit* (Steve Box and Nick Park, 2005)? These two types of animation certainly have different relationships with reality. Photorealism strives to be indistinguishable from filmic representations of reality and motion capture is a means of creating realistic movement and expression in animated characters. Stop motion animation retains, similarly to live action, a physical connection between image and profilmic and physical marks, such as fingerprints in clay, point, in the manner suggested by Hosea, to the hand of the animator and to the process of production.

When viewing an animated documentary, colour palette, texture, movement, shape, and character design for example, are all qualities that inform our interpretation of the images we see. As Vivian Sobchack (2006: 176) has put it, all cinema is iconic, but '*one* of its poles – the indexical photograph or the symbolic emblem – usually tends to dominate' (emphasis in original). So, while the animated image often resembles what it is referencing – Disney rabbits look like real rabbits, we recognise that Gromit is a dog and that Bart Simpson is a young boy – it also looks very different. It is from this difference that much of the pleasure of animation derives, be it aesthetic, comedic, ironic or so on. This also means that when animation is used in a documentary context, the image is doing more than representing, or transcribing, reality. The graphic novel aesthetic of the animation in *Waltz with Bashir*, with its strong colours and clearly outlined characters, has little aesthetically in common with the washed-out pastel quality of *The Light Bulb Thing*, a short film about manic depression that is part of the 2003 *Animated Minds* series. These differences are not insignificant and they have a bearing on how the films come to have meaning for the viewer. Indeed, a significant quality of much animation is that:

> the physical qualities of the materials from which the imagery is made, processed by the animator's frame-by-frame construction of a separate temporal reality, can help viewers access a sense of the original experience and/or story that inspired the work (Hayes, 2012: 217).

Animated images, in their non-indexicality (or alternative indexicality) do not directly point to or connect to reality. Even if, as in the case of mimetic substitution, the animation strives to photorealism, we are still aware that this is not a filmed image of reality and that lack of analogy combined with the striving for the look of analogy becomes a factor in our interpretation and reception of the images we see. More commonly, 'unrestricted by the dictates of photographic realism and traditional narrative, animation can make [...] experience palpable via visual imagination, metaphor, metamorphosis' (National Film Theatre programme for 'Textures of Reality' symposium, Feb 2004, quoted in Pilling, 2012: 2). It is this potential of animation, its affinity with metaphor and metamorphosis for example, that must be taken into consideration when interpreting and understanding animated documentary. In addition, as these are animated *documentaries*, we must consider the relationship between the means of representation and the reality to which it refers.

The contradictory nature of film has been frequently observed. John Ellis puts it eloquently when he says:

> The cinema image is marked by a particular half-magic feat in that it makes present something that is absent. The moment shown on the screen is passed and gone when it is called back into being as illusion. The figures and places shown are not present in the same space as the viewer. The cinema makes present the absent: this is the irreducible separation that cinema maintains (and attempts to abolish), the fact that objects and people are conjured up yet known not to be present. Cinema is present absence: it says 'This is was' (Ellis, 1982: 58–9).

Laura Mulvey (2006) associates this uncanny quality with film and photography's indexical quality. For Mary Ann Doane (2007a: 2) the 'dialectic of the empty and the full' comes from the indexical's dual qualities as deixis and trace. If in film we can talk of a present absence and presence/absence, in animated documentary we have a visual dialectic of absence and excess. This, I would argue, is one of animation's strengths as a representational strategy for documentary. As Paul Ward (2008: para. 9) has observed, 'the very *constructedness* of animation might be the key to a specific mode of address that can elude live action documentary filmmaking, precisely because of the expectations that the indexical link – and apparent transparency – can raise' (emphasis in original). This means that astute and imaginative creative choices of how to visually represent, interpret and infer reality can enable truth claims of a different order to live-action documentary. Photorealism, metaphor and metamorphosis, for example, can allow us to see or imagine aspects of reality that cannot be shown through conventional means. And while animation may not provide a direct connection to a moment passed, it does allow temporal and spatial expression that is beyond live action and permits us to explore the past, present and future of the world out there of shared experience and the world in here of subjective experience. Over the following chapters, the different strategies of representation available to animated documentary, and what these strategies imply for the representation of reality, will be explored.

2
Digital Realities

Battle 360, a 2008 History Channel series, combines digital animation with archival material and interviews to construct a kinetic and at times spectacular representation of the exploits of a US naval aircraft carrier during World War Two. The credit sequence begins with a number of breathtaking animated 'aerial shots'. We swoop down the side of the computer-generated *USS Enterprise* before swiftly zip panning up to see a squadron of enemy aircraft zeroing in on the ship and, just as quickly, we are in the position of the pilots, seeing the *Enterprise* as we nosedive towards the sea. This digital visual overload manifests in other ways. Frequently, the photorealistic imagery is superimposed with outlines of grids, charts and compass bearings, which lend the underlying images the official air of navigational charts and military documents. As we are introduced to new ships or airplanes, factual information, such as maximum speed and bomb carriage capacity, is imprinted on the screen.

Perhaps less attention grabbing is the way digital animation is frequently treated to resemble the deteriorated look of the archival footage and photographs with which it is integrated. Here, the sharp clarity of the digital image gives way to sepia tones and a grainy, blotchy texture, one that mimics the look of decaying film. At one point digital animation and live action are even combined to form a single image. This approach – of using animation that mimics the look of live action as a means of representation within a documentary – seems to blur the ontological distinction between animation and live action. If the primary basis for this differentiation is the relationship between image and reality, what does it mean that animation is increasingly able, as Dan North (2008: 20) has observed, to 'imitate[s] those properties of the photographic image which signal its indexicality – the photographic idiosyncrasies which remind us of the photochemical reactions required to record on celluloid'?

One response is to suggest that *Battle 360* is claiming its validity as a history documentary by copying the properties of the types of image – in this case archival film from World War Two – that carry the weight of evidence and the connection to reality in that type of programme or film. This claim is being made via what Rosalind Galt (2008: 63), in her Bazanian analysis of the Dutch experimental fantasy film *Forbidden Quest* (1993), has termed 'indexical affect'. In that film, problems with the footage such as graininess, blurring, missing sections and damaged film become markers of its authenticity. In Galt's example, indexical affect is put to the service of reinforcing the fictional narrative in which the deteriorated documentary footage is placed. In *Battle 360*, the faked markers of indexicality, such as graininess and other imperfections of celluloid exacerbated by the passage of time, are used to authenticate the digitally created images, and the text in which they are placed, as documentary.

This act of authentication is premised on assumptions of what certain types of documentary footage should look like. Such assumptions are in part grounded in the beliefs regarding the ontological uniqueness of film, discussed in Chapter 1 – that its indexicality quality demands resemblance, and resemblance, in turn, guarantees indexicality. As Mary Ann Doane (2007a: 2) has observed, the iconicity of 'the index as trace has, unfortunately, suggested for many theorists an alliance with realism as both style and ideology.' She later clarifies realism in a way that is useful for thinking about animated documentaries, particularly those that use animation for mimetic substitution, as 'a mimetic copy, an illusion of an inhabitable world' (Doane, 2007a: 4). Our idea of what a mimetic copy, or realist image, should look like on film is again influenced by Bazin. In several of the essays collected in the two volumes of *What Is Cinema?* he seems to promote a somewhat essentialist theory of film aesthetics that is implied by the medium's ontology. Bazin extolled the virtues of non-interventionist filmmaking because these techniques, he argued, were best suited to the fundamental nature of the cinematic form. Conversely, he was critical of montage editing, which he called 'anticinematic', because it distracted from the reality in front of the camera (2005 [1967]: 46). The power of the film image, for Bazin, arises from its ability to 'lay bare the realities' (Bazin, 2005 [1967]: 15), and this could best be done in a style that maintained the physical and spatial as it is in our own direct experience, rather than the juxtaposition of shots that disrupt space and time.

But, just as realism is a style it is also something that is culturally specific and conditionally accepted, rather than an absolute. Manovich (2002: 186–7) indicates this quality when he examines how the look of cinematic realism, and thus audience conception of what counts as realist, has changed with developments in the technology of filmmaking and production. We have to learn the codes of cinematic realism, even if we are not aware we are learning them, not least because, as Joel Snyder (1980) has pointed out, and as discussed in Chapter 1, the photographic does not look like reality as we perceive it. The cultural specificity and acceptance of the codes of realist representation are also true of documentary. Brian Winston has noted that with the rise of Direct Cinema in the 1960s and early 1970s that style of fly-on-the-wall documentary filmmaking became established as 'the dominant model for contemporary Anglo-Saxon documentary' (Winston, 1995: 206). Theatrically released documentaries that offered a glimpse into the life of rock stars and politicians led to an increased popularity of the form among the general audience. As a result, viewers came to associate non-interventionist, realist style with what a documentary should look like. Thus, through a variety of cultural and rhetorical means, the 'notion of particular aesthetic devices being perceived as "more real" or "more truthful" than others is a pervasive one' (Ward, 2008: 12). This dominance of a certain style of documentary realism is made manifest in mock-documentary. With the intention of humour and satire (and occasionally trickery), mock-documentaries demonstrate how easy it is to fake the documentary codes of shaky camerawork, talking-head interviews, grainy image quality, production sound and a filmmaker positioned as impartial observer. The ease with which documentary realism can be faked reveals that these documentary codes are not necessarily markers of authenticity, but rather norms that have come to be accepted as representing reality in a truthful way.[1]

The examples examined later in this chapter – the BBC television series *Walking with Dinosaurs* (1999) and *Planet Dinosaur* (2011), the feature film *Chicago 10* (Brett Morgen, 1997), and a selection of short films made by Bob Sabiston in the 1990s and 2000s – are all animated documentaries that use animation in mimetic substitution. They demonstrate the importance of various visual and aural tropes of non-fiction style for asserting documentary status for a text, despite the fact that the look of a documentary, and realism in particular, does not guarantee a connection between filmed and profilmic. They also show how the material qualities of film can be emulated, as the possibility of verisimilitude increases with the development of technologies of computer image generation. The fact is that we cannot necessarily distinguish between a 'real' documentary and a 'fake' one on the basis of what it looks like, either in terms of filming style or the quality of the image. This means, as Bill Nichols (1991: 153) has pointed out, that while 'indexicality plays a key role in authenticating the documentary image's claims to the historically real [...] the authentication itself must come from elsewhere'. This is echoed by Philip Rosen's (2001: 261) observation that 'the documentary tradition has rarely supposed that the photographic/cinematic "impression of reality" is, in itself, sufficient for knowledge.' In order for us to afford images' documentary status, verification that an image is genuine, must come from another source. This can take the form of authentication embedded in the text via on-screen titles or voiceover, the latter being a key authenticating element for *Walking with Dinosaurs* and *Planet Dinosaur*, for example. Usually, though, some degree of extra-textual information, such as that contained in publicity and marketing material, is required in order for the viewer to know for certain that the film is a documentary.[2]

Animated documentaries that use mimetic substitution have no indexical validity in their own right. Their imagery may be 'indistinguishable from traditional photo and film images', but 'on the level of the "material" they are quite different' (Manovich, 2002: 180). Craig Hight (2008: 28) has suggested that such ontological complexity is elided so as not to trouble the viewer. This elision can occur, as we shall see, in the texts themselves through mimetic, sometimes photorealistic, animation that is marching towards being 'indistinguishable from traditional photo and film', in which images resembling their real-world counterparts are presented within a framework of documentary indicators that include the tropes of documentary style, such as certain camera angles and movement. This validation is echoed in the paratextual, for example in filmmaker interviews that emphasise the evidence-based nature of a film, or via websites and other promotional materials that demonstrate the factual basis for the animated visuals.

The textual and paratextual are not, however, entirely about validating documentary status. Despite Manovich's claims regarding computer-generated images and film being indistinguishable, we are usually aware that what we are seeing is not imagery that was captured with a camera. The documentary presentation is rarely entirely seamless and there are moments where the excess of animation is irrepressible and attention is drawn to the ontological difference between it and live action. The aesthetic quality of the animation carries meaning in its own right, exceeding its role as a simple substitute. Sometimes, for example, the imagery seems to be making a claim for its own aesthetic value as beautiful or breathtaking, especially considering its fabricated nature. The paratextual often draws attention to the animation, breaking the illusion of realism, through behind-the-scenes footage of how the images were created and filmmaker interviews and websites that reveal the painstaking process of reconstructing reality using digital animation techniques.

While we might not necessarily argue that *Battle 360* is an animated documentary, its use of computer-generated imagery exemplifies the tensions and contradictions within animated documentaries that use digital animation to copy the look of reality, or reality as we are used to seeing it via film, video and television. While at first glance we could consider the digital animation as making up for an absence of filmed material, it soon becomes apparent that the animation goes beyond mere substitution. The animation draws attention to itself, by virtue of both its visual similarities and differences to film. In addition, our attention is drawn to it by the paratexts that surround these animated documentaries. Such texts and paratexts encourage us to question the presumptions of documentary realism, along with the privileged relationship between documentary film and reality.

Dino-docs and strategies of visual and aural authentication

In 1999 the BBC set a new benchmark for natural history programming with *Walking with Dinosaurs*. The six-part series used digital animation techniques to reconstruct prehistoric life that were, for their time, cutting edge. *Walking with Dinosaurs* spawned a *Walking with...* franchise of two further series on prehistoric animals (*Walking with Beasts* (2001) and *Walking with Monsters* (2005)), one series on the evolution of mankind (*Walking with Cavemen* (2003)), as well as several one-off specials and spin-off series on dinosaurs and prehistoric beasts.[3] All of the series and specials employ a combination of digital animation, animatronics and live-action backgrounds to reconstruct the world of the dinosaurs and cavemen. The *Walking with...* franchise occupies a pivotal position in television science documentary. Historically, it is ensconced in a long tradition of quality natural history broadcasting on the BBC, one cemented by David Attenborough in the 1970s, that allows viewers a privileged view of the animal kingdom. The series also established digital animation as a valid means of representation for natural history and science television to the extent that its use is now ubiquitous. In

2011 the BBC revisited the territory of *Walking with Dinosaurs* with their *Planet Dinosaur* series, this time relying solely on computer technology to produce the images of prehistoric life.

Walking with Dinosaurs was conceived by producer and ex-zoologist Tim Haines, who, several years earlier, had been impressed and inspired by *Jurassic Park* (1993) and the way that film used technology to bring dinosaurs back to life (BBC Worldwide, 2004). The intention for the television series, however, was to go beyond fictional fantasy and to 'create the most accurate portrayal of prehistoric animals ever seen on the screen' (BBC, n.d.). This involved the help of a consultant palaeontologist and myriad other scientific experts who advised on all aspects of prehistoric life, from climate to plant life. The animation was created by a small team at the London-based company FrameStore, whose work was composited with footage of animatronic models that had been filmed at suitably prehistoric-looking locations, such as New Caledonia and the Redwood National Park in California. The endeavour involved two year's worth of research, filming, animation, and post-production, and the reported budget of £6 million made the series the most expensive documentary series produced by BBC (BBC, n.d.; K D Scott & White, 2003: 316).

The six episodes take the viewer on a chronological rise-and-fall journey from the evolution of the dinosaurs during the late Triassic period to their extinction in the late Cretaceous, 150 million years later. Each episode focuses on a few major dinosaurs of the period, as well as spotlighting a particular type of habitation environment, an approach that gives viewers specific insight as well as a general overview of the subject matter. In particular, one of the selling points of the series was the opportunity to gain the type of knowledge traditionally offered by natural history programming, such as intimate views of animal life. For example, episode four looks at the giant flying dinosaur ornithocheirus and its mating cycle and episode six shows us the social habits of the leallynasarus, who survived through freezing Antarctic winters.

When the BBC revisited the world of the dinosaurs over a decade later in *Planet Dinosaur*, *Walking with Dinosaurs* was an inevitable point of comparison, in terms of the way the dinosaurs looked as well as narrative structure and content.[4] *Planet Dinosaur* differentiates itself from its predecessor in two key ways – by using 'the latest CGI and cutting-edge research' (BBC, 2012). By describing itself as 'groundbreaking' (BBC, 2012), *Planet Dinosaur* implies that it will be offering something that we did not see in *Walking with Dinosaurs*. *Planet Dinosaur* certainly takes a different approach to visualising prehistory. Instead of the proscenium-arch style static framing of *Walking with Dinosaurs*, the 'camera' is more mobile and shot lengths are much shorter. The later series is not chronological, but rather organized thematically according to the type of dinosaur. Significantly, *Planet Dinosaur* limits its subject matter to dinosaur activity that can be more readily proven by the fossil record. This means there is more focus on the impact of environmental factors and activities such as hunting and killing and less on mating and social behaviour.

Both *Walking with Dinosaurs* and *Planet Dinosaur* employ a photorealistic style of animation whereby the animation is designed not only to look like reality as we experience it, but more importantly to mimic reality as it is re-presented on film. This verisimilitude has several different visual references. Firstly, the dinosaurs in both series look, move and sound as science would expect them to. The series' producers paid great attention to fossil evidence in bringing their dinosaurs to life, often dispelling previously held misconceptions.[5] Physical elements such as skin tone and texture, as well as auditory characteristics, of which no or little evidence exists in the fossil record, are extrapolated from contemporary wildlife.[6] In this way, the digital dinosaurs are made to look and sound realistic, based on evidence and reasonable assumption, and correspond with audience expectation.

Additionally, the look of the dinosaurs is consistent with already existing representations of prehistoric creatures and the series' visual style mimics that from relevant film, television and other media. For *Walking With Dinosaurs*, the key visual references were the dinosaurs in the Hollywood blockbuster *Jurassic Park* and the filming style of television nature documentaries. *Planet Dinosaur* has more contemporary visual references, most notably losing the style of natural history filming in favour of a more dynamic documentary style, including more 'camera' movement and a high cut rate. The later series also alludes to computer games with frequent pauses in the narrative with HUD-like[7] information graphics that tell us about recent fossil discoveries and provide more specific details such as dinosaur dimensions and the geographical location of finds.

When *Walking with Dinosaurs* was first broadcast *Jurassic Park* would have been relatively fresh in viewers' minds.[8] Producer Tim Haines was keenly aware of this and the importance of his dinosaurs not departing 'too radically from their digital predecessors as envisioned by Spielberg' (Scott & White, 2003: 321). If the dinosaur 'protagonists' of *Walking with Dinosaurs* resemble the creatures seen on the big screen in the early 1990s, the style of 'filming' takes its cues from the traditions of small screen television nature documentary. During episode four (*Giant of the Skies*) we are afforded the ornithocheirus eye view of a herd of iguanadon ambling along a sandy beach identified in the voiceover as the 'southern tip of North America', mimicking the aerial shots familiar from countless wildlife films. The telephoto lens camerawork frequently used in natural history programming to reveal detail from a distance is similarly copied throughout the series. For example in the first episode we see, in intimate close-up, the carnivorous coelophysis preying on a cynodonts' burrow, successfully catching and devouring one of the young, a shot that could only have been captured (in a traditional natural history documentary) using a telephoto lens so as not to disturb animals in the wild. These techniques implicitly knit *Walking with Dinosaurs* into the canon of natural history documentary and, in so doing, covertly claim that these images are as authentic as anything one might see in any other wildlife programme.[9]

This sense of authenticity is further amplified through moments that imply a co-presence of camera and living dinosaur. Episode five of *Walking with Dinosaurs* features a section where we see the laellynasaura feeding during the arctic winter. The narration tells us that the filmmakers are utilizing 'image enhancement' to better see the behaviour of the animals under the cover of darkness. As this is said, the style of animation changes instantly, as if at the flick of a switch, to mimic the look of a night vision camera, with grainy, green-tinged black and white footage. In the next episode the 'camera' tracking the fearsome T-rex catches the full force of the beast's roar as its spittle splatters the 'lens'. This visual embellishment becomes a trope in *Planet Dinosaur*, through multiple uses in each episode, and to the extent that it is used as part of the title sequence in which blood splatter on the screen from a maimed dinosaur morphs into the letters 'Planet Dinosaur'.

These visual cues to authenticity are entirely unnecessary within the schema of the individual episodes and overall series and could, in *Walking with Dinosaurs* in particular, potentially jolt the viewer out of the seamless narrative of an episode's story. However, whereas a participant directly addressing the film crew or camera in a fly-on-the-wall observational documentary disrupts the pretence of the invisibility of the filmmakers and their non-intervention in events, these moments in the digital dinosaur documentaries intentionally draw our attention to the imagined filmic apparatus and in so doing mask the presence of the computer software responsible for the scene. They are a covert claim that this is what 'real' footage of dinosaurs would have looked like had cameras been around to film them in the first place. As such, they operate similarly to 'markers of indexicality', to borrow Philip Rosen's (2001: 20) term, which testify to the authenticity of indexical traces such as photographic and filmic images. Whereas a genuine indexical trace 'derives its current authenticity from the fact that it was present in the past yet survives to the present' (Rosen, 2001: 239), the effect of this faked indexicality is to add authenticity to constructed imagery through our association of these types of devices – the use of night vision and an unexpected interaction of animal subject and camera – with genuine documentary footage.

In addition to adopting the trope of shared space of camera and dinosaur, *Planet Dinosaur* uses alternative stylistic strategies to authenticate its documentary status. Perhaps in an effort to mark it out as more than '*Walking with Dinosaurs* part two', a different documentary style, one not traditional to natural history filming, is mimicked in this later series. This is established from the outset of the series, where the images of an encounter between a herd of lumbering duck-billed ouranosaurus and a spinosaurus resemble those captured by a hand-held camera. Shaky movement, tracking shots, frequent changes in camera angle and position, many of which assume the point of view of the dinosaurs in a shot-reverse-shot fashion, give a sense of intimacy with the action. This privileged viewing position, one that persists throughout the series, would be unusual for a natural history documentary due to the practical restrictions of filming in the wild, but is familiar from reality television, with its use of hidden cameras, or observational documentary. It also helps immerse the viewer in the episode, although one could argue that immersion is interrupted by the frequent use of HUD-like displays.

These information graphics create pauses in the action of the episode by supplying corroborating evidence regarding the dinosaur currently featured. For example, after watching an epidexipteryx escape from the predatory grasp of a juvenile sinraptor by scampering up a tree in episode two, the image freezes and the small feather-tailed creature is highlighted in a white outline, accompanied by a computer data type sound effect (see Figure 2.1).[10] The full-screen image immediately shrinks down and spawns two further info screens, one giving the age, weight and length of the dinosaur, the other showing an image of the epidexipteryx relative to a human figure. This third screen then shows images pertaining to a fossil discovery in 2008. As this happens, the words and numbers on the second screen change to give information about the fossil discovery (such as location, discovery date, age of fossil) at the same time as a fourth screen appears giving close-up images

50 *Animated Documentary*

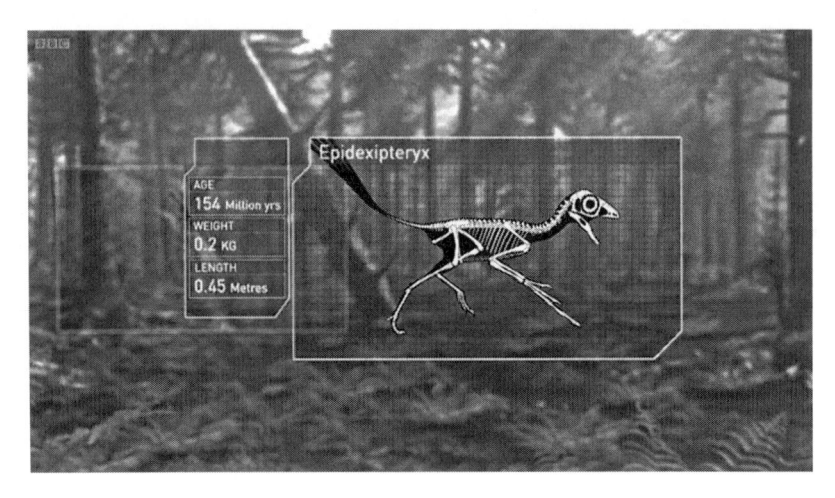

Figure 2.1 HUD-like displays in *Planet Dinosaur* (dir. Nigel Paterson, prod. Sara Cropley, BBC, 2011)

of the discovered fossil. While one could take the HUD-like displays in *Planet Dinosaur* as pandering to its desired audience through imitating a populist conception of mediated information, José van Dijck's reading of science documentaries offers another interpretation. She suggests that 'computer graphics and animatronics are to twenty-first-century physicists and palaeontologists what the microscope was to nineteenth-century biologists: new instruments allowing for new claims, but also for a retooling of the imagination' (van Dijck, 2006: 20). We could conclude from this that the differing visual strategies of *Walking with Dinosaurs* and *Planet Dinosaur* are reflective of changing cultural norms in documentary style and the mediation of information in factual and fictional contexts.

In *Walking with Dinosaurs* and *Planet Dinosaur* the soundtracks' voiceovers carry a significant amount of the burden of verifying the documentary veracity of the images and are vessels of both information and authentication. Both series use voice-of-God narration, delivered by the disembodied, gravitas-filled voices of, respectively, British thespians Kenneth Branagh and John Hurt. First used extensively in the Griersonian documentaries made in Britain from the 1930s onwards, and a key feature of what Bill Nichols has termed the 'expository' mode of documentary, the voice-of-God commentary is most commonly understood as a device of instruction, guiding the audience as to the meaning of the images and how they should be interpreted. In such

Digital Realities 51

expository documentaries, sound dominates and the voice-of-God speaks for the images. Stella Bruzzi (2006: 49) has characterised the dominant reading, in particular that of Bill Nichols, of these types of documentaries as follows:

> by blending omniscience and intimacy, they address the spectator directly; they set out an argument (thus implying forethought, knowledge and the ability to assimilate); they possess a dominant and constant perspective on the events they represent to which all elements within the film conform; they offer a solution and thereby a closure to the stories they tell.

The documentary voiceover is afforded a position of authority, over the images, over the narrative and over the viewer.

Kenneth Branagh's voiceover for *Walking with Dinosaurs* offers such a 'dominant and constant perspective' (Bruzzi, 2006: 49) on the events the series portrays and works in tandem with the various strategies of visual authentication discussed earlier to elide the ontology of the computer-generated images. The narration mostly just ignores this ontology, treating the images as if they were actual natural history footage filmed in the usual way. There are some instances, however, where the voiceover more overtly denies their non-photographic status. For example, towards the end of episode five, Branagh utters the following: 'under the sleeping trees it is almost pitch black, but with image-enhancement it is possible to get a laellynasaura's eye-view of the clan' as the image on screen switches from darkness to a green-tinged, grainy black-and-white image of a group of diminutive dinosaurs foraging under the arctic forest ferns. There is no indication here that these images were not captured using a camera on image-enhancement mode, even though we know this cannot have been the case, and narrator and audience collude in this denial. Similarly, Branagh's script never acknowledges the hypothetical basis of much of the material presented and there is no suggestion that, for example, mating rituals and other dinosaur behaviour is extrapolation and guesswork rather than fact.

Just as fact and hypothesis and film and CGI are conflated, the voiceover, by speaking in the present tense, also denies any temporal distance between image, narration and subject matter. Each episode begins, after a brief introductory sequence, with Branagh concertinaing time by directly positioning the viewer in the period covered, for example, in episode two, 'this is the Jurassic period', in episode six, 'it is the end of the Cretaceous period.' This denial of temporal disjuncture between viewer and image is established in the opening sequence of episode one, which contains the only aurally reflexive or meta-commentary of the series. Here, over filmed footage of a road running through a semi-rural area, Branagh instructs viewers to 'imagine you could travel back in time, to a time long before man, back across 65 million years'. As images of the landscape morph and change, and cars and road disappear, he says, 'now you've reached a remarkable period in Earth's history, known as the Cretaceous period. It is a different world.' Branagh then describes the images of the Cretaceous presented on screen before stating 'you will *witness* how the forces of nature conspire to drive these animals to extinction' (my emphasis). By evoking the concept of time travel, the series requests a suspension of disbelief that involves conflating the temporal distance between viewer and prehistory. This pretence of the 'constant perspective' (Bruzzi, 2006: 49) of present-tense witnessing is maintained throughout the series by Branagh's narration, which as well as situating viewers in the now of then, also presents the images of dinosaurs as if they were live-action, captured footage.

In her discussion of voiceover narration in documentary, Stella Bruzzi (2006: 57) suggests that this device tends to be demonised and distrusted by scholars of documentary because it 'is assumed to be undemocratic and inherently distortive. There is therefore the suspicion that a voice-over has the capacity to violate the "truth" revealed in the image.' Such a fear is based on the ontological assumptions underlying most of documentary studies – that of the privileged relationship between film and reality. However, to what extent is this fear short-circuited in a CGI documentary such as *Walking with Dinosaurs*, where the images do not have the same sort of capacity as live action? On the one hand, the voiceover guides audience interpretation of the 'truth' of the content of the images, explaining what we see – it is feasible that without the voiceover a viewer might believe, at least for a moment, they are watching a fictional programme, TV's answer to *Jurassic Park*. On the other, the narration also perpetuates the well-meaning deception of the images by denying their true ontology as constructed, computer-generated images the design of which was guided at times by scientific fact, but at others by science-based hypothesis and guesswork. If *Walking with Dinosaurs*' voiceover does 'violate the "truth"' of the image, this truth is not the same as that of live-action imagery.

John Hurt's voiceover for *Planet Dinosaur* is more transparent than Branagh's. The words spoken at the beginning of episode one, as in *Walking with Dinosaurs*, immediately work to orient the viewer temporally in relation to the series' subject matter, although this is a different position from the one adopted in *Walking with Dinosaurs*. Hurt's first words are: 'We are living through a golden age of dinosaur discoveries – all over the world, a whole new generation of dinosaurs has been revealed.' Rather than trying to position the viewer in the now of then, or the present tense of prehistory, *Planet Dinosaur* acknowledges, and even celebrates, the distance between present and past by emphasising the series' basis in the modern science of recent fossil discoveries and the 'latest imaging technology'. The implication in Hurt's words is that it is the 'cutting-edge research' of current developments in palaeontology and imaging that allows the programme to 'probe deeper and reveal more than ever before'. It is the technology and knowledge of the present that afford us this view of the past.

The narration maintains this attitude of reflexivity throughout the series, acknowledging the historical nature of the subject matter as well as the means of determining the information presented. Rather than pretending we are witnessing dinosaur behaviour as it happens, as in *Walking with Dinosaurs*, *Planet Dinosaur* makes it clear that the prehistoric creatures being recreated on screen lived in the past and Hurt often talks of them in the past tense. It also makes overt the evidence on which the images are based. The HUD-like digital displays discussed earlier are accompanied by explanatory voiceover from Hurt, which speaks of when and where fossils were discovered, as well as the deductions made from the finds. This series is as much about the process of discovering dinosaurs and understanding how they lived and died, as about the actual creatures themselves.

Although both series take different approaches to their narration, each voiceover is equally authoritative. Information is presented clearly, assertively and with little space for alternative interpretations of the images. Both fit the description of the didactic, expository voiceover narrations characterised by Bruzzi. This authority comes from the content of the scripts, the way the words are delivered and that they are delivered by disembodied voices that speak from above and beyond the content on screen. The voice becomes a 'guarantee of knowledge', Mary Ann Doane (2009: 325) suggests, because of 'its irreducibility to the spatiotemporal limitations of the body'. It is, she says, 'precisely because the voice is not localizable, because it cannot be yoked to a body, that it is capable of interpreting the image, producing its truth' (Doane, 2009: 324). However, while we may not see the bodies from which the voiceovers emanate, the identity of the voices' owners in *Walking with Dinosaurs* and *Planet Dinosaur* is important. The voices are disembodied, but not anonymous. They are male voices, a 'crucial component' of the traditional voiceover narration that carries with it the 'traditional tones of authority and universality' (Bruzzi, 2006: 64). The 'possession of knowledge' and 'privileged, unquestioned activity of interpretation' is, as Mary Ann Doane (2009: 324) observes, most often the preserve of the male speaker.[11]

These two specific male speakers also have clear, resonant voices, are trained in vocal delivery and carry a certain reputational baggage that reaffirms their all-seeing, all-knowing role. Prior to *Walking with Dinosaurs*, Branagh was better known for his Shakespearean adaptations and, more latterly, roles in quality historical television docudramas such as *Shackleton* (2002) and *Conspiracy* (2001), both of which reconstructed significant events from history. Prior to *Walking with Dinosaurs* Branagh established his narrator credentials on both sides of the Atlantic by lending his voice to the joint CNN–BBC television mini-series *Cold War* (1998).[12] In addition to his long and successful stage and screen career, Hurt's rich voice, now pleasingly gravelled by age, has guided audiences through several documentaries as well as the feature films *Dogville* (Lars von Trier, 2003), *Manderlay* (Lars von Trier, 2005) and Tom Tykwer's *Perfume* (2006). Branagh and Hurt, with their clearly identifiable voices, lend their respective dinosaur series the legitimacy and prestige gained through long and successful careers as serious and feted actors.

Walking with Dinosaurs was a resounding success for the BBC, gaining record viewing figures for a documentary (of any type) on the BBC.[13] The series received a great amount of press coverage, much of which positively reviewed the visuals as both spectacular and realistic (Banks-Smith, 1999; Hanks, 1999). Criticism of *Walking with Dinosaurs* was mostly due to the way it 'finesses the line between fact and speculation' (Hanks, 1999) and was levelled more against suppositions of dinosaur behaviour, and the definitive tone and content of Kenneth Branagh's narration, which Banks-Smith (1999) complained sounded 'surer of itself than the facts warranted', rather than the way the series looked. However, one expert critic did take issue with the representational style of the series, complaining that 'verisimilitude [is] fine when dealing with the present but not so acceptable when dealing with the very distant past' (McKie, 1999). Presumably this critic's consternation is driven by the impossibility of verifying much of the information presented in the series and that, as such, its realist visual style is potentially misleading. At the root of such a complaint is a point emphasized by Anneke M. Metz (2008: 336) when she criticises the use of CGI in primetime television documentaries because 'there is no telling whether the subject in question was actually photographed directly (thus providing a direct indexical linkage to the subject) or computer-generated (with the concomitant possibility that what is depicted is pure fiction).' This disquiet can help explain the need for the series' frequent recourse to markers of authenticity and faked indexicality in order to justify its status as documentary rather than CGI fantasy.

By 2011 such disquiet over the ontological blurring of CGI and live action seems to have all but disappeared. *Planet Dinosaur* created a much smaller splash than its predecessor. It was less popular with audiences and hardly registered with press or expert critics.[14] This more muted response was perhaps due to the fact that by 2011, the use of CGI in factual television programming was ubiquitous to the point of being unproblematic. To my eye, the animated visuals in *Planet Dinosaur*, while glossy and at times impressive in their verisimilitude, are in less danger of crossing the ontological line feared by Anneke M. Metz, and I would find it surprising to hear of a viewer mistaking the images, particularly the backgrounds, for filmed material. Perhaps, somewhat counter-intuitively, because the imagery in the later series is so clearly computer generated, a quality that I would argue is highlighted by the use of HUD-like displays, and because CGI is now a more familiar means of documentary representation, there is less need for *Planet Dinosaur* to authenticate its documentary agenda. Tropes such as the splatter of dinosaur bodily fluid on the 'camera lens', therefore, can be read as a nod to its predecessor and a way of knitting *Planet Dinosaur* into the tradition of BBC natural history programming, rather than a bid for documentary authenticity.

Tracing the sights and sounds of reality in Rotoshop and *Chicago 10*

Unlike live-action film, the ontology of digital animation does not imply an aesthetic, and photorealism is not the only option when using computer animation for mimetic substitution as a representational strategy in documentary. The 2007 feature documentary *Chicago 10* (Brett Morgen) and Bob Sabiston's short animated interviews use digitised, computer-aided versions of rotoscoping, or tracing over live-action film. *Chicago 10* uses animation to reconstruct witnessed historical events for which no filmed record exists. Combining animation, archival footage and photographs, the film details the run-up to the 1968 Democratic Convention in Chicago and the subsequent trial of members of the anti-war movement, including Yippie leader Abbie Hoffman and Black Panther Party co-founder Bobby Seale, who were accused of inciting riots during the convention.[15] Bob Sabiston has used his proprietary rotoscoping software, Rotoshop, to animate talking-head interviews, and between 1997 and 2007 made five short films of this type.[16] *Chicago 10* and Bob Sabiston's interview documentaries are not photorealist in the sense of *Walking with Dinosaurs* or *Planet Dinosaur*, and there is no danger of mistaking their animated images for film. They are, however, realist by way of being mimetic copies in their imitative representation of a reality that is recognisable from the animation. They also utilise a variety of visual and aural cues to confirm their status as documentaries.

Chicago 10 uses animation to make up for missing live-action material. The filmmakers had no shortage of footage for most of the events leading up to the trial, including gatherings of anti-war protesters and the convention itself, as much of this was covered in local and national news. However, the trial was not filmed, as cameras were not allowed in the courtroom, and these and other key scenes for which no filmed record exists were reconstructed using animation. These reconstructions of the trial were 'adapted from' the 23,000-page court transcript.[17] The film also reconstructs from aural evidence, such as the speeches given by the defendants at various public speaking engagements undertaken at the time of the trial and the aired phone calls between Abbie Hoffman and DJ Bob Fass on New York City's WBAI Radio.

Almost all of the animation in *Chicago 10* was created using the motion capture technique. Better known through its use in mainstream, high budget feature films such as *Avatar* (James Cameron, 2009) and the *Lord of the Rings* trilogy (Peter Jackson, 2001–03) this device is a technological descendent of the Rotoscope, which was invented by Max Fleischer in 1917. The Rotoscope enabled the animator to trace over live-action footage in order to create lifelike movement of animated characters. Motion capture is similarly about verisimilitude in movement and character design. Multiple sensors are placed on a performer's body to capture key points of movement and these data are mapped onto a 3-D character in order to translate a live performance into a digital one (see Menache, 2000: 1). The final animation can take any form and while it enables verisimilitude of movement it does not necessarily dictate a photorealistic style. Whereas fiction films often use motion capture to help attempt to create characters that are indiscernible from humans, *Chicago 10*'s animation is more stylized (see Figure 2.2). The film's visual references are taken as much from comic books and graphic novels as from reality and film.

Figure 2.2 Stylised, cartoon-like animation in *Chicago 10* (dir. Brett Morgen, Participant Productions, River Road Entertainment, 2007)

Chicago 10's relationship with the indexical is not as clear as the cut-and-dried mimicking of indexical media we see in *Walking with Dinosaurs* and *Planet Dinosaur*. The characters in *Chicago 10* look human, in fact they closely resemble their human counterparts. There would, for example, be no mistaking Abbie Hoffman for Judge Julius Hoffman or defence attorney Leonard Weinglass as each is distinctly recognisable. It was for this reason that director Brett Morgen used animation, instead of the more conventional dramatic re-enactments, as he felt the frequent intercutting between archival material and courtroom would draw attention to differences in appearance between an actor and the real person and be disengaging for viewers (Roadside Attractions, 2007: 17–18). However, there would also be no mistaking the animated image for film as the animation looks nothing like indexical imagery. It is bright, colourful and has a cartoon-like quality in which characters and objects are clearly outlined. Despite being created using motion capture, the characters' movement is sometimes blocky and jerky. Even more distracting is that their lip movement is rarely in synch with the dialogue. In short, it does not look like film and, contrary to the concerns Anneke M. Metz has about digital imagery in science documentaries, there is little danger of inciting ontological confusion.

This is not to say that *Chicago 10* does not contain some moments of visual verisimilitude that nod towards photorealism. When Abbie

58 *Animated Documentary*

Hoffman talks to Bob Fass from a telephone box on a snowy Chicago night, the condensation on the glass, through which we see Hoffman on the phone, is strikingly realistic. The droplets of water draw our attention because their photorealism is in stark contrast to the cartoony look of the rest of the animated scene. In general, however, the film is not attempting to fake indexicality in the manner of the BBC dino-docs. It instead uses other devices to visually and aurally endorse the animation as a viable means of reconstructing unfilmed events.

Visual links are often made between the animation and the archive material used in the film by matching the clothing on an animated embodiment of a character to that which they wore in a scene shown in archival footage, even if those two scenes are not necessarily contemporaneous. We cut, for example, from a courtroom scene in which Jerry Rubin wears a distinctive yellow-and-red striped shirt to archival footage of a press conference of him wearing the same shirt. This match on clothing happens throughout the film and it makes a mental connection between the animated reconstructions and the 'genuine' documentary news footage from the time. Other devices are used to subtly back up the animation. After the animation of Allen Ginsberg giving testimony, in which he recites his poem about a wet dream, we cut to original footage of a news anchor describing that event. This second scene is narratively unnecessary, as it offers no more information than we have already gained in the animated sequence. However, it corroborates both the previous scene and, by association, all of the animated reconstructions.

Another sequence in the film goes further than these editing and structural techniques by compositing live action and animation. On day four of the convention leaders of the anti-war movement, including Dave Dellinger and Jerry Rubin, addressed the gathered crowds from the band shell in Lincoln Park prior to the fateful march to downtown. This is depicted through a composite of animation and live action as Rubin and Dellinger are animated over the filmed footage of the surroundings and the crowds. The animation is blended with the live action to the extent that it matches the grainy quality and washed-out colour of the original material. Unlike the courtroom scenes, these moments of animation are more photorealistic and at times it is hard to discern the animation from the blurry live-action footage in which it is placed.

The piggy-backing of the animation onto live action in *Chicago 10* does two things. As previously mentioned, it works to establish the animated sequences as sincere reconstructions. It also works to legitimate questionable moments in the animated portion of the story. Even though the animation of the court scenes, for example, is based on transcripts, there is still a certain amount of hypothesising that went into their reconstruction. For example, any parts of the reconstruction that were not recorded in the court transcript must have been guessed at or extrapolated, such as the physical gestures of the defendants. One wonders, for example, if Jerry Rubin really did fly a paper airplane across the courtroom as a witness gave testimony against him. Similarly, we could question whether a party scene, where Hoffman and Rubin discuss ideas for protesting the convention and form the Yippie group, is based on the same sort of oral or written evidence as the trial. Or is this just an imagining of an event that the filmmakers knew to have happened?

The extrapolated or hypothesised nature of these moments is potentially elided by presenting them in the same way as the rest of the animated sequences, animation that is framed as a genuine documentary tool of reconstruction. The film even goes so far as to reposition the relative fictional status of animation and live action in one courtroom scene. When undercover police officer Robert Pierson gives evidence about working as Rubin's bodyguard, he recalls an incident in Lincoln Park. As he retells the events, the animation simulates a camera pushing tight into his face and moving around the side of his head. As we pass his left ear, the animation segues into live-action black-and-white archive footage from the park. In this way, animation and live action switch their traditional roles. As will be discussed in later chapters, animation has often been used to 'get inside' someone's head and to show their point of view. In this instance, though, it is through live action that Robert Pierson's memory is conveyed.

All these devices add up to give the animation the same status, in terms of representing reality, as the 'genuine' documentary material. The framing of the animation within a documentary context of unproblematic photographic-based imagery and the easy slippage between the animation and the original footage works to justify its inclusion as a tool to retell the events surrounding the convention and trial. The animation is, the film implies, showing us things as they happened and is offering us the same knowledge that we would have gained had we been eyewitness to the events as they occurred.

The epistemological parity of animation and live action is mirrored in the soundtrack of the film, which does not distinguish between indexical and non-indexical material. Some of the voice recordings heard are original, that is, taken from the time of the trial – most obviously, during the sequences of archival footage in which we see and hear characters speaking. Some of the animated sections are also accompanied by oral documentary material, such as the radio show conversations between Abbie Hoffman and Bob Fass. Most of the trial, however, is vocally reconstructed by actors, many of whom took pains to achieve oral verisimilitude. Hank Azaria, a skilled voice mimic, plays both Abbie Hoffman and Allen Ginsberg. Hoffman in particular had a distinctive Boston accent, one that Azaria convincingly imitates. Morgen has also discussed how Roy Sheider took particular care to match the inflections and ticks of the presiding judge. This oral mimicry became possible when the filmmakers uncovered a sound recording of the trial, evidence not previously known to exist (Morgen, 2008). In a further move to oral/aural authenticity, Morgen recruited defence attorney Leonard Weinglass to re-voice his original words. Morgen has mentioned that he was particularly pleased when he heard that Weinglass, nearly forty years later, still sounded much as he did in 1969 (Morgen, 2008).

While Morgen shunned the use of actors and filmed reconstructions in *Chicago 10* for fear of the disruptive juxtaposition of real person and actor, he showed no such reluctance in terms of the film's soundtrack. The film shifts between the aurally indexical and the aurally mimicked, with no indication to the audience as to whether they are hearing, for example, Hoffman or Azaria-as-Hoffman. This aural indeterminacy reinforces the parity suggested visually between animation and live action, in terms of viable means of documentary representation. The smooth elision of original recording and oral reconstruction works to validate the latter, just as the integration of animation and live action implies the suitability of animation for reconstructing the past.

This elision presumes, perhaps, that audiences are less attentive to what they hear than to what they see, or at least less adept at telling the difference between the real Abbie Hoffman and Azaria's impression. Somewhat at odds with this, however, is the casting of known actors to voice the key roles, including Nick Nolte, Liev Shreiber, Mark Ruffalo and Jeffrey Wright. For those who recognise these performers from their voices, there is the threat of a viewing experience where 'animated bodies [a]re haunted by the specter of (often non-matching) "real" bodies' (Beckman, 2011: 271). Mary Ann Doane (2009: 324) has suggested that in narrative film, voice and image are matched so that the 'voice serves as a support for the spectator's recognition with and his/her identification of, as well as with, the star.' This suggests that if the voice–body match is slightly off-kilter, speaker identification becomes difficult, or fails entirely. Such disjuncture in *Chicago 10* is potentially heighted by the poor lip-synching in the animated sections. As Steven Connor (2000: 20) has observed:

> in cinema, we appear to need the specific verification of seeing a speaking mouth at the very moment of its utterance in order to manage the magic or scandal of an unattributed voice; the confirming obverse of this being the uneasiness induced in us by inexpert dubbing, or the faulty synchronization of image and sound.

In *Chicago 10*, the technical shortcomings of the animation mean that while voice is synched to body, the synchronisation of lip movement to spoken word is far from perfect and could potentially undo the film's efforts towards visual and aural cohesion.

Bob Sabiston developed Rotoshop in the 1990s and first used it in 1997 to make a ninety-second short for an MTV competition. Inspired by Nick Park's animation of 'real people' in the *Creature Comforts* series (1989 onwards), Sabiston wanted to 'capture something [he] liked about people's personalities'.[18] After filming interviews with people in Austin, Texas, Sabiston looked for a computer programme that would allow him to trace on top of frames of video footage. When his search proved futile, he developed the software himself. The interpolation process, Sabiston's hi-tech answer to the in-betweening of traditional hand-drawn cel animation, evolved when he realized the tracing process would go more quickly if he did not have to painstakingly draw all the lines that barely changed between frames. Instead he programmed the software to best guess the movement between key frames based on information it had already been given.

The five animated interview films made by Sabiston and colleagues at his Austin-based company, Flat Black Films, document exchanges between filmmakers and subjects. Several of the shorts (*Project Incognito* [1997], *Roadhead* [1998] and *Grasshopper* [2003]) feature interviews with people met in public spaces and two (*Snack and Drink* [1999] and *The Even More Fun Trip* [2007]) are encounters with Ryan Power, a young man with autism. The aesthetics of Rotoshop, while recognisable across the five films, change considerably in the decade between *Project Incognito* and *The Even More Fun Trip*. The former displays a simple, monochrome style, featuring characters drawn in black outline on a white background. By 2007, the software had developed to allow use of colour, fill and shadow to create a more detailed, and relatively, photorealistic representation of the interview scene. It is the two more photorealistic shorts, *Grasshopper* and *The Even More Fun Trip*, that are of most interest to the discussion of visual realism in animated documentary.

The fourteen-minute long *Grasshopper* is an unedited interview in which 'park-bench philosopher AJ Vadehra expounds on astrology and more productive avenues of contemplation.'[19] The film is animated using a consistent green–grey colour palette, which contrasts to the visual style of earlier films, for example the vibrant psychedelia of *Snack and Drink* and the black-and-white figuration of *Project Incognito* and *Roadhead*. It also displays a depth of field comprising planes of background, filling in the park behind Vadehra with trees, grass, people and so on. This, combined with the use of shading on Vadehra's features, creates an illusion of three-dimensionality. Often, Vadehra's features are clearly distinguishable and the shading and fill on his face realistically resemble the shadow and light that would have fallen on him in the park that day (see Figure 2.3). This photorealism is also apparent in *The Even More Fun Trip*, Sabiston's second film featuring Ryan Power, in which Sabiston, Ryan and a group of friends visit a Texas theme park.

Figure 2.3 Photorealism in *Grasshopper* (dir. Bob Sabiston, Flat Black Films, 2003)

Rotoshop animation is created by digitally tracing over previously filmed video footage, and in the final version only the animation remains. Much like *Chicago 10*, however, there would be little risk of a viewer confusing *Grasshopper*, or any of Sabiston's rotoshopped interviews, with the original video footage on which it was based. Rather than mimetic substitution of animation being necessitated by a lack of original filmed material, for Sabiston it is a creative choice to represent reality in this way. Similarly, rather than glossing over the ontology of the image, as *Chicago 10* and the dinosaur documentaries could be accused of doing, Sabiston's films draw attention to their means of construction, leading a viewer to puzzle over how they were created and the nature of their relationship with reality. In fact, there is little in the look of Sabiston's animation that implies its documentary status, especially as the same animation technique has been used in wholly fictional films. An irony given that of all the films discussed in this chapter, Sabiston's have the most direct visual and aural relationship with reality by virtue of being so closely based on video footage and using soundtracks of documentary interviews.

Instead, the documentary veracity of Sabiston's interview shorts is confirmed through adhering to many of the visual and aural codes of documentary realism. Interviews often start and finish abruptly, with some of the technical tasks of filmmaking appearing on screen or being heard on the soundtrack, and all of the films begin *in media res*. *Roadhead* and *The Even More Fun Trip* both begin in a car travelling down the highway, looking out of the windshield at the road ahead, halfway through a conversation between the passengers, which we hear off-screen. *Grasshopper* begins with the very last few seconds of a previous interviewee onscreen. This smiling woman laughs to the words 'she is very wise' heard from off-screen before Vadehra steps into frame and takes a seat on the park bench. A hand then protrudes into the screen as another voice, also off-screen says '... just going to clip this to your collar' as Sabiston attaches a microphone to Vadehra's coat. The interview context is similarly established in *Roadhead* when we see Colleen, the first interviewee, fumble over clipping on her microphone. After introducing herself ('ok...umm...my name is Colleen White...and I work at ...') she hesitates and asks for confirmation of the filmmakers' intentions and Sabiston reassures her that she does not have to say exactly what she does for a living. In these films, we not only see interview documentaries, but also hear elements of their production, which works to authenticate them as documentaries.

Further authentication comes from the presence of the shaky and handheld camera and the inconsistent, imperfect framing that results, familiar from observational documentary. When Sabiston and his friends arrive at Ryan's house in *The Even More Fun Trip*, we see the front door from a low, canted angle, as if the camera is being held loosely down at the cameraman's side. A sense of 'being there' is captured in the roller-coaster sequence, in which we get a front row view, alongside Ryan, of the hair-raising swoops and drops of the ride. This sense is amplified by accompanying production sound of rushing wind and the yells of the roller-coaster passengers. The sound in these films is significant as a confirmation of their documentary status. It often has a rough production aesthetic, which reminds us that this element of the film retains its indexical link with reality. Often the mix of different sound elements is slightly off, as in the fast-food restaurant sequence in *The Even More Fun Trip*, where the background noise of the music being played in the restaurant threatens the clarity of the dialogue. We often, also, have the sense of eavesdropping on a conversation that is not being spoken directly into the microphones. Many of the films begin and end this way and often the visuals cut out at the end of a film while the conversation continues. For example, in *Snack and Drink*, we can hear Sabiston talking to someone in Ryan's apartment as the credits roll. The visual impression of filming-on-the-fly works in tandem with this happenstance sound recording.

The lip-synching issues present in *Chicago 10* are avoided in Sabiston's films, where presumably the Rotoshop technique allows for accurate tracing of lip movement as characters talk. Invariably, whenever characters' mouths can be seen as they talk, the lips move in synchronisation with what they say. Even in the more expressive iterations of Rotoshop such as *Snack and Drink*, which are discussed further in Chapter 3, when a mouth is seen and moving, it is in step with the dialogue. Ian Garwood (2012: 55) has observed that while there is no requirement for lip-synching in Rotoshop, Sabiston's films tend 'to accept lip-sync ideology as the taken-for-granted norm'. This has an effect, as Garwood suggests, of reminding viewers of Rotoshop's close relationship with the original filmed material that forms its foundation. The primary effect of lip-synching in live-action cinema is, as Mary Ann Doane (2009: 320), Rick Altman (1980: 59) and Steven Connor (2000: 20) have observed, to obfuscate the heterogeneity of image and sound, the latter coming from a completely different source than the illusion of cinema would have us believe. In a format such as Rotoshop, lip-synching has the same effect, but it also helps to assert the sound's indexicality, a characteristic that in turn helps reaffirm the interview shorts' status as documentaries.

However, as mock-documentary shows us, the visual and aural stylistic traits of documentary filming do not necessarily guarantee a film's non-fictional status. The unequivocal authentication must come from beyond the text itself. In the case of Sabiston's shorts, a viewer might come across these films via Sabiston's website, flatblackfilms.com. Here, the animated documentaries are clearly identified as such, along with production information revealing, for example, how interviewees were sourced or the background context to the films. While aspects of the films' visual presentation indicates their status as documentary, this can only be confirmed from a paratext such as the filmmaker's website and other extra-textual sources.

Paratextual authentication

The need for paratextual authentication is demonstrated by the BBC's release of such material simultaneously with the broadcasts of *Walking with Dinosaurs* and *Planet Dinosaur*. For the first series, a fifty-minute special, *Making of Walking with Dinosaurs* (1999), was aired two days after the premiere of the first episode on BBC1. The timing of the broadcast, the fact that it was shown before episode two and would also coincide with any reviews of episode one, indicates the intention for the special to validate the scientific information being given in the series as well as to justify its style of presentation. In fact, the episode indirectly responds to many of the points raised in the critics' initial response to episode one, which appeared in press the day before the *Making of* episode was aired.

The opening voiceover reiterates the claims of the series when narrator Kenneth Branagh states:

> If a film crew ventured back 65 million years they would be among dinosaurs in their natural habitat; they could bring back unique images of a time when reptiles ruled on earth; images we thought we'd never see. This is exactly what the makers of the TV series *Walking With Dinosaurs* wanted to achieve: a portrait of a lost world as it really was.[20]

The claim that *Walking with Dinosaurs* is showing dinosaurs as they would have been filmed, had that been possible, is emphasised by the images the voiceover accompanies. As we hear Branagh's assuring words, we see live-action footage of a film crew carrying equipment into a clearing. The crew stops in their tracks as they hear an ominous distant roaring, only continuing when the coast seems clear. As the crew set up their camera, a computer-generated tyrannosaurus walks into the clearing, and into the frame of their shot. The feeling of eyewitnessed material that is evoked by the series' photorealistic animation is reinforced in this, albeit light-hearted, opening sequence of the behind-the-scenes documentary.

The veracity of the information presented in the series is corroborated by the opinions of several expert advisors featured in the *Making of* episode. Segments that describe the creation of the animation and the animatronic models are cut together with scenes of palaeontologist Peter Larson and his team excavating a T-rex skeleton in South Dakota. Larson lies in the dust as he gently scrapes away dirt from a prehistoric bone and tells us that contemporary palaeontologists are now using evidence from excavations like this to theorize dinosaur behaviour. Another advisor, Dr David Norman, sits in a lab and claims 'it's not unreasonable to suspect that many dinosaurs were colourful in many ways and used colour in various aspects of their behaviour – so there's no harm in introducing colours to reconstructions.' Through the words of these two scientific experts the BBC astutely offsets one of the major criticisms of the series: the assertive presentation of hypotheses regarding dinosaur behaviour and appearance.

James Moran (1999: 265) has suggested, in an examination of the documentary nature of animated dinosaur imagery, that 'what seems most necessary to the credibility of dinosaur imagery rests not so much upon its perception as an unmediated record of reality as upon the spectator's trust that the images, as documentary, were generated in good faith.' The *Making of Walking with Dinosaurs* reinforces this idea, confirming to a potentially sceptical audience that the images were created 'in good faith' and under the advice of leading scientists undertaking cutting-edge palaeontology research. *Planet Dinosaur*, perhaps in a response to the reception of *Walking with Dinosaurs*, contains much of this assurance of good faith within the text itself. The frequent recourse to the fossil record, through the use of the HUD-like displays, corroborates what we see in the CGI sequences of dinosaur action. Yet, the series' key paratext, its website, includes six behind-the-scenes clips that detail the making of the series. Several of these clips work to further authenticate the documentary status of the series itself, a status that is re-confirmed in written text on the website as well as that on the website of Jellyfish Pictures, the London-based visual effects, animation

Digital Realities 67

and motion graphics company that partnered with BBC Science to make *Planet Dinosaur*.

For example, in the *Finding Stories* clip, producer Nigel Paterson goes to some length to emphasise the factual basis of the series. After acknowledging that you can create anything using CGI, he reiterates the need for *Planet Dinosaur* to be 'based on things that are reasonable', and infers that the determination of 'reasonable' in the case of these dinosaurs included an involved research process of 'collating papers'.[21] This is echoed on the Jellyfish website with the comment that '[A]s usual with a BBC factual series, it was essential that the quality of the information and science was second to none and so Paterson and his team had to be extremely thorough in ensuring the veracity of their stories' (Jellyfish Pictures, 2012). The implication in the BBC clip and the Jellyfish website text is that *Planet Dinosaur* is based on bona fide research and, as such, its images can be taken as an as accurate a portrayal of dinosaur life as permitted by contemporary scientific knowledge.

The reassertion of the factuality of *Planet Dinosaur* can be understood in the context of the criticisms of guesswork and supposition levelled against *Walking with Dinosaurs*. Nigel Paterson refers to this as the 'perennial problem' of the earlier series that left people questioning 'how do they know that?'[22] He cites this as the reason for including the fossil record HUD-like visualisations in the series. It might also be what leads him to spend a certain amount of time, in the *Finding Stories* clip, clarifying the nature of the evidence on which the series is based. Here he justifies the recourse to natural history, in the absence of significant evidence in the fossil record of dinosaur behaviour. He acknowledges this as a 'grey area', but then asserts that it is reasonable to extrapolate from contemporary wildlife these 'fundamental instincts' and include them as part of the 'cocktail of evidence' for the series. Thus Paterson assures sceptics that even the parts of the series that are not directly backed up within each episode via fossil record evidence displayed in the HUDs, such as some aspects of behaviour and characteristics like skin colour, tone and texture, are based on fact.

The excess of animated realism

The paratexts for these animated documentaries that use animation in mimetic substitution do not work solely to reassert their factual status. At the same time as working to authenticate the animated documentary as a representation of reality, they also frequently invite us to marvel at the animated documentary image, and its technological and artistic construction. This reasserts the sense of spectacle that is often found in the images themselves. *Walking with Dinosaurs* is packed with sweeping vistas, aerial and wide-angle shots and images that we can assume are intended to provoke awe and, as Karen D. Scott (2003: 30) has termed it, 'wonderment'. The critical response to the series seems to confirm this. The *Guardian*'s Nancy Banks-Smith (1999) applauded the visual grandeur of the show, saying, 'visually, it's a bobby dazzler', admiring that 'the dinosaurs are computer generated down to the rippling twitch of their diminishing tails'. Similarly, Robert Hanks (1999) called the series 'simply marvellous'. The kinetic, dynamic style of *Planet Dinosaur* seems equally designed to draw our attention to the imagery, which is realised in glossy, 'polished and jazzed up' CGI (Sutcliffe, 2011).

Perhaps in a less overt way, *Chicago 10* and Bob Sabiston's interview documentaries also invite us to notice the image as a thing in itself, to take pleasure in it, and to enjoy its spectacle. For both *Chicago 10* and the Sabiston interviews, animation provides a more visually appealing option to the conventional alternative. While Sabiston has asserted no commercial aim for his short films, it is hard to deny the attraction of the imagery in these interview shorts. Indeed, as Caroline Ruddell (2012: 18) has observed of the rotoshopped feature film *Waking Life*, 'the visual stylistics of the film are surely the most noticeable aspect on viewing.' One could question, therefore, whether *Grasshopper* and *The Even More Fun Trip*, for example, would be as visually appealing if presented as the original video interviews.

Appeal was a guiding factor in choosing animation for *Chicago 10* in the hopes that it would draw the youth of the late 1990s to a story of activism and protest. Animation was thought as something that would attract that demographic and Morgen wanted to 'do the film in a way that resonates with kids today [...] in a language they understand [...] without talking heads and a narrator and those trappings' (Roadside Attractions, 2007: 16).[23] The animation in *Chicago 10* can be also read as more than a commercial tactic. For Karen Beckman (2011), aspects of the film's visual and oral aesthetics override the parts, described earlier, where documentary and animation are more seamlessly interwoven into a realist whole. Here I would agree with Beckman, and indeed in a previous analysis of *Chicago 10* (Honess Roe, 2009), I drew attention to Morgen's comment that he was motivated to use animation after reading Jerry Rubin's description of the court case as a 'cartoon show' (Roadside Attractions, 2007: 18). Morgen says that for him it was 'so obvious. By animating the trial I would not only avoid all the clichés [...] but I was able to make a statement about the circus-like nature of

Digital Realities 69

the courtroom' (Roadside Attractions, 2007: 18). Indeed, much of the film's thematic resonance comes from an aesthetic that combines elements of realism and elements of the cartoon. The animation helps, as Beckman (2011: 270–1) observes, to represent the trial as the theatrical spectacle that it was at the time.

Spectacle is something more usually associated with fiction film than documentary. In fiction film its typical function, as suggested by Laura Mulvey (2009: 716), is as a moment of excess than stands outside the cohesive progression of the narrative. Andrew Darley (2000: 191) points out that spectacle is 'largely vision-centred and is about direct and immediate sensual pleasures'. Although Tom Gunning has disagreed with the opposing of narrative and spectacle, he does characterise the 'cinema of attractions' of pre-1906 film as being based on an 'ability to show something' and an 'exhibitionist cinema' (Gunning, 1990: 57). These descriptions imply a depthlessness that goes with spectacle. Spectacle is about surface pleasure that activates us on the level of sensation, rather than activating us cognitively on the deeper level of meaning and knowledge.

Bill Nichols (2010: 128) has observed, spectacle is generally distrusted in documentary studies scholarship, treated as 'an embarrassing fellow traveller rather than as a central component'. This is something Keith Beattie (2008: 23), following Brian Winston, attributes to being due to the looming shadow of the Griersonian approach to documentary as a sober, expository tool of education and persuasion. However, Elizabeth Cowie (2011) and Beattie (2008) have opposed this position, suggesting that documentary spectacle has epistemological potential. In particular, they make links between spectacle, pleasure of the visual and a desire for knowledge. Such a link is also suggested by Gunning (1990: 58), with his claim that 'the cinema of attractions directly solicits spectator attention, inciting *visual curiosity*' (emphasis added). The visual appeal of animation in the films discussed in this chapter can be thought of as provoking a desire to know about the films' subject matter. This is clearly the case for *Chicago 10*, with the producers' expressed aim that the film's aesthetic presentation would prompt younger viewers to take an interest in activism and feel encouraged to express political discontent around the time of the US invasion of Afghanistan. In addition to the surface attraction of animated visuals, animation also appeals to audience interest in the technologies of production. This interest is longstanding, and Gunning (1990: 58) tells us that early cinema-goers went as much to see the means of exhibition as the exhibition itself. Animation, in particular, seems to draw such interest, and Paul Ward

(2000: n.p.) notes that 'the tension between animated films as, on the one hand, a novelty in terms of technique (or process) and, on the other hand, a novelty in terms of presentation, is something that resonates throughout the history of animated films.'

In the case of the substitution of mimetic animation in documentary, I would suggest that the spectacular appeal is not just of the images themselves and of the means of their production, but also their sometimes unclear ontology. Michael O'Pray (1998: 435) has compared photorealistic animation to *trompe l'oeil* painting, in that part of the appeal of these films comes from our 'thrill to the virtuosity of the means of representation itself'. This is something Vanessa Schwartz (1999: 153) has noted, in her discussion of panoramas in *fin-de-siecle* Paris when spectators marvelled not at the subjects represented, but at the means of representation and its technological illusionism. A similar kind of pleasure is elicited in particular in *Walking with Dinosaurs* and *Planet Dinosaur*. Robert Hanks (1999) praised *Walking with Dinosaurs* as 'staggeringly real' and 'full of striking details', and Tom Sutcliffe (2011) seems to be implying an impressive realism in *Planet Dinosaur* when he says in describing the 'digital star treatment' of the spinosaurus that 'every ripple of its flank and every gluey strand of its saliva registered on screen'. There is a pleasure to be taken in *Walking with Dinosaurs* and *Planet Dinosaur* in knowing that the images are not real (i.e. filmed or videoed) but appreciating quite how real they look. This, Paul Ward (2005b: 162) claims, amounts to the paradox 'where CGI is admired for its ability to mimic with amazing accuracy the surface details of phenomenal reality. "Look how *real* this looks! (though I know, *really*, that it isn't real)" is arguably what passes through viewers' minds' (emphasis in original). In the Sabiston shorts that lean towards the photorealistic, there is a similar thrill in the ontological obliqueness of the images – that they retain something of the filmic despite so clearly being animation. Similarly, *Chicago 10* could be praised for how much the animated likeness of Abbie Hoffman captures the essence of the original or how seamlessly animation and archive footage are interwoven.

Paratexts surrounding these films amplify the idea that the realism of the image is a source of spectacle and something to be admired. They do this by offering insights into the complex processes and technologies of production and inviting viewers to marvel at the means by which the prehistoric world is brought back to life in such a realistic way. The *Making of Walking with Dinosaurs* special devotes some time to revealing the efforts of the animators as they strive to make the digital footage of the dinosaurs look as realistic as possible. Animator Virgil Manning talks of the difficulty of animating the tyrannosaurus in motion as the dinosaur's large size means he has to use lots of squash and stretch, a traditional animation technique in which a part of a character or object are manipulated, squashed and stretched to simulate natural movement, around the feet and ankles to convey a sense of its five-ton weight. We also see visual effects supervisor Mike McGee showing how computer technology is used to seamlessly blend the animated dinosaurs into the filmed backgrounds. McGee expertly manipulates the computer software to match the colour of the dinosaurs to the surroundings as well as to create shadows and to break up the shafts of light that are filtered through the trees as a dinosaur moves through a forest setting, all actions that make the animated scene appear more realistic.

The revelation of the labour and effort involved in realistically reconstructing reality via digital animation occurs again in several of the behind-the-scenes clips available on the BBC's *Planet Dinosaur* website. Three clips, *Selling the World*, *Creating the Action*, and *Building a Dinosaur*, detail the highly involved production process, from creating the backgrounds to modelling, painting and rigging the dinosaurs. The process appears intricate, protracted, and one that can only be carried out by highly skilled experts. This is reiterated on the Jellyfish Pictures website, which explains the pipeline that facilitated the organisation and streamlining of the demanding production emphasised 'efficiency, specialism and precision' in order to deliver more than 2,500 CGI shots in just over a year. The website goes on to list the vast range of departments and skills required, asserting that 'every person in the pipeline [is] absolutely proficient in their area of expertise' (Jellyfish Pictures, 2012).

The enigmatic ontology of Bob Sabiston's animated interview shorts also engenders curiosity as to their production. Caroline Ruddell (2012: 18) has observed that 'any discussion of Rotoshop [...] automatically incorporates the question of the role of technologies.' A page on Bob Sabiston's website implies how the visual indeterminacy of the rotoshopped image leads to incorrect assumptions regarding its production process. 'Despite some appearances to the contrary', it informs readers, 'this software does not use filters, image-processing or any kind of motion capture technology' (Flat Black Films, n.d.). Furthermore, it is stressed that 'the process is user-driven and can be extremely time consuming' (Flat Black Films, n.d.). This tells us there is manual labour and human hand required to create imagery with such a mutable relationship with reality. Such paratextual information heightens the paradox of real and spectacle that is apparent in the films' imagery, an excess that compounds the absence of indexical link between these photorealist and realist animated images and reality.

In animated documentaries in which animation functions as mimetic substitution, the representational strategy of mimesis frequently works to validate the factual content of these films and programmes, and asserts their status as a documentary text. This factual status is something that is often reasserted in the paratextual, for example in 'behind-the-scenes' material, websites, or press interviews. At the same time, and paradoxically, the animation exceeds its role as a simple stand-in for live action. Aspects of quality, aesthetics and style means the animation draws attention to itself, even in efforts to appear indistinguishable from indexical imagery. Often, the films seem to be inviting viewers to marvel at the spectacle of their visual presentation and its means of production, be it through kinetic animated cinematography or animated images that are increasingly indistinguishable from film. The constructed and spectacular aspect of these animated documentaries is re-emphasised in extratextual material that draws attention to the complexities and technical wizardry of the production process.

In this way, the extratextual articulates a tension between surface and meaning, spectacle and knowledge, wonder and authenticity – a tension that is already present in the films. This tension, I would argue, is a pleasurable one. There is a delight in knowing those dinosaurs are animated, and quite how tricky it was to do so, while at the same time marvelling at quite how *realistic* the whole thing is. We know these images are not 'real', in the documentary-indexical-evidence sort of way, but they still have a very real impact on what we take away from these films.

What this adds up to is animated documentaries that are far from the closed texts suggested of *Walking with Dinosaurs* by Andrew Darley (2003). For all attempts to seamlessly integrate animation and live-action imagery, or to elide any ontological difference between the two visually and aurally, I would argue that we can always tell the difference. The attempts at elision may work to smooth over differences between animation and documentary, but the excess of animation always breaks the surface. Be that in the spectacular verisimilitude of photorealism of *Walking with Dinosaurs* and *Planet Dinosaur*, the ontological elusiveness of Sabiston's Rotoshop, or the overt cartoonish aesthetic of *Chicago 10*. These films, by borrowing the aural and visual tropes of documentary realism and mimicking the material appearance of indexical imagery, show us that animation can be a valid tool of documentary representation. In so doing, they query the presumptions of documentary realism, along with the privileged relationship between film and reality. Yet at the same time, the animation demands attention in its own right, both in the texts themselves and via the paratexts that surround them. The animation is something that must be contended with in our reception of these documentaries.

3
Animated Interviews

Documentary and testimony are so intertwined that we rarely question the inclusion of the latter in the former, or even the substitution of the former for the latter. In *The Politics of Documentary* Michael Chanan (2007) recalls being summoned to a 1978 trial to present footage shot at an anti-Fascist rally. The layout of the courtroom demanded the projector be set up in the witness box in order that the court could see the image. This ironic anecdote demonstrates how documentary footage can unquestioningly be taken as evidence – in this case the footage speaking for itself and giving testimony from the witness stand.

Talking-head interviews have become the primary way to facilitate documentary subjects' testimony. This documentary trope, which is now so familiar, was first explored by Grierson's cohort of young filmmakers in 1930s' Britain. The successful inclusion of interviews in *Housing Problems* (Arthur Elton, Edgar Antsy, 1935) cemented this device as a tool of documentary production. Jack C. Ellis and Betsy A. McLane (2005: 68) have pointed out that the use of direct interviews was experimental at the time and while director Arthur Elton had previously explored the journalistic approach of asking documentary subjects to speak their interview responses directly to the camera in *Workers and Jobs* (1935), it was *Housing Problems* that 'more clearly defined the potential values of the device' (Barnouw, 1993: 95). The words of the slum dwellers, who describe their poor living conditions and anticipate the prospect of better, healthier lives in the new mass housing, back up the film's argument of slum clearance in favour of modern, high-rise housing estates (these ones fuelled by the Gas Board, who sponsored the film). The Griersonians continued to use interviews in their films and established testimony and first-person oral accounts as an accepted, even integral part of the documentary. This is true to the extent that, as Chris Holmlund and Cynthia Fuchs (1997: 4) have pointed out, the interview is now one of the recognisable markers of documentary on film and television.

To testify to something, and to give testimony, is synonymous with bearing witness, giving evidence and asserting and affirming the truth. Brian Winston (1995: 140) has noted, 'the law is the source of a critical documentary technique – the interview.' Once the interview was accepted and naturalised as legitimate legal procedure it was 'borrowed for journalism and [...] then borrowed again for radio and the cinema' (Winston, 1995: 140). The legal origin of this now integral part of documentary results in the documentary interview carrying the evidential weight of a legal testimony. Just as testimony is evidence in a court of law, so it becomes evidence in a radio or screen documentary. In the same way the interview is a legitimate source of the truth in a legal trial, it becomes a marker of truth, proof and authenticity in a documentary. This is despite documentary interviews being, as Jane Chapman (2009: 105) describes them, 'problematic'. While interviewee intentions may be genuine, 'witness contribution in the form of memories can be unreliable – people tend to invent and embellish, usually unintentionally' (Chapman, 2009: 105).

Whether or not what is being said is factually accurate, the 'default function' of documentary viewers, according to Bill Nichols (1993: 178), is to 'trust those who speak to the camera unless given a reason to do otherwise'. Our tendency to trust those who testify in a documentary film is something that can be capitalised on by filmmakers. Predominantly, it underlies the assumption that the audience will take a documentary speaker at her word. However, our trust can also be drawn on for ironic, humorous or reflexive purposes. Mitchell Block exploits the audience's belief of a young woman's revelation of a rape in *No Lies* (1973) to comment on the manipulative possibilities of a format (documentary) and aesthetic (observational filming). The pact of honesty and trust among filmmaker, participant and viewer is satirised through the earnest, ridiculous interviews with a fake heavy metal band in *This Is Spinal Tap* (1984). In Errol Morris' *The Thin Blue Line* (1985), the interweaving of interviews and stylised re-enactments encourages reflection on the credibility of witness testimony.

That the interview is open to such exploitation and manipulation is indicative of its assumed status and use within documentary film. For something to be imitated, satirised or spoofed, it must already exist as a tendency or recognisable characteristic. This status is established and perpetuated through stylistic traits of framing and setting, for example, editing together talking heads with other corroborating evidence such as archival or observational footage. Another common strategy to enhance the speaker's credibility, and thus encourage the default tendency to trust, is through what Bill Nichols (1993: 178) calls 'iconic authentication'. This includes positioning the interviewee in front of shelves of relevant books, or other objects or locations that establish the status of their testimony as truthful, dependable and authoritative.

While the veracity and authenticity of filmed testimony is asserted through elements of style and filming, the body of the interviewee has been theorised as significant in the way we gain knowledge from documentary interviews. Nichols claims we learn as much from what we see as from what we hear in interview documentaries when he says, 'it is not simply the knowledge possessed by witnesses and experts that needs to be conveyed through their speech, but also the unspoken knowledge that needs to be conveyed by the body itself' (Nichols, 1993: 175). Here he is emphasising the importance of embodied knowledge in the audience's perception of documentary interviews, and the interpretation of meaning being conveyed by the interviewee. Similarly, Michael Renov discusses the power of the testimony in Claude Lanzmann's *Shoah* (1985) as coming from the body of the interviewee when he says 'the kernel of trauma, buried and of the Real, erupts less as language, more as signs of bodily distress – grimacing, tears, the cessation of activity' (Renov, 2004: 127). What Renov and Nichols draw our attention to is that the epistemology of testimony, at least in the case of audiovisual documentary, is not only entailed in the words of the speaker. Rather, it is how these words are delivered and, more specifically, the actions of the body and the gestures of human behaviour that betray the truth of the testimony. However, if the body is so central to how we gain knowledge from interview-based documentaries and if the 'documentary film insists on the presence of the body' (Nichols, 1991: 232), what happens when the body is no longer present? Animation is becoming an increasingly familiar way of representing the interview scene, a means of reconstructing talking heads in a way that may or may not resemble the interviewee. What are the implications of this type of non-mimetic substitution, where the human body is replaced with an animated one, one that has either no tangible physical presence, or a presence to which the body of the interviewee bears no physical relationship?

Perhaps the most familiar example of substituting animated figures for physical bodies in an interview scenario is *Creature Comforts* (1989), one of several short 'claymation' films made by the United Kingdom's Aardman Animations.[1] *Creature Comforts* was made in a style already established by Aardman in their 1978 *Animated Conversations* films produced for the BBC. *Confessions of a Foyer Girl* and *Down and Out* were based on eavesdropped conversations and pair documentary sound with stop-motion animation of Plasticine figures. These two films led to a commission from Channel 4 to make five more shorts that 'demonstrated how real people's voices could be characterised with insight, humour and sensitivity' (Aardman Animations Ltd, 2010).[2] Ultimately, this trend in Aardman's work led to 1989's *Lip Synch* series, one of which was the *Creature Comforts* short film of zoo animals animated to the musings of interviewees on their living conditions and domestic amenities, which won the studio its first of many Academy Awards.[3] *Creature Comforts* is an anomaly among Aardman's non-fiction animations in its use of non-human characters to embody the soundtrack's voices. The film substitutes Plasticine animated animals for corporeal human bodies for comedic effect, and is peppered with amusing visual flourishes, often occurring in the background behind the primary 'interviewee'. These looks between characters and amusing, seemingly irrelevant, gestures lend the film a light-hearted and at times silly tone. The embodiment of human voice via animated animal also often adds poignancy to the short, such as when a long-faced big cat laments the differences in amenities between the UK and Brazil or an ape, pictured in a tiled room evocative of a prison cell, with marks scratching off the days on the wall, complains of being 'stuck indoors'.

The creatures in Aardman's short have no direct visual relationship with their human counterparts and the choices of representation are determined by how the animators interpret the voices of the interviewees. This interpretive and creative freedom is the foundation of the success of *Creature Comforts* (and its subsequent sequels and spin-offs), something that has often been credited to animator Nick Park's ability to capture the essence of a speaker's personality through the type and behaviour of the animal to which their voice is lent. The film's attention to detail in rendering the animal characters helps communicate something about the realities of life for their homo sapien counterparts as well as emphasising the ironies and foibles of human predilection. Aardman co-founder David Sproxton has attested to the dialogue-led creative process of their animation. Even in the early films that animated interviewees or speakers in human form, the animators 'avoided meeting the people wherever possible taking [their] cues purely from what [they] heard' on the sound recordings (Sproxton, 2008). The result is that the 'body language and the verbal language in the documentary type films seem to match very well' (Sproxton, 2008). The deferral of image to sound means that the two work hand-in-hand to express the sentiments of the speakers. Moments of non-linguistic vocal expression, such as natural pauses and hesitations of speech, are reflected in animated, stop-motion body language. The importance of the aural in these Aardman films is emphasised at the beginning of each of the *Conversation Pieces* through a pre-title shot of a reel-to-reel tape recorder, a visual cue to the authenticity and significance of the soundtrack.

Bodies and voices go together, one requiring the other, but, as Steven Connor (2000: 35) tells us, 'voices are produced by bodies: but can also themselves produce bodies'. The voices heard in animated interview documentaries are produced by corporeal human bodies, bodies that are visually absent from the viewer. The bodies that are visible are instead, via the creative work of the animators, inspired by the words spoken and the way those words are spoken. The animation is influenced by sound and it is 'the voice which seems to colour and model its container' (Connor, 2000: 35) in animated interview documentaries. Connor (2000: 35), in his study of ventriloquism, suggests the notion of the 'vocalic body':

> the idea – which can take the form of a dream, fantasy, ideal, theological doctrine, or hallucination – of a surrogate or secondary body, a projection of a new way of having or being a body, formed and sustained by the autonomous operations of the voice.

We can think of the animated embodiments of interview subjects as vocalic bodies, ones that emphasise the autonomy of the voice as expressive and meaningful in its own right at the same time as adding a dimension of interpretation, and sometimes juxtaposition, to what is heard. For while animated bodies may seem to astutely 'match' the voice of the speaker, they are also fundamentally a mismatch by virtue of not being the body of the speaker. The voices in *Creature Comforts* are indeed 'skillfully matched to an appropriate animal' (Wells, 1998: 60), but it is still an animal speaking the words uttered from a human body. Even if the speaker is animated in human form the very difference between corporeal and animated, and the way the animation is realised, is something that must be contended with in interpreting the bodies and voices in an animated interview documentary. As Michel Chion (1999: 172) points out, 'the alteration of bodies [...] can engender entirely new possibilities in the relation between body and voice.'

The use of animation to represent documentary interviewees has gained increasing currency since *Creature Comforts* was released over two decades ago. There are frequently situations in which the identity of interviewees must be protected and the standard device in live-action documentary is to silhouette their face and the body. Animation is a more creative way of achieving such anonymity. Most often, this anonymity is necessitated when a film is on a sensitive subject or something that interviewees would not otherwise be willing to discuss on film. Dutch filmmaker Mischa Kamp directed six short films under the series title *Naked* (*Bloot,* 2006) in which pre-teens talk about the physical and emotional changes of puberty. One could imagine that these adolescents would not be as forthcoming on subjects such as sex, menstruation and pubic hair without the veil of animation. Similarly, Harrie Geelen's 1984 film *Drawn People,* an animated documentary about the impact of drug abuse on 1980s' Dutch society, protected the anonymity of participants by basing animation on sketches made on the basis of their voices (IDFA, 2007: 45). Makers of a more recent film for the BBC about relationships, *The Trouble with Love and Sex* (Jonathan Hodgson, 2012), believe that their interviewees, clients of the UK relationship counselling service Relate, would not have agreed to take part in a conventional documentary. The use of animation, and promises that the on-screen alter egos would not resemble real-life counterparts, 'gave them enough privacy to feel able to talk freely about infidelity, erectile dysfunction, and their deepest family secrets' (Beattie, 2011).

As animation is not forced to resemble that which it represents, it offers freedom to explore possibilities for not only masking identities, but also interpreting the words of interviewees and illustrating and conveying a film's themes and issues. *Stranger Comes to Town* (Jacqueline Goss, 2007) is an animated documentary about how visitors and immigrants to the United States experience crossing the border into the country. Goss animates her interviewees as characters from the videogame *World of Warcraft,* chosen and created by the interviewees. These representations belie audience assumptions of someone's physical appearance based on their voice and offer commentary on US government attitudes towards non-resident 'aliens'. At the same time, the removal of the indexical imagery of live-action talking heads amplifies the importance of the soundtrack in animated interview documentaries. In particular, the voice of the interviewee takes on additional significance when their face and body remains hidden. As Goss points out (2011: 249), someone's voice, and the way they use verbal language, reveals a lot about who they are. Animation can also encourage questions regarding the status of the interviewee and of the relationship between reality and what is seen on screen. The fact that interviewee participation requires the promise of anonymity, or that filmmakers feel animated, vocalic bodies can be more meaningful than physical ones, often speaks loudly about the subject matter of a film and the realities experienced by those participants.

Uncanny bodies

In animated interview documentaries the absence and excess that characterises all animated documentaries manifests most acutely in the body of the interview subject. This is accentuated in animation that has, inherent in its means of production, an additional ontological complexity. Rotoscoping, or the production of animation by tracing over live-action images, has a causal link with reality that is absent in most animation. This mode of animation, similar to stop-motion animation, requires the existence of profilmic objects and bodies in a way that, for example, drawn, cel-based animation does not. Rotoscoping relies (along with its computer-based descendants such as motion-capture techniques and Bob Sabiston's Rotoshop) on the presence of the body in the original film or video footage on which the animated representation is directly based. When such techniques are used to create animated documentaries, they add complexity to the already ambiguous relationship between the animated documentary image and reality.

The Rotoscope was invented by Max Fleischer and patented in 1917. The device enables a process of tracing live-action footage frame by frame and these traced illustrations are then filmed to create the final animation. The development of the process was motivated by the Fleischer Brothers' desire for greater naturalism in the movements of their films' characters, the presumption being that a tracing of human movement would look more realistic than movement created solely by the animator's hand. The Fleischers used the Rotoscope to animate many of the 'stars' of their studio, including Betty Boop and Koko the Clown (whose movement was based on filmed performances by Max's brother and fellow animator Dave). Walt Disney, in his pursuit of his own brand of realism later used the device to draw the leading lady in his first feature film, *Snow White* (1937). With the advent of computer animation, the Rotoscope has spawned many digital descendants, including the Motion Capture process that was used in *Chicago 10* (Brett Morgen, 2007) and the software programme Rotoshop.

Rotoshop software was developed by Bob Sabiston in the 1990s and first used in 1997's *Project Incognito*, a series of twenty-five animated films, each thirty-seconds long, that grew out of Sabiston's entry to an

MTV competition the previous year. Rotoshop is, most basically, a computerised version of the Rotoscope. Live-action footage is shot using digital video cameras, and this footage is then input to a computer where it is converted into Quicktime files. The footage can then be traced over, one frame at a time, via Wacom graphics pads and pens using the Rotoshop software,[4] and the pressure sensitivity of the pads enables both subtle and dramatic variations in line and shade (see Ward, 2006a: 116). It is the 'interpolation' feature, however, that most clearly differentiates Rotoshop from other computerised rotoscoping programmes and that lends the finished product its distinctive 'smooth-yet-undulating' look (Ward, 2004: 34). Interpolation is Sabiston's high-tech answer to the in-betweening process of traditional animation. Both processes are a means of filling in the movement between key frames of action. In Rotoshop, the animator can trace an image in one frame and then jump forward several frames to trace the same object in its new position. The computer then fills in the frames in between, interpolating the movement from the information it has been given.

Rotoshop also has a feature that enables the separation of planes of the image, updating another established device of traditional cel animation. This means certain aspects of the image (such as the background) can be animated and then 'fixed in place by the push of a button', so that the animator can work on other planes (such as characters in the foreground) relative to the parts of the image that have already been isolated and 'fixed' (see Ward, 2004). This is similar to cel animation where only the moving parts of the image are re-drawn on clear cels that are laid over the static parts of the frame (such as backgrounds and non-moving body parts). This separation of the image into layers gives Rotoshop the potential to add depth and dimension to the finished animation. This depth and dimensionality is not a pre-determined feature, however, as the aesthetic of Rotoshop is dictated both by the technological features of the software, which continue to develop over time, and the hand of the animator. This can be seen in the changing look of the four short animated documentaries made after *Project Incognito* by Sabiston and colleagues at Flat Black Films in Austin, Texas, between 1998 and 2007. All of these films combine Rotoshop animated visuals with documentary soundtracks of interviews conducted by Sabiston. *Roadhead* (1998) looks similar to the *Project Incognito* shorts, with interviewees shown in black outline on a white background. *Snack and Drink* (1999) has a more abstract, expressionistic style, and is the first Rotoshop short to be made in colour. The two later films, *Grasshopper* (2003) and *The Even More Fun Trip* (2007) are more photorealistic, making full use of the software's developed capacity for adding dimension and depth to the image.[5]

It is Sabiston's later interview shorts, which move towards the photorealistic, that most acutely draw attention to the fact that animated bodies '[gain] "body" by drawing on (and being drawn on) other bodies that boast more flesh and substance' (Bouldin, 2004: 7). In her discussion of body politics in rotoscoped films, Joanna Bouldin claims that due to maintaining an indexical connection to the real world, the 'reality and materiality of an original body' is transferred to the animation via the filmed image on which the animation is traced (Bouldin, 2004: 13). This can create a strange viewing experience of being aware at the same time of both the realness, and non-realness, of the final product. In particular, due to the appearance of depth and dimensionality in *Grasshopper* and *The Even More Fun Trip*, these films seem to carry the ghost of their original footage.[6] There is a temptation to believe that if we could just peek behind the animation, or scrape back its layers, the filmed image would be there to view. There is in these two films an uncanny sense of reality haunting the animated image.

When viewing fictional animation, a hiccup occurs when reality ruptures the veneer of the make–believe world. These moments occur when the suspension of disbelief required for viewing fictional animated stories is momentarily hijacked by a visual representation that is either too real, or not real enough, in its given context. These moments have been variously theorised, but are generally acknowledged as arising from a dissonance between viewing expectations and viewing experience, as well as between what we know and what we feel while watching animation. This was observed by Sergei Eisenstein (1988: 55) when he marvels about Disney animation:

> We *know* that they are ... drawings and not living beings
> We *know* that they are ... projections of drawings on a screen
> We *know* that they are ... 'miracles' and tricks of technology, that such beings don't really exist
> But at the same time:
> We *sense* them as moving, as active
> We *sense* them as existing and even thinking!

What Eisenstein points to with these comments is the epistemological–phenomenological dichotomy created by animation that occupies the liminal space between reality and make–believe.

The psychological concept of the uncanny has been applied from Freud's psychoanalysis to animation, particularly in cases where animation contains elements of realism at odds with the diegetic world of the film. The uncanny, according to Freud (2003 [1919]: 24), occurs when we experience something that is both familiar and unfamiliar, as indicated by the original German word, *unheimlich*, the opposite of *heimlich* or homely. Puppet animation has been associated with feelings of the uncanny because it brings inanimate objects to life, an action that implies concepts of the return and doubling. Such repetition and doubling are representative of our own death and remind us of our own potential, eventual, inanimateness. By bringing to life that which is inanimate, animation evokes 'Freud's notion of the Death Drive – that drive of animate beings to return to the inanimate state from which they came' (Cholodenko, 2007: 504). Thus certain kinds of animation can arouse the feeling of familiarity yet strangeness that, according to Freud, evokes fear, or at least the sense of being unsettled.

The concept of the uncanny is also frequently applied, via the notion of the uncanny valley, to photorealistic CGI animation.[7] Here the uncanny arises in characters that look too human, yet not human enough. Whereas we might identify with an anthropomorphised animated animal because we focus on the aspects of the character that look human, such as facial features and expression, with animated human characters that look highly photorealistic we focus on the facial and other features that are not quite right. These characters are both familiar and unfamiliar at the same time. So, somewhat paradoxically, viewers find talking cars less troubling than very photorealistic computer-generated animated humans.[8]

Aardman Animation's David Sproxton (2008) has suggested that an uncanny oddness arises from traditionally rotoscoped images because they contain an excess of information due to the ability to too faithfully transcribe the movement and behaviour of a subject.[9] He notes: 'there [is] often too much detail in the movement – necessary for the human form to keep upright or to balance itself or simply idiosyncratic action' (Sproxton, 2008). Similarly, Paul Ward (2004: 36) has noted that the historical discomfort with the rotoscoped image is due to the realness of the movement feeling out of place in a highly constructed, and often highly unrealistic, animated world. The lifelike movement created via the Rotoscope becomes, following this argument, something that transgresses our (pre-)conception of animation, and something we cannot square with the style of the images and story we see on screen.

84 Animated Documentary

Vivian Sobchack (2006: 176) makes a similar suggestion regarding viewers' perennial dissatisfaction with photorealistic CGI human characters. Discussing the 2001 film *Final Fantasy: The Spirits Within*, she proposes there is a disconnect between its narrative and its visual semiotics. That is, 'the film attempts to achieve indexical, photorealistic "human characters" in a world that is emblematic, symbolic, irreal.' She goes on to assert that the hyper-real characters on the one hand, and the fantastical storyline on the other, evoke from the viewer conflicting emotional and phenomenological responses. Whereas the eyes of the motion-captured CGI characters in a film such as *The Polar Express* are noticeable because they are lifeless, the characters in *Final Fantasy* are disturbing because they seem too real, and real in a way that is not justified by the film's sci-fi fantasy narrative.

Sabiston's five animated interviews also present a complex viewing experience, one that is of an epistemological/phenomenological order, rather than rooted in our subconscious fear of death. This is evoked in part by the fact that these films are animated documentaries, and the tension between absence and excess that this type of film always entails. But, more specifically to Sabiston's films, the absence of the body of the interviewee combined with the materiality of the Rotoshop style of animation also creates an ambiguity for the viewer. As a digital version of the Rotoscope, Rotoshop threatens the same response of the uncanny from spectator. This occurs, I would suggest, because the fabric of Rotoshop is neither consistently emblematic nor indexical, to use Sobchack's distinction.

The sense of being able to peel back the surface of Rotoshopped animation to reveal the indexical image underneath occurs alongside moments that are on the other end of the spectrum, at the symbolic–emblematic pole. Sabiston's third animated interview, *Snack and Drink*, is an animation of a short encounter between Sabiston, his producer Tommy Pallotta and thirteen-year-old Ryan Power. Sabiston and Pallotta accompany Ryan on his routine trip from his apartment to the local 7-Eleven store to buy candy (a snack) and soda (a drink). The film is the first full-colour Rotoshop interview documentary and the palette is filled with bright, solid hues. In comparison to the black-and-white drawings in the earlier *Project Incognito* and *Roadhead*, *Snack and Drink* has a relatively high degree of realism in its representation of the mobile interview scene. The previously white background is now filled in with the detail of trees, roads, cars and buildings as Ryan walks down the street. This adds a dimensionality to the space occupied by the interviewee that is absent in previous films and that will be further developed in *Grasshopper* and *The Even More Fun Trip*.

There is, however, an overriding sense of expressionism in *Snack and Drink*. The style of animation constantly fluctuates, at times pared down to geometric shapes and primary colours. When Ryan is filling up his cup at the soda machine, a ritual that involves dispensing a small amount of each soft drink in turn until his cup is full, the individual drinks buttons are animated with arms, hands and eyes as they vie for his attention. During this sequence, which lasts for about a third of the film, the animation style changes approximately thirty times, to coincide with Ryan repetitiously hitting each button on the machine. The representation of Ryan switches from psychedelic to sober in a matter of seconds, cycling through a variety of styles from black and white to bright neon.

In *Snack and Drink*, the emblematic–symbolic pole dominates and we learn about Ryan in part through the artistic expression and impression of the animated visuals. In particular, as Paul Ward (2006a: 120) has noted, the drinks dispenser sequence is 'an amusing and strangely touching visual rendering of just how obsessively focused an autistic person can be'. Sabiston is here using the animation to interpret Ryan's experience of interacting with the world. We understand that the world, for Ryan, is a contrast between some things that intensely retain his focus and others that are noise or distractions. This sequence in *Snack and Drink* also demonstrates the importance of the individual animators' interpretation of reality for Rotoshop's aesthetic. This is emphasised by Sabiston when he observes that the animated image always starts with something that is hand-drawn by the individual animator. Thus, as Sabiston (2012: 79) points out, 'there cannot help but be the smallest stamp of the artist in every line. From the beginning, before it even enters the computer, the artwork is coming from someone's hand.'

This is particularly apparent in *Roadhead*. In this road movie of Sabiston's drive home from New York to Austin after working on *Project Incognito*, he stops off in cities along the way and interviews the people he meets. Once Sabiston returned to Austin with the video footage he, along with thirteen others, animated the material.[10] Each interviewee is drawn by three or four different artists, something that is apparent from the first interview, with 'Colleen' (Washington, DC). Very quickly, the initial clear outline and contours of her face give way to a Picasso-esque rendering that fractures her visage into disconnected lines and accentuated features (see Figure 3.1). While the differences in style may

86 *Animated Documentary*

Figure 3.1 Two interpretations of 'Colleen' in *Roadhead* (dir. Bob Sabiston, Flat Black Films, 1998)

not always be extreme, it is easy to tell when we have switched from one animator's work to another, and this prevails through the three subsequent animated interview shorts, all of which are animated by Sabiston in collaboration with a number of others.[11] *Roadhead*, as with all of the interview shorts, is not just a representation of reality, but also a multiple-authored interpretation of it.

The presence of interpretation is emphasised in the way the interviewees' words are reflected in the animation. When Elton (Athens, Georgia) explains that he has only met seven other Eltons and they were 'all pretty old', the body of this young man is animated as someone far more advanced in years, shrunken in relation to the size of Elton's head and balancing its infirmness on a wooden cane. Similarly, the 'mysticism' of a tarot card reader (New Orleans) is accentuated by placing a turban on his head and giving him other stereotypical accoutrements of a fortune-teller such as a long curled moustache and pointy beard. The choice regarding which elements of an interview to highlight, and how to interpret those words through the representation of the interviewee's face and body, remains at the discretion of the individual animator. The animated bodies in the film are 'vocalic bodies' (Connor, 2000: 35) instigated by the voices of real people. But, they are also produced by other bodies, those of the animators who draw them, a process of interpretation that gives body to voice and meaning to the words that are heard.

The mutability of Rotoshop's aesthetic within the individual films affords, for example, more acute interpretations of aspects of an interviewee's physical presentation or what they said in their interview. In *Snack and Drink*, a style of animation that embraces the symbolic and emblematic becomes a means of drawing our attention to how Ryan interacts with the world and how this might differ from our own experience. Similarly, in *The Even More Fun Trip* the switch from the monochrome grey–beige colour palette of the car journey to the bright colours once the group reach the theme park visually echoes Ryan's exhortation of 'come on, let's have some fun'.

The uncanniness of the rotoshopped animated documentary image due to the ontological obtuseness of the image creates a strange viewing experience, as viewers are aware of and must constantly negotiate the spectral presence of the physical body and the ontological status of the final image. This negotiation is further heightened by the often surreal and highly expressive nature of the animation style. The tangibility of the animated character is often at odds with their visual representation – for instance, Ryan's hair cycles through a shock of fantastic colours in *Snack and Drink*. In *Grasshopper*, the existentially philosophical interviewee, AJ Vadhera, periodically morphs into a Buddha-like version of himself, sitting in lotus position and floating several feet above the park bench upon which he sits. As in *Roadhead*, the depictions of Vadehra change often throughout the film and his face in particular is drawn in a variety of styles. This reminds us that these Rotoshop animated documentaries are not merely a computer-generated product; they not only bear the trace of the original filmed material, but also the imprint of the animator's hand. These films, then, are doubly indexed, pointing to the presence of the interviewee in front of the camera, and the presence of the artist in the process of translating the video image to animation. This indexicality, as with all indexical signs, emphasises the absence of the original (see Mulvey, 2006; Doane, 2007b).

Absence as representational strategy

Chris Holmlund and Cynthia Fuchs (1997: 1) have pointed out that 'to see and be seen is a matter not only of visual representation but also of social acceptance and political clout.' There is a politics associated with visibility and, conversely, invisibility. To have a presence, you must be visible. To have a say, you must be both seen and heard. Much activist film and video from the 1970s onwards works from this premise of raising awareness through raising visibility. Similarly, other politically motivated documentary-making, such as the Workshop Movement in the United Kingdom in the 1980s, sought to rectify the lack of representation of certain ethnic, racial and social groups in mainstream media (see Dickinson, 1999). The suggestion in this type of politically motivated filmmaking is that there is power in having a presence in and on audiovisual media.

Jane Gaines (1999) has argued that the power of political documentaries to effect change is carried in the presence of the onscreen body and the response of the body of the audience member. Following Linda Williams, Gaines posits that political action by the documentary spectator is spurred by the action of the body in the documentary itself. This 'political mimesis', in which the audience is prompted to mirror the physical actions of the documentary participants, occurs when viewing films that make us 'want to kick and yell, films that make [us] want to do something' (Gaines, 1999: 90). Documentary has a particularly potent political power because 'its aesthetic of similarity establishes a continuity between the world of the screen and the world of the audience' (Gaines, 1999: 92). Gaines is suggesting that the presence of the onscreen body is an essential ingredient in motivating the body of the viewer into political (re)action. Moreover, this motivation is bound up in documentary's particular representational relationship with the 'real world'.[12]

Documentary's role in the political sphere seems intrinsically bound up with the presence of the body. To enter the debate on identity politics, the embodiment of that identity must be present on the screen. To motivate (socio-)political action and reaction, there must be a body onscreen for the body of the viewer to mirror. Yet, this relationship between documentary, embodiment and visibility is called into question by the increasing number of animated interview documentaries that engage with socio-political issues. The absence of the physical body of the interviewee initially seems at odds with such films' themes and issues. Animation masks the 'real' people, making them invisible to viewers. This very suggestion seems to only exacerbate their under-representation and lack of voice in mainstream media. This notion becomes even more acute in light of claims regarding the importance of the presence of the body in documentary, both in terms of Gaines' theorisation of political efficacy and Nichols and Renov's suggestions regarding epistemology. How much power can we say is being claimed, or afforded to, people who remain invisible to us? Films that replace the bodies of those who are already marginalised in society with animated characters could be open to criticism of depoliticising and disempowering their subjects through the animated aestheticisation of their physical form. Similarly, if meaning is conveyed through the physical actions and gestures of the documentary interviewee and the 'documentary film insists on the presence of the body' (Nichols, 1991: 232), what sort

Animated Interviews 89

of things can we know about documentary interview subjects that are represented via animation?

When David Aronowitsch and Hanna Heilborn interviewed a young Peruvian refugee and his family in 1999 for their animated documentary *Hidden* (*Gömd*, 2002) there were concerns for the interviewees' anonymity. Their status as illegal immigrants meant their identity had to be kept secret to protect them from deportation, a threat constantly looming over their life in Sweden. This concern, which gives Aronowitsch and Heilborn's film its name, is flagged prior to the film's beginning, via an intertitle informing us that Giancarlo and his family live in hiding and that the interview was recorded at 'an undisclosed location'. In the short, eight-minute film, animated by Mats Johansson, the subjects, which include Giancarlo, his parents and two younger siblings, the two interviewers and a translator, are animated in a simple, two-dimensional style. They are drawn in a childlike fashion, with bold outlines demarcating their bodies and facial features. The family sits around a large table in an otherwise empty room. Giancarlo's younger sibling sits next to him, drawing quietly with a felt-tip pen. His mother stands in the background, silently rocking a young baby.

The film is based on an audio interview recorded by Aronowitsch and Heilborn, rather than taking any filmed material as its source. As such, *Hidden* eschews one of the traditional conventions of anonymity in documentary – silhouetting the face and body of the interviewee. Instead, animation becomes a way of preserving the subjects' anonymity as well as conveying the film's themes of isolation, loneliness and desperation. Giancarlo's physical absence mirrors his lack of legitimate physical presence in Sweden. This idea is further emphasised in the two live-action sections of the film. When Giancarlo speaks of the difficulty of fitting in at school, we see images of schoolchildren running through a hallway before taking their seats in a classroom. In these scenes, Giancarlo is superimposed onto the live-action images in animated form, a flimsy 2-D figure in a bustling 3-D world. Later, when he describes the year he spent on his own in Peru before his parents could afford the plane fare for him to join them in Sweden, he is again inserted in the scene in animated form. The contrast between live action and animation is highlighted when Giancarlo retells the fate of the other Peruvian street children who were not as lucky as him in fleeing the local police who would patrol the city for truant minors. A giant (live-action) hand grasps an animated young child between its thumb and forefinger, a tiny figure dwarfed in the clutches of authority. The paper-thin child dangles precariously until it is finally dropped, as Giancarlo timidly tells us how these captured children were sent to orphanages.

If, as Gaines and Holmund and Fuchs suggest, political power is dependent on physical presence, then *Hidden*'s visual mode of address can be read as a metaphor for the disempowerment of a young, illegal immigrant who has little control over his destiny.[13] The absent bodies in the film speak to Giancarlo's plight as an invisible member of Swedish society. The Australian film *It's Like That* (2003), made by the female collective: the Southern Ladies Animation Group (SLAG), takes up a similar theme. Here a variety of animation styles are used to depict young children being kept in an asylum centre. The film is based on telephone interviews between the young subjects and journalist Jacqueline Arias. SLAG member Nicole McKinnon first heard Arias' interviews in May 2002 on the ABC (Australian Broadcasting Corporation) radio documentary, *Un-Australian Behaviour, Part 3: The Children*, about children detained under the Australian Migration Act of Mandatory Detention of Asylum Seekers (Documentary Australia Foundation, n.d.). The group then worked through the six hours of Arias' original audio material to choose three of the interviewees, all boys aged eleven and twelve, to focus on in their seven-minute film (Webb, 2003).

The film's variety of animation styles, which include stop-motion puppet animation, computer 3-D animation, flash and hand drawn on paper, reflect the input of the thirteen animators who worked on the project (Documentary Australia Foundation, n.d.). The three boys are primarily represented by three knitted figures of small birds (see Figure 3.2) and also in 2-D drawn animation, in the same birdlike form. The metaphor here is clear, incarcerated children being likened to caged birds. The innocence of the children is further expressed by the design of the soft, knitted puppets, which are reminiscent of simple, old-fashioned stuffed toys. The texture of the fabric reveals the puppets' construction and makes them seem fragile and at risk of being unravelled. Like Giancarlo, the boys in the Australian detention centre are physically absent from the film, replaced by puppets or drawings. They are further absented by not being rendered in human form, giving us no indication of these boys' actual physical manifestation. Once again, the absence of the body of the documentary subject can be seen as representative of their lack of power or control over their world.

These questions of power and the politics of absence become more complex when one remembers to consider the films as audiovisual, rather than just visual, texts. There is a sense of Giancarlo and the boys in the Australian detention centre being given a voice through these films, a

Figure 3.2 Child asylum seekers animated as knitted birds in *It's Like That* (dir. Southern Ladies Animation Group, 2003)

concept that reinforces the notion that testimony is a form of speaking out and of bringing hidden truths and secrets to light. Testifying can be thought of as a means of taking epistemological control of a past event or present situation through the possession of knowledge that is then expressed through spoken language. Foucault (2008 [1969]: 58) tells us 'Western societies have established the confession as one of the main rituals we rely on for the production of truth.' The interview testimonies in *Hidden* and *It's Like That* share traits of the confession. Giancarlo and the boys in Australia speak openly about their deepest fears and, in the process, reveal their vulnerability.

The mechanisms by which these revelations are facilitated, however, recall Foucault's theorisation of the power relations of confession. Here, he suggests, it is the inquisitor, not the speaker, who holds the dominant position. The one asking the questions and receiving the answers is the one who holds it in his or her power to 'judge, punish, forgive, console, and reconcile' (Foucault, 2008 [1969]: 62). Rather than being freeing for the subject, interviews are instead the 'vehicle of a kind of incessant back-and-forth movement of forms of subjugation and schemas of knowledge' (Foucault, 2008 [1969]: 98). Indeed, 'interviews are a form of hierarchical discourse deriving from the unequal distribution of power, as in the confessional and the interrogation' (Nichols, 1991: 47). Not only does articulation through interview depend on the uneven balance of power between interviewer and interviewee, but the results of the process also give power to the recipient of the testimony, as it is they who decide on how to use the knowledge gained from the words spoken. This emphasises that the telling of these children's stories is being facilitated by others and that the subjects had little or no control in the process of production, distribution and exhibition. Their visibility and voice is beholden to those who are in greater control of the media and have the ability, through considerably higher social status, to reveal their plight.

While *Hidden* and *It's Like That* can be read as socio-political allegories through the absence of the bodies they represent, it is also true that their aesthetics strike an emotional note. Giancarlo is animated with enormous, sad eyes. He looks down as he speaks, keeping his arms by his sides, gestures that heighten his vulnerability. His animated form is differentiated from the 3-D live-action images of the other children in the classroom scene because he lacks the physical substance of his peers. As a result, a feeling of protective sympathy is evoked for Giancarlo through his representation as both helpless and hopeless. In a similar fashion, *It's Like That* relies on metaphor to generate emotional resonance. The cuteness of the knitted puppets works to evoke sympathy for the plight of these juvenile asylum seekers. The detention centre in which they are held is animated with a boundary fence that is drawn as both sterile and forbidding. The use of perspective in this sequence creates a looming, vast prison in comparison to the diminutive birds, which tend to be shot from an elevated angle. This emotive animation is augmented by the voices of the children on the soundtracks of these two films. They are softly spoken and sound sad and vulnerable. In *It's Like That*, the broken English and thick accents of the interviewees, combined with occasionally poor sound quality, makes it sometimes hard to discern what they are saying. This failure of communication makes the child subjects of this documentary seem even more at risk.

Liz Blazer's *Backseat Bingo* (2003) tackles an issue that, while not the political lightening rod of asylum and immigration, is one that is still to a certain extent a social taboo. The senior citizens interviewed in this film talk frankly about their sex lives, challenging the perception of the aging body as a desexualised one. The short film evokes both the confessional and dating agency videos as the different characters speak directly 'into the camera' of their desire for intimacy and describe their ideal partner. Our presumptions regarding sexual activity in old age are dispelled in the first moments of the film when we hear David ('born in 1918') talk about the 'most romantic' moment when he asked his partner if she would go to bed with him. Quick cuts to four other residents of

David's retirement community reveal a cast of characters aged between 79 and 92. Sunge (84) says she believes sex keeps you young. Feisty Ruth Cooper admits that her desires in a partner have changed ('at 18 you just wanted a sex object; at 75 you may still want sex, you're not sure you're going to get it, but you're looking for comfort').

The animation design in *Backseat Bingo* reflects the youthful attitudes of the interviewees. The colour palette is painted in bold, primary tones and objects and bodies are demarcated by clearly defined outlines. The facial features of the residents belie their age. Their skin is smooth and unblemished with just a few lines to indicate wrinkles and other signs of aging. Their body language is open and their movements indicate a youthful vigour to match their attitudes. The style of simple cut-out animation (where different body parts are animated individually) is reminiscent of the movement of characters in the television series *South Park* (1997–ongoing) and the design of the lay-outs recalls stylised retro cartoons such as the *Jetsons* (1962–3 and 1985–7). The overall aesthetic of the film is one of youth and energy, colour and life. This reflects the attitudes we hear on the soundtrack and works to confront commonly held attitudes about old age as depressing or lonely. These residents show no indication of the slowing down associated with retirement.

It could be argued that the film fails to overcome the stereotype of the geriatric body as a desexualised one. The cartoony style, along with the jaunty music, gives the film a comedic tone. The use of animation, and this particular style of animation, could be considered sidestepping the underlying issues the film alludes to. Society's disavowal of old-aged sexual activity is wrapped up with conceptions of beauty and body image, prejudices that privilege young bodies. By hiding her subjects behind a mask of colourful, humorous representation, one that belies many of the physical signs of aging, Blazer could be accused of simply making a joke out of the idea of sex in our twilight years.

In a similar way, *Hidden* and *It's Like That* sidestep issues of identity politics. The racial and ethnic identities of Giancarlo and the asylum seekers in Australia are completely erased via animation. The animation that makes them anonymous to protect their identity also deracializes them. On the one hand, this avoids the stereotyping that has so pervaded the animated representation of non-white, non-Western characters, as well as the construction of the interviewees as 'other' (see Wells, 1998: 215–21). There is very little, for example, other than hair colour, to distinguish Giancarlo and his family from one of the film's directors Hanna Heilborn, who is also represented in animated form in *Hidden*.

Heilborn is drawn with flaxen hair, and Giancarlo and his family have dark hair. In *It's Like That,* the use of anthropomorphism of the children as birds makes any guess as to their ethnic origin impossible. However, it also means that in both films race and ethnicity are ignored, or even denied, as factors affecting the interviewees' current situations.

To a certain extent, the closing credit sequence of *Backseat Bingo* overcomes the criticisms of absenting the participants and ignoring the identity politics of old age by showing still photographs of the interviewees, subtitled with their names. Any notion of the animation being used to protect the anonymity of the participants is dispelled at this point. The photographs reveal faces and bodies much older, much more decrepit than the animation suggests. The elision of wrinkles and aging physical presence in an animation style that matches the lively voices is revealed to be an illusion. The actual bodies of the speakers reveal all the signs of aging and the photographic images lack the bright, playfulness of the animation that helps lend the film its light tone. As such, the film can be read as asking audiences to look beyond the prejudices regarding the corporeality of the aging body and to see, instead, the physical desires such bodies hide. This point is emphasised by David's partner who comments that, although he may not look it, he is a 'very sensual man'. While their bodies may not be, the attitudes and opinions of the interviewees are youthful and sprightly. Blazer's aesthetic style could be argued to represent more truthfully the reality of physical intimacy for these senior citizens, more so than their photographic likenesses.

Hidden, It's Like That and *Backseat Bingo* demonstrate how animation can complicate the relationship between visibility and testimony in interview documentaries. This complexity does not, I would argue, necessarily depoliticise or disempower subjects who already lack visibility, and thus agency, in the social world. Animation is used as a means of hiding the identity of the interviewees, sometimes because such anonymity is necessary for their safety and sometimes because it encourages participation from otherwise reluctant subjects. David Aronowitsch (2010) points out that Giancarlo and his family would never have agreed to appear on film for *Hidden* and that the filmmakers did not even provide the animator with a picture of Giancarlo on which to base the animated representation. In *Backseat Bingo* the subjects felt free to express themselves frankly and openly because Blazer promised to only use the audio portion of the interviews she had filmed (Blazer, 2009).[14] In *Hidden* and *It's Like That*, the physical absence of the interviewees is not a choice of the filmmakers. In these two films, a conventional documentary approach of filming the interviews, even as a basis for the animation, was not an option. As in *Backseat Bingo*, the animation becomes a solution for an absence that is demanded. That such absences are necessary reflects the realities of the socio-political environment in which the films were made, ones in which children must remain hidden for fear of political and legal repercussions and adults feel unable to discuss their sexual behaviour and personal relationships in public.

Bill Nichols (1993: 174–5) has made a distinction between disembodied knowledge, which is primarily conveyed through speech, and embodied knowledge that is conveyed by the body. While disembodied knowledge, which he claims is the type most favoured in documentary, is externalised from human experience and thus generalised in the way we understand it, embodied knowledge is situated and specific and 'cannot be separated from the body in which [it] resides' (Nichols, 1993: 184). The insistence here is that specific, personal knowledge is carried in and communicated through the body of the documentary subject. Nichols' assertions are called into question by films such as *Hidden*, *It's Like That*, and *Backseat Bingo*. These films do convey knowledge and experience that are personal and specific to their subjects. The words spoken by the interviewees are not disembodied, they are neither externalised from human experience nor generalised. The knowledge being conveyed is very much situated and specific. Visually, this situated and specific knowledge is not transmitted via the human body, as there is no physical gesture, no witnessed body language to hint at the subtext of the words spoken. Instead, such hints come from how the bodies, and the spaces they occupy, are realised through animation.

Jose B. Capino contests the suggestion that an absence of physical body in animation precludes a very real response in the viewer. In an essay on animated pornography, he comments on the ability of animated bodies to elicit physical responses in spectators. This demonstrates our 'recognition of the corporeality of these bodies (i.e., acknowledging these bodies as being somewhat like our own) and our willingness to project upon them similar values that we assign real bodies (i.e., bodies like our own)' (Capino, 2004: 55–6). The sadness of Giancarlo and the young boys in *It's Like That* and the *joie de vivre* of the senior citizens in *Backseat Bingo*, which can be heard in their respective vocal intonation, are conveyed to us through the animated body much as it would be in the cinematic body of a live-action film. This exemplifies Capino's suggestion that animated bodies can evoke a response just as live-action bodies can. A viewer can respond to Giancarlo's down-turned gaze and timid body language much as one would respond to this behaviour if it were seen on a physical, 'real' body.

Yet, the animation styles of *Hidden*, *It's Like That* and *Backseat Bingo* go beyond trying to copy the look of a conventional interview documentary or trying to dutifully reconstruct the bodies and gestures of their real-life interviewees. In this going beyond the animation is adding something to the words we hear, just as the corporeality of the body goes beyond words in the documentaries of embodied knowledge discussed by Nichols. What the animation adds lies in its power to suggest and imply ideas and themes through its expressive capabilities. Where the body might be able to non-verbally communicate 'pain, pride, doubt' (Nichols, 1993: 187), animation can also convey emotional states and attitudes. Giancarlo's feelings of helplessness and abandonment are shown through the flimsy two-dimensionality of his animated counterpart. The fears of the boys in the Australian detention centre, something that may have been written on their bodies had viewers been able to witness their physical demeanour, is implied through the metaphor of the knitted birds. The youthful attitude of the seniors in *Backseat Bingo*, which may have been observable in a bodily gesture or physical delivery of speech, is instead represented in the lively, irreverent animation style. What these three films suggest is that animation has a power of its own, a capacity to evoke the type of specific, local knowledge that Nichols theorises is carried by the body.

With Capino's claims in mind, I suggest that the animated documentaries discussed here have a tripled potential. The physical absence of the bodies from the film adds a layer of metaphorical meaning regarding the socio-political power of the interviewees. The absence of the physical body does not, however, entail an absence of political meaning and affect. Not only do animated bodies have the power to evoke a response similar to the one we have to physical cinematic bodies, because 'spectators appraise and evaluate animated bodies in terms of real ones' (Capino, 2004: 56), but meaning is also evoked in these films through the style and techniques of the animation and the metaphorical absence of the bodies that are heard speaking. These animated bodies are vocalic bodies, 'a surrogate or secondary body, a projection of a new way of having or being a body, formed and sustained by the autonomous operations of the voice' (Connor, 2000: 35). Such vocalic bodies 'colour and model [their] container' (Connor, 2000: 35), by guiding the style and look of the animation by which they are represented. The relationship between the absence of the body and the excess, in terms of potential for metaphor and interpretation, of the animation has the capacity to deliver a strong, yet complex political message regarding the roles and positions we ascribe certain people in society.

The animated embodiment of documentary interview subjects challenges the way talking heads, and the visibility of documentary testimony, has been theorised. In conventional documentary, visual elements such as body language, physical gesture and the iconography of interview location are suggested as adding meaning and authenticity to the words we hear the interviewee speak via the soundtrack. Rendering these visual elements in animation, whether it is based closely on filmed imagery or not, requires audiences to engage with what they are seeing, potentially leading to questions regarding the nature of the image itself or the significance of the absence of the human body. At the same time, the way human voice is embodied via animation to create animated vocalic bodies becomes a factor in understanding and interpreting the films' meaning.

The expressive power of the disembodied voice

Dennis Tupicoff's *His Mother's Voice* (1997) animates a radio interview given by Kathy Easedale in which she describes the night her teenaged son Matthew was shot and killed. The interview, which was broadcast on Australia's ABC Radio in 1995, is heard twice through, each time accompanied by different animated visuals offering two alternative points of view of the events. The first hearing goes back to April 1995, reconstructing the scene of Kathy rushing through the night to the location of the shooting and expectantly waiting for news of her son. The second hearing offers a reconstruction of Kathy being interviewed in her home in suburban Brisbane and the camera roams around her house, viewing the interiors of the home as well as the quiet neighbourhood in which it is situated. The two halves are rotoscoped by hand, but in different styles. The first half simplifies the frame into clearly demarcated areas of shadow and colour, and resembles a comic book or graphic novel. In the second half, the filmed image is traced in charcoal and the colour palate is pale and washed out (see Figure 3.3). The image in this second half jitters and wobbles, an effect partially achieved by animated on twos, or filming each drawing for two frames (Tupicoff, 2009).

His Mother's Voice illustrates several of the issues raised in this chapter. It questions the importance of the body in delivering supplemental knowledge in documentaries, knowledge that is embodied, rather than the disembodied knowledge usually associated with documentary voiceover. The film also articulates the epistemological–phenomenological dichotomy prompted by rotoscoping, with its uncanny presence and

Figure 3.3 Two styles of rotoscoping in *His Mother's Voice* (dir. Dennis Tupicoff, 1997)

absence of the original profilmic material. This is amplified by the participation of actors, rather than the documentary's subjects, and the use of reconstructions. The techniques of production and animation that completely absent the speaker's body, visually, from *His Mother's Voice*, combined with the film's powerful and moving impact, stress the significance of the interviewee's voice in testimony-based documentaries.

Viewers are used to learning things via a documentary's soundtrack. As discussed in Chapter 2, the Griersonians raised documentary sound to a level of importance that meant it frequently took precedence over the visuals as the voice-of-God commentary often communicated the didactic message of these films while the visuals work to 'illustrate, illuminate, evoke, or act in counterpoint to what is said' (Nichols, 2001: 107). As Nichols has pointed out, the type of knowledge gained through documentary voiceover is usually disembodied and generalised, seeking to make a broadly applicable argument. When Nichols states that 'it is not simply the knowledge possessed by witnesses [...] that needs to be conveyed through their speech, but also unspoken knowledge that needs to be conveyed through the body itself' he is suggesting that this unspoken knowledge is conveyed only by the body (Nichols, 1993: 175). Nichols is proposing the epistemological potential of the body in interview and testimony documentaries (what he would term the 'interactive' or 'participatory' mode) as an antidote to the epistemological hierarchy of the voice in the 'expository' mode (See Nichols, 1991, 2001). What this formulation denies, however, is the expressive potential of the voice to convey more than the information communicated through words. Disembodied voices, as Michel Chion shows in *The Voice in Cinema* (1999), are not necessarily without body or soul.

Dennis Tupicoff says of Kathy Easedale's recounting that 'this is an interview which delivers not just the basics: [...] factual information in the first person, more or less intelligibly', but that it is also 'a song of lament, a mother's song that describes time and space unfolding as she searches for her son' (Tupicoff, 2003). There is something more than information being conveyed in Kathy's words. Her delivery, her hesitation as she tries to describe her feelings at hearing Matthew has been shot ('my head and my body disconnected'), her faltering voice as she talks about the period between learning of the shooting and finally being told he was dead, the timbre of her voice, tell us more than the facts. Her voice evokes and embodies her emotional response to the events, yet this emotional knowledge is, in its own way, unspoken. It is less through her words that we get a sense of the awfulness of that night, but more through her inability to say them – the hesitations and shallow breaths between the words. It is the voice, rather than the words it speaks, that conveys Kathy's experience.

Michel Chion draws attention to this distinction between voice and speech when he observes that 'from the speech act we usually retain only the significations it bears, forgetting the medium of the voice itself' (Chion, 1999: 1). The power of the voice to express and communicate gets forgotten because we tend to conflate it with speech. Mladen Dolar stresses the distinction when he says of the voice:

> it is *what does not contribute to making sense*. ... It is there, in the very act of saying, but it eludes any pinning down, to the point where we could maintain that it is the non-linguistic, the extralinguistic element which enables speech phenomena, but cannot itself be discerned by linguistics (Dolar, 2006: 15, emphasis in original).

The voice is something that goes beyond the language we hear it speak, the voice gains supplemental meaning through tone, delivery, timbre.

This element of the human voice that goes beyond language is what Roland Barthes might term the 'grain' of the voice (Barthes, 1977a). Although Barthes was talking about the singing voice in his essay on this topic, his ideas translate readily to the expressive, emotive speaking voice as heard in Tupicoff's film.[15] What we can discern from Barthes, Dolar and Chion is that the voice has expressive potential that goes beyond what we might be able to interpret from the words it speaks. That the meaning of the voice goes beyond language is illustrated in the films discussed earlier in this chapter. We might discern quite quickly in *Snack and Drink* that Ryan has an autism spectrum disorder from the way he delivers his words in response to Sabiston's questions and his patterns of vocal tone. The vibrant, colourful animated bodies in *Backseat Bingo* are vocalic bodies by virtue of representing the youthful and playful voices heard on the soundtrack. The vulnerability, and lack of agency, of the juvenile interviewees in *Hidden* and *It's Like That*, is conveyed in part through their childlike intonation.

In *His Mother's Voice* we learn as much about Kathy's experience from how (or, in some cases, how not) she says as what she says. She recites the events without interruption from interviewer Matt Brown. Even when she seems to be on the verge of breaking down, and Brown can be heard attempting to intervene or reassure, she continues as if determined to evacuate from her mind in one go the memories of that night. Tupicoff has described this delivery as 'like a metronome, or a heartbeat, minute after minute, the rhythm of her song beats out: every 28 frames' (Tupicoff, 2003). Contrasting with this are moments when remembered hope or still raw grief threaten to puncture the stream of recitation. Kathy's voice wavers as she remembers the agonising wait for Matthew to be brought out of the house where he had been shot. A policewoman tells her they are 'probably stabilising him', and Kathy recalls asking 'does that mean ... that he's alive? That there's hope?' The grief that is always present beneath her retelling of the events comes to the surface when she speaks of the moment she was informed of Matthew's death. She speaks of the 'most agonising part' as watching Matthew's brother react to the news and describes it as 'having one son die, and then watch the other one ...' Throughout the interview, Kathy never openly breaks down in tears, but at this moment and many others they can be heard threatening to rupture the surface of her speech.

Michel Chion distinguishes between different types of off-screen voices in cinema. The disembodied voice most commonly associated documentary as heard in *Walking with Dinosaurs* and *Planet Dinosaur* is what Chion would class as 'offscreen commentary' and is one that is 'triaged to another place, an imaginary one, comparable to a proscenium' (Chion, 1999: 3). Such a voice stands outside of the narrative in fiction film, and above reproach in documentary. The *acousmêtre*, on the other hand, is a voice that 'has not yet been visualized – that is, when we cannot yet connect it to a face' (Chion, 1999: 21). Such voices can be distinguished from voiceover commentators in the following way:

> We may define it as neither inside nor outside the image. It is not inside, because the image of the voice's source, the body, the mouth, is not included. Nor is it outside, since it is not clearly positioned offscreen in an imaginary 'wing', like a master of ceremonies or a witness, and it is implicated in the action, constantly about to be part of it (Chion, 1994: 129).

This concept of voices of absent, soon-to-be or nearly present bodies, is significant in understanding the power of Kathy Easedale's voice in *His Mother's Voice*. It is also what distinguishes the expression of grief from that heard in *Prayers for Peace* (Dustin Grella, 2009), a film narrated by Grella's disembodied voice in the first person, which features another significant disembodied, non-visualised voice.

Grella tells of how, walking one day in Manhattan, he found a church whose railings were covered with yellow ribbons, memorials for soldiers killed in Iraq. Viewers learn that Grella's brother died in such circumstances when he talks of searching for, and finding, the ribbon bearing his brother's name. The animation, created by pastel markings drawn, erased and re-drawn on slate, reconstructs the church and Grella's subsequent walk through Central Park, followed by scenes from Iraq as well as the funeral home as Grella remembers his brother's memorial service. The animation, by virtue of its process of production, is ephemeral, and as such the few representations offered of Grella's brother are nebulous.

As the narrator, Grella speaks in a consistent, almost measured tone. He is presumably reading from a script he has prepared earlier, and his words are clearly articulated, with none of the pauses or hesitations of spontaneous speech. In this way, his voice is closer to the traditional disembodied documentary voiceover, as he imparts his experience of grief and loss, revealing information about his brother and the circumstances of his death. As Grella is never visualised in animated form in *Prayers for Peace*, he is to a certain degree a 'master of ceremonies or a witness' (Chion, 1994: 129), and he guides the viewer through this personal family story. The absence of any animated embodiment of the narrator is also an effective way of illustrating the absence of Grella's brother and, to a certain extent, a comment Grella makes early on in the film that he does not think of his brother that often anymore. But, in many ways, the film is as much about a sound file made by Grella's brother shortly before his death, as about Grella's grief and loss. Grella talks of how his family huddled round his brother's laptop, returned to them after his death, in the funeral home and of how they played the file over many times, listening to 'his innocent, 21-year-old voice, oddly more mature since he'd left for Iraq three months ago'. For the last ninety seconds of *Prayers for Peace*, this audio file is played over a smeary brown–black background on which the words heard are handwritten on the slate over a barely discernible animated representation of a photograph of Grella's brother in dress uniform. Gunfire can be heard in the background and Grella's brother's voice is at times distorted as he speaks too close to the microphone. He talks, somewhat aimlessly, as if to himself, about the background noise, about feeling excited to be part of such a 'big mission'. In *Prayers for Peace*, Grella's brother is the *acousmêtre*, voice of the absent body that is fleetingly glimpsed in hazy, dark animation. It is his voice that is the significant one in this film, given precedence by having the last, unedited word.

Mladen Dolar (2006: 71) has suggested that:

> one could use a French pun, and say that the voice is *plus-de-corps*: both the surplus of the body, a bodily excess, and the no-more-body, the end of the corporeal, the spirituality of the corporeal, so that it embodied the very coincidence of the quintessential corporeality and the soul.

Here Dolar emphasises the specificity of the voice to the body it inhabits, yet also that the voice is not simply reducible to the body – it is something more, a surplus, an excess. This is echoed by Steven Connor (2000: 23) when he says that 'sound, especially sourceless, autonomous, or excessive sound will be experienced as a lack and an excess; both as a mystery to be explained, and an intensity to be contained.' Furthermore, when he cites Aristotle's differentiation between sound and voice as 'a difference between unsouled and ensouled entities' (24), he emphasises the connection between the voice and the self. Rather than the disembodied voice being one of power and authority, Dolar and Connor point towards recognising the voice as a means of expressing the internal and the subjective. The voice, as the soul, speaks from within and, as such, has the capacity to reveal what is specific to the particular body it inhabits. It also has the potential to live on, in the form of audio recordings, once the body no longer exists.

Dolar suggests that the evocative capacity of the voice is heightened in those that are acousmatic. When the voice is separated from the body it is 'powerful because it cannot be neutralized within the framework of the visible, and it makes the visible itself redoubled and enigmatic' (Dolar, 2006: 79). This power is divested once the *acousmêtre* becomes visualised sound, that is a voice whose source can be seen on screen.[16] The power and potential of the acousmatic voice is complicated in *His Mother's Voice*, as it is in *Prayers for Peace*, because the voice is de-acousmatised, but via a body other than Kathy's.[17] Kathy's voice is assigned to a body to which it does not belong (an actress) and then animated and brought to life in a process that further removes it from its original embodiment. The uncanniness of the rotoscoped image is amplified by a voice that is acousmatic, yet at the same time, briefly, synchronised, visualised sound.

The evocative nature of Kathy Easedale's voice is amplified by her status as an *acousmêtre* and also by the style of animation in *His Mother's Voice*. The stark contrasts, bold colours and clear outlines of the reconstruction of the night of Matthew's death give way to the monochrome charcoal depiction of the interview in Kathy's home. In the former, the harsh horror of that evening is shown through the graphic animation style and shots that accentuate key moments and object. The telephone on which Kathy receives news of Matthew's death is animated in bright, blood red, a solitary objects casting a dark shadow on a beige background. As Matthew's brother falls to the ground upon news of his death, he is a lone blue figure in a sea of blue background. The camera pans around and underneath him as he rises up in a silent roar of grief. The only break from the re-enactment of that night's events is for moments of 'wish-fulfilment', as Michael Renov (2002) has described them, in which Matthew appears alive and well. When Kathy speaks of the glimmer of hope when she is informed that Matthew is being stabilised, he is seen brought out of the house on a stretcher, his eyes open and responsive. At other moments throughout this first half, Matthew momentarily appears, embodied by an actor and animated in a softer style with a pastel colour palate and none of the harsh, black shadow of the rest of the animation in this section.

By the second time the interview is heard, the words and events are now familiar. This time the visual scene begins with Kathy being interviewed in her home by Matt Brown. The camera then pans off to begin its roam around Kathy's house, scanning over the Jimi Hendrix poster in Matthew's room, the 'M' emblazoned mug in the windowsill, looking over the fence at the neighbours' house. Eventually it returns to Kathy at the end of her interview, fighting back tears as she recalls being told her son was dead. The soundtrack in this half is layered with diegetic sounds of the surroundings – birds are heard cawing, wind chimes tinkling, dogs barking. The mundaneness of what is seen, the everydayness of this suburb in which 'nothing much is happening' (Tupicoff, 2003) is at odds with the story being told, a story of lives changing irrevocably or ceasing altogether.

Kathy barely talks directly of her emotional response to the events and her recounting is restricted mostly to the descriptive. Yet, the film still conveys palpably and acutely her loss. This loss, conveyed through the voice, is also reflected in Kathy and Matthew's physical absences from the film. Tupicoff has never met Kathy Easedale and actors were used to reconstruct the events Kathy describes and the interview scene. The interview was not filmed at Kathy's house and neither did Tupicoff have any indication of the type of house she lived in nor the objects contained within.[18] Tupicoff describes the final animation as being 'twice removed from the events being described' (Tupicoff, 2003), first by the re-enactments, and then by the animation itself. This is a disembodied voice, although that does not necessarily entail that only disembodied and impersonal knowledge is gained from this film. In *His Mother's Voice*, Kathy's voice exceeds the animation and the animation exceeds the voice. The grief-filled voice is more than the body seen on screen, while what is seen on screen is Tupicoff's interpretation of the radio interview. The soundtrack is of the world of Kathy's personal experience, the animation is a reconstruction of the world, twice interpreted by Tupicoff.

The importance of sound, and its primacy as a documentary indicator, is acknowledged in several of the films discussed in this chapter. In *Hidden*, the interviewers are included as characters in the scene and co-director Aronowitsch is adorned with the paraphernalia of sound recording – headphones, tape deck and microphones. Aardman's *Conversation Pieces* and Tupicoff's *His Mother's Voice* begin with shots of audio devices. The pre-title shot of a tape recorder in the Aardman films acknowledges the source of the documentary material as does Tupicoff when he segues into the first animated re-enactment of Kathy's story from a live-action shot of the old radio in his kitchen on which he first heard her interview (Tupicoff, 2003). These images are hints to how animated interview documentaries assert the significance of sound, and in particular the recorded voice. These are voices of absent bodies, bodies that are represented in animation that reflects, interprets and imagines the participants as vocalic bodies. The use of animation as a representational strategy for documentary interviews both responds to and exceeds the present voices and absent bodies of interviewees. In keeping the identities of participants hidden it also adds meaning and significance to the testimonies heard on the soundtrack.

4
The World in Here

One of the contentions of this book is that if you look at the subject matter of animated documentaries and think about why animation is used in place of the live-action alternative, a tendency can be traced wherein animation compensates for the shortcomings of live-action footage. Either the footage does not exist (as in *Chicago 10*, because cameras were not allowed into the courtroom in 1968) or it is impossible to film the subject (such as *Walking with Dinosaurs*, where the prehistoric subjects precede the existence of humans let alone motion picture cameras, or in many of the interview documentaries discussed in Chapter 3, due to considerations of anonymity). There are reasons that go beyond logistics and participant privacy, however, for why animation is chosen as a representational strategy in documentary.

Live action, especially within the confines of documentary convention, is limited when it comes to visually conveying subjective, conscious experiences such as feelings and states of mind. There are various devices familiar to fiction film, for example distorting the image quality to imply a mind-altering drug experience. In documentary, even subjective documentary filmmaking, conscious experiences are usually communicated aurally to the audience via first-person narration from the filmmaker. Animation, however, is becoming an increasingly popular means by which to visually express the internal worlds of documentary subjects. Sometimes this happens in a relatively direct way, with animation offering a visualisation of a feeling or experience described by an interviewee on the soundtrack. At other times, animation works in more oblique and metaphorical ways to evoke experiences that may be unfamiliar to viewers. Frequently these types of animated documentary are seeking to raise awareness by breaking down taboos surrounding unspoken feelings or offering insight into, for example, mental health issues such as depression or brain states such as autism. We all ostensibly live in the same world but, as these animated documentaries show, we all experience that world differently. Animated documentaries often seek to dispel these differences, offering audiences access to 'conditions or principles which are hidden or beyond the comprehension of the viewer' (Wells, 1998: 122).

The suitability of animation for conveying subjective states is a quality that has been readily observed. Michael Renov (2002) comments that animated documentaries stir the imagination and evoke reality, rather than re-presenting it. Paul Ward (2005: 89) has suggested that animated documentaries have the potential to reveal more of the reality of a situation than live action, and goes on to discuss documentaries that 'use animation techniques to explicitly represent and interpret the thoughts and feelings of their subjects'. Paul Wells makes similar claims when he tells us that the use of animation to create documentary enables 'the film-maker to more persuasively show *subjective reality*'. He goes on to state that animation 'effectively shows the *perception* of reality as it is experienced' by a documentary subject and that 'this is a more truthful reality and one which is only possible to document in animation' (1998: 27 emphasis in original). Wells borrows the term 'penetration' from John Halas and Joy Batchelor to describe the way animation can 'evoke the internal space and portray the invisible' (Wells, 1998: 122). Thus, 'abstract concepts and previously unimaginable states can be visualized through animation in ways that are difficult to achieve or which remain unpersuasive in the live-action context' (Wells, 1998: 122). It seems that documentary and animation scholars alike acknowledge the potential for animation to offer viewers knowledge of what it is like to inhabit someone else's specific position and experience of the world. In addition, this knowledge is facilitated through the *evocative* capacity of animation to stimulate the *imagination* of the viewer, two concepts that will be key for this chapter.

Paul Wells highlights the power of animation to express certain aspects of human experience when he says 'it is often the case that difficult concepts or unusual codes of existence can *only* be expressed through the vocabulary available to the animator' (Wells, 1998: 122). What is it about the 'vocabulary available to the animator' that makes it uniquely suited to this task in a way that live action is not? It is, perhaps, animation's lack of indexicality that facilitates its expression of subjective, conscious experience, because, as Bill Nichols (1991: 153) claims, subjectivity eludes indexicality and you cannot deduce someone's state of mind or motivations from evidence that is visually indexical. James Elkins (1998: 252) has suggested that there are many things that are 'unrepresentable', from the forbidden (such as child pornography) to those things that one cannot bear to see (he gives the example of images of the Holocaust) and things that are technically impossible to represent. Additionally, and significantly for the animated documentaries under discussion in this chapter, 'dreams, evanescent entopical displays, hallucinations, and half-forgotten notions of pictures' come under the unrepresentable (Elkins, 1998: 252). While Elkins' comments were made about non-art and sacred images from the Renaissance, his claim that pictures get less mimetic when they try to visualise the unrepresentable is particularly useful for thinking about how animated documentaries work to visualise feelings and states of mind. For, as Elkins (1998: 253) says, 'the unrepresentable can only be experienced as something that resists presentation while also lending itself – partly and with forms held in reserve – to actual pictures.' While mimetically representative media, such as photorealistic animation and indexical live action may not be effective at conveying subjective, conscious experiences, images, in some other form, are.

Scott McCloud's work on comics can help us understand this capacity of non-mimetic animation, in particular, his line of questioning as to why humans 'respond to a cartoon as much or more than a realistic image' (McCloud, 1994: 30). He attributes this, in part, to an abstract image's tendency to emphasise specific details and that 'by stripping down an image to its essential "meaning", an artist can amplify that meaning in a way that realistic art can't' (30). Neuroscience has confirmed McCloud's instinctive belief that the human brain responds differently to abstract and realist images. Patrick Power (2008) cites a study in social psychology that, via fMRI (functional magnetic resonance imaging) scans, compared the brain activity of people viewing examples of the rotoshopped animated features *Waking Life* (2001) and *A Scanner Darkly* (2006) to when they viewed the original live-action video footage on which the animation was based. The scans revealed that the two different sets of footage prompted different types of brain activity. Live-action images 'triggered agency and intent', whereas the animation 'caused more activity in the bilateral orbitofrontal cortex (associated with emotion and reward)' (Power, 2008: 40). The study suggests that viewers respond in a more intellectual way to realistic images and in a more emotional way to non-realist ones. That is not to say that animated documentaries about subjective, conscious experience do not make viewers think, and by turn, learn something about their subject matter. It is, rather, that this knowledge, in the case of these animated documentaries, is not of a factual nature. It is not the same type of knowledge that one might learn, for example, about prehistoric life from *Walking with Dinosaurs*. It is knowledge of a different order, the acquisition of which requires empathy and imagination, something that non-mimetic animation can help evoke.

Bill Nichols uses the term 'evocative' with reference to what he calls the performative mode of documentary, films that 'stress the evocative quality of the text' (Nichols, 1994: 100). The evocative, for Nichols, is contrasted with qualities more traditional to documentary – representationalism and description. To evoke, according to the *Oxford English Dictionary*, is 'to call (a feeling, faculty, manifestation ...) into being' and 'to call up (a memory) from the past'. In this way, performative documentaries signal an epistemological shift away from logic and evidence derived from indexical images, towards knowledge that is called up through the 'poetic, expressive and rhetorical' of an 'experimental domain, expressively substantiated' (Nichols, 1994: 99, 100). I am not suggesting that the animated documentaries discussed in this chapter should be categorised as performative documentaries.[1] Nichols' suggestions of the evocative's potential for knowledge acquisition is, however, a useful concept for understanding how and why animation has staked a somewhat unique claim on documentaries about subjective, conscious experience.

The term to 'evoke' has etymological roots in magic and spirituality and it once meant to summon up spirits and later alluded to magical operations. This is apparent in Stephen A. Tyler's (1986) use of the word in an essay on ethnography that has useful applications for understanding how evocation might work in animated documentaries. Here Tyler suggests that 'evocation is neither presentation nor representation' (123) and that 'since evocation is nonrepresentational, it is not to be understood as a sign function, for it is not a "symbol of", nor does it "symbolize" what it evokes' (129). Furthermore, he stresses that 'the whole point of "evoking" rather than "representing" is that it frees ethnography from *mimesis*' (130, emphasis in original). When something has no visual equivalent it is impossible to mimetically represent it. Neither depression nor autism 'look' like anything and, as such, cannot be re-presented, nor can they be fully understood by reduction to facts. In order for those who do not have such experiences to better know what they are like, some other means of facilitating understanding is required.

One such means is through soundtracks in which those who have experienced certain subjective conscious states can be heard talking about them first-hand. These soundtracks are a vital component of the animated documentaries under discussion here, providing an aural indexical link with the realities being described. Yet, these films are more than just radio documentaries or oral testimonies. In each case, the animation adds something vital to the soundtrack, enhancing the potential understanding of the experiences being discussed. We process words and images differently, with pictures having a 'perceptual immediacy that is lacking in language' (Forceville, 2008: 463). As children, we know how to interpret images, something that requires no formal education, before we understand and can communicate via language (see: McCloud, 1994: 49; Berger, 1972: 7). As a result, the pictorial has a 'stronger emotional appeal than [the] verbal' (Forceville, 2008: 463). This allows 'images [to] plunge us into the depths of experience itself' because they 'reach the emotions before [they are] cognitively understood' (Barry, 1997: 75, 78). Those who cannot read words can often understand the meaning of an image, and images have a greater affective potential than language, something that is capitalised upon in animated documentaries that travel in the nebulous areas of subjective, conscious experience.

Animation, as image rather than word, encourages viewers to imagine, and to empathise with, that which is spoken. Aristotle, in *De Anima*, claims that images are integral to the process of imagination when he says 'imagination is that in virtue of which we say that an image occurs to us' (Aristotle, 1986: 428a). This association of image and imagination still has currency today, with the *Oxford English Dictionary* defining the latter as forming a mental concept of what is 'not actually present to the senses' with the process resulting in a 'mental *image* or idea' (emphasis added). The significance of image for imagination is indicated by philosopher Nigel Thomas (2002) when he notes that imagination 'is what makes perception more than the mere physical stimulation of sense organs. It also produces mental imagery, visual and otherwise, which is what makes it possible to think outside the confines of our present perceptual reality.' Furthermore, 'imagination makes possible all our thinking about what is, what has been, and, perhaps most important, what might be' (Thomas, 2002). Thomas' words imply that viewer imagination is a significant aspect of an animated documentary successfully communicating what it is like to experience a certain subjective, conscious state that may not be universally familiar because such a process usually requires the viewer to imagine what it is like to experience something that is entirely alien to them.

The reason non-mimetic animation, as opposed to live-action or photorealistic animation, may be particularly adept at facilitating this imagination and understanding can be extrapolated from Scott McCloud's (1994: 35–6) claim as to why readers so readily identify with comic book characters. The abstract and symbolic style of most comics makes the cartoon image more universal, allowing a greater number of people to identify with that image. Everyone can see him or herself in a simplified cartoon face of a circle filled with two dots and a line, whereas arguably only a few (or just one) can identify with a photograph, or photo-realistic image, of a face. McCloud explains this as arising from the human tendency to see one's own face, in the mind's eye, differently from the faces of others. Whereas I might see another person's face in vivid detail when I interact with them, my 'mind picture' of my own face is 'just a sketchy arrangement...a sense of shape...a sense of general placement. Something as simple and basic as a cartoon.' Thus, 'when you look at a photo or realistic drawing of a face you see it as the face of another. But when you enter the world of the cartoon you see yourself.' McCloud's implication that readers more readily empathise and identify with non-realist images of bodies and faces can be translated to animated documentaries, which frequently use non-figurative, non-specific and non-realist animation in an attempt to evoke empathy for unfamiliar states of being.

Another reason animation facilitates imagination is its affinity with visual metaphor. Bill Nichols (2010: 108) suggests that documentary topics that do not lend themselves to 'straightforward description', such as love, war and family, are better communicated via metaphor. This is because 'metaphors help understand things in terms of how they look or feel; they establish a likeness that involves our own physical or experiential encounter with a situation' (Nichols, 2010: 109). Something unique to animation, compared to live action, is the malleability and mutability of the image – an animated image can take any form and that form can easily be changed and morphed into another. This quality means animation has a stronger capacity to act as visual metaphor for ideas and other abstract notions that may be understood differently by different individuals. As Paul Wells (1998: 84) states, 'the use of metaphor simultaneously invites interpretation but insists upon openness', and 'metaphors make the literal interpretation of images ambiguous and sometimes contradictory.' The non-specificity of metaphorical animated images means they are well suited to evoking empathetic responses and identification from the audience, even for subjective, conscious experiences that are different from their own. The variety of animation techniques available means that an animated documentary's materiality and means of production can become another way of metaphorically communicating the reality expressed by the documentary subject. The different ways animation does this are explored over the following pages.

More than the interview seen: Sheila Sofian's illustrated interviews

Animator Sheila Sofian has created several animated documentaries based on recorded interviews.[2] In *Survivors* (1997) and *A Conversation with Haris* (2001), Sofian explores an approach of using 'visual metaphors and abstract animation to illustrate the interview' (Sofian, 2004). Through a style she describes as 'surreal, expressionistic drawn animation' (Sofian, 2004) she visualises the words spoken by the interviewees as well as interprets their meaning. Unlike the films discussed in Chapter 3, Sofian's animated interviews do not offer a representation of the interview scene, and any representation of the interviewee is either fleeting or gives no indication of being a likeness of the person heard on the soundtrack.

In *A Conversation with Haris*, Sofian interviews Haris Alic, a young Bosnian boy from Sarajevo who moved to the United States with his family after the Bosnian War in the 1990s. Haris describes the destruction the conflict wreaked on his hometown and the death of members of his extended family at the hands of Serbian forces. Sofian interprets his spoken words in two ways, via direct illustrations of events or objects mentioned by Haris and by giving a visual equivalent to the states of mind and emotions he describes experiencing. For example, when Haris remembers how he hoped to see the Statue of Liberty as he flew into New York for the first time, we see an animated image of the statue. Similarly, when he talks about his family members who were killed, we see figures disappear, one by one, from an animated version of a family photograph. This illustration is at times metaphorical, such as when Haris accuses the Serbians of wanting 'the whole country for themselves' and the hand of a Serbian soldier comes into frame and grasps up a mass of land that symbolises former Yugoslavia. Sofian also uses animation to express Haris' emotional experiences, such as when he talks about moving from New York to Baltimore. Here the colour palette becomes dark and ominous in shades of black. An image of a lone white figure receding into a vast black background, becoming smaller and smaller until it is swallowed up entirely, evokes Haris' description of feeling alone.

For *Survivors*, Sofian interviewed victims (or 'survivors' as one speaker corrects early on in the film) of domestic violence, along with professionals who work with such women, and the men who habitually abuse and attack their partners. Sofian edited together portions of these separate interviews to create the audio track of the sixteen-minute film. This seamless aural insight into domestic violence is illustrated through imagery that relates both directly and indirectly to what is heard in voiceover. In a similar style to *A Conversation with Haris*, the animation alternates between picking out elements or words of the interview as they are heard and evoking more abstract concepts such as fears and social attitudes. When one survivor describes how she was punished for returning home late one day, we see a woman's hand turning a door handle as a fist comes straight towards the camera. Here the animation picks out a key element of the speaker's account – arriving home and the unexpected act of violence that comes from behind the door. At another point in the film, the images visualise ideas that are alluded to by an interviewee. Brian, who works with men who have abused their partners, describes how these men often have very fixed ideas about gender roles. The animation that accompanies his statement illustrates the point with a female figure that metamorphoses between the traditional female roles of secretary, housewife and mother.

Sofian also uses animation in a less direct way so that images are not always simply giving visual form to what is heard, but are also evoking abstract concepts such as emotions. As one woman describes how her mother refused to let her move back home, admonishing that she had 'made her bed', a figure can be seen trapped underneath a sheet on a bed, struggling to break free. In addition to visualising this metaphorical turn of phrase, the figure's desperate, futile straining at the oppressively smothering bedclothes that keep her pinned in place evoke this woman's frustration of being imprisoned in her domestic situation. This feeling of being trapped is further evoked by the animated bed sheet first being pulled across the screen, filling the frame and obliterating the face that had previously been 'speaking' the mother's words. The vastness of this inescapable prison is amplified in the following frames as the bed on which the woman is pinned occupies almost the entire frame with only a black emptiness surrounding it (see Figure 4.1). This expressive use of animation to evoke linguistic metaphors spoken by the interviewees and the more abstract ideas heard discussed is a prevalent feature of *Survivors*.

As in several of the films discussed in Chapter 3, the women interviewed for *Survivors* wished to remain anonymous, so their animated

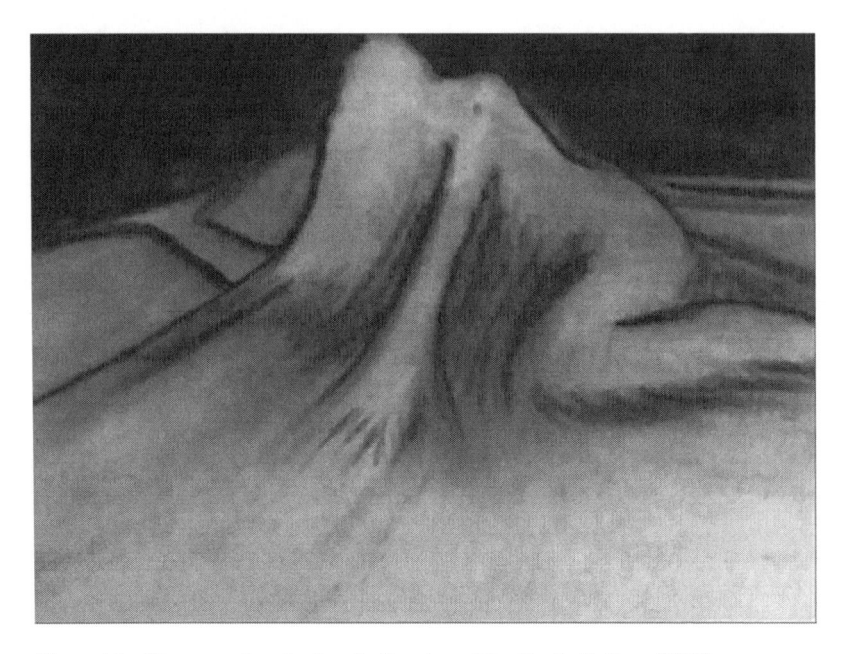

Figure 4.1 The use of metaphor in *Survivors* (dir. Sheila Sofian, 1997)

counterparts bear no likeness to their real selves. Sofian also found that audiences responded positively to this anonymizing act, and viewers reported that the use of animation instead of live action prevented them from making judgements about the women based on their appearance (Sofian, 2004). Sofian also sought to make the animated realisations as universal as possible so that a wide audience would be able to empathise with the situations of the women whose accounts are heard (Sofian, 2009). This approach resonates with McCloud's suggestions that the more abstract and less specific a figure or face is, the more people can identify with it. To further achieve this, Sofian animated multiple characters to represent each woman's point of view, thus no one animated figure is identified with any one voice heard on the soundtrack. So, while the figures are recognisable as women, they do not resemble the actual women heard speaking. The universality of the image is aided by the representation of different races and physical characteristics so that no one type becomes associated with domestic violence.

The materiality and aesthetic of the animation techniques chosen by Sofian for each film come to have thematic and metaphorical resonance. For *Survivors* she hand-drew the images using crayons, a medium usually associated with children's drawings. The waxy, grainy texture of the crayon's mark becomes more conspicuous through Sofian's choice to create the animation using a four-field, or an area that measures four-inches square. The lo-tech simplicity of the animation technique and its associations with the innocent play of childhood works a double effect in the film by making the visuals accessible and 'friendly', as Sofian has described them, as well as counterpointing the harshness and brutality of the women's stories (Sofian, 2004). *A Conversation with Haris* was created through the painting-on-glass technique of animation. In this technique, an image is painted onto opaque Plexiglas and then photographed with a camera before it is re-painted, altering it by varying degrees, and shot as the next frame. This is a process of filming that requires the destruction of the artwork as it is created, so unlike other forms of drawn animation, in which individual images continue to exist after they have been filmed, the images that make up *A Conversation with Haris* are ephemeral. The painted images transition into each other via a series of fades to and from what looks like a blank canvas. The delineation of the painted form dissolves and disappears into a block of hazy colour, or sometimes no colour at all, before evolving into the next clearly identifiable object or figure. This animation technique, and the process of progression through dissolution, becomes a metaphorical signifier of Haris' world repeatedly being collapsed and re-built as well as the ongoing experience of upheaval that Haris has endured since the Bosnian conflict.

In both *Survivors* and *A Conversation with Haris*, Sofian chooses techniques that allow a certain fluidity of movement and transition between images. Therefore, it is not just the metaphor of the static, isolated image that comes to evoke and have meaning in her films, but also the metamorphosis of one image to another. Metamorphosis is a process to which animation lends itself particularly well and is something that cannot be achieved in live-action cinema without the aid of digital animation techniques. In fact, Paul Wells considers metamorphosis so integral to animation that he has called it the 'constituent core of animation itself' (Wells, 1998: 69) while Sergei Eisenstein celebrated the 'plasmaticness' (Eisenstein, 1988: 21) he considered unique to animation. Wells defines metamorphosis as 'the ability for an image to literally change into another completely different image, for example, through the evolution of the line, the shift in formations of clay, or the manipulation of objects or environments' (Wells, 1998: 69). Sofian's use of hand-drawn and painted techniques in *A Conversation with Haris* and *Survivors*, ones that allow complete freedom to alter the image in both subtle and extreme ways, lend themselves to this type of seamless visual evolution of the image.

While in *A Conversation with Haris* the image evolves via a series of fades, the images in *Survivors* often move in a more traditionally metamorphic way, transforming from one clear object to another in a 'fluid linkage of images through the process of animation itself rather than through editing' (Wells, 1998: 69). One woman describes turning to her pastor as a last resort and receiving the advice that she must stay with her husband because 'God does not want people to be divorced.' As we hear her say this, figures of a man and woman can be seen standing in front of a large cross, the horizontal strut of which folds inwards, forcing the couple together. The couple disappears under the pressure, and falls out from the folds of the cross as a blob of unidentifiable matter before the cross itself morphs into a couple bound tightly together by rope. As the woman struggles to break free, two hands close in prayer around them. The smooth transition between these stages and objects is a clear metaphor for the uselessness of the Church's counsel as the physical binding of woman to abusive partner leads to their eventual destruction and her disappearance from the frame.

Scott Bukatman (2000: 226) has said of digital morphing that it 'holds out the promise of endless transformation and opportunity to freely make, unmake, and remake oneself'. This echoes Eisenstein's much earlier suggestion that our attraction to the metamorphosis found in US studio animation is due to 'its trait of all-possible diversity of form' (Eisenstein, 1988: 21). There is something primal, Eisenstein claims, about our attraction to the metamorphic, plasmatic form. Wells (1998: 69), however, points out that 'in enabling the collapse of the illusion of physical space, metamorphosis destabilises the image, conflating horror and humour, dream and reality, certainty and speculation.' Wells' reading of metamorphosis gives a better understanding of the symbolism of the fluidity of transition in *Survivors*, where the instability of the human form can be seen as implying the lack of security in these abused women's lives. We can see this in one sequence in which a woman describes being beaten so badly by her husband while she was pregnant that it induced early labour. Her heavily expectant form morphs and transforms, reflecting the fragility of her body in this physical state. Metamorphosis, in this example, is less an opportunity to 'freely [...] remake oneself' and more a metaphor for uncertainty and the destruction of self-identity that comes with persistent physical and mental abuse.

The fluidity of bodily transformation in Sofian's film illustrates Vivian Sobchack's (2000: xiv) suggestion that morphing is a 'representational practice whose specific material means radically interrogate certain traditional notions of coherence and self-identity in space and time'. Morphing thus 'breaks down ontological and epistemological boundaries' by leading viewers to question the very things previously thought unquestionable – the physical presence of the body and knowledge of one's own identity (Sobchack, 2000: xvi). Here the metaphor of absence comes into play with consideration of Norman M. Klein's theorisation of the moments that occur between the two extremes of an animated metamorphosis, or 'ani-morphing' as he calls it (Klein, 2000: 22). The ani-morph is the 'lapse or hesitation' between the extremes (22). It is 'solid and absent at the same time. It is like a scar that narrates, a Braille of absences' (24). The present absence of the animated image is exacerbated through the process of metamorphosis, in which the image transitions through a brief period of non-presence as it transforms from one recognisable thing to another. As the image de- and re-forms we are forced to consider the meaning of this visual transience. Such visual instability mirrors physical instability while the process of metamorphosis must also be reconciled as an excessive gesture that goes beyond the mere representation of two different objects. Their connection through a transformative progression of destruction and reconstruction is a process of both too much and not enough, one that in the case of *Survivors* reflects the physical and mental experiences of the abused women.

Inside out: animating subjective experience

The potential of animation to evoke subjective, conscious experiences by encouraging us to imagine and empathise means that expressive, non-realist animation is frequently used in films about mental health issues, feelings and brain states that may be unfamiliar to the majority of viewers. The *Animated Minds* series, directed by clinical psychologist-turned-documentary director and producer Andy Glynne, was the first to extensively exploit and explore this capacity of animation in a documentary context, first in 2003 and again in a second series in 2009. The first series was commissioned by the United Kingdom's Channel 4 as part of a season on mental health, and each of the four three-minute films tackles a different issue. The second series, originally called *Troubled Minds*, was made for the UK cable channel Teachers TV and funded by the Wellcome Trust; it focuses on mental health issues amongst young people. Each of the eight films comprises animated visuals accompanied by testimony from one person (with the exception of one film in the second series, *My Blood Is My Tears*, which features testimony from three young women) talking about their experience. The films have distinct animation styles, in part because each one was created by a different animator, but also, importantly, revealing the way animation can be designed and manipulated to reflect and reinforce the subject's voiceover.

The films have been described as allowing viewers to 'climb inside the minds of the mentally distressed' (Mosaic Films, 2012b), and they demonstrate certain characteristics of the penetrative power of animation delineated by Paul Wells. Through this *'revelatory* tool, used to reveal conditions or principles which are hidden or beyond the comprehension of the viewer', animation 'becomes a *mediator* of possibilities, offering as close to a visceral revelation of the condition as a medium of expression can offer' (Wells, 1998: 122, emphasis in original). In *Animated Minds*, animation mediates by means of visual metaphor. As the films' makers say, '[we know] that it can never be fully understood what it feels like to actually experience some of the difficulties covered in these films, but – as far as metaphors go, it was felt that it would be a good starting point' (*Animated Minds*, 2012b). In fact, *Animated Minds* tends towards the visually illustrative as much, if not more than, the metaphorical. That is, the animation frequently gives a direct visualisation of a physical experience or event described by the interviewee and, in general, the series' animation closely mirrors the words heard in the voiceovers. Many of the moments of visual metaphor are similarly prompted by a metaphor or simile used by the documentary subject to describe their experiences. There are, however, also instances of the animation working in a less direct relationship with sound and more obliquely evoking the mental health issue under discussion.

In *An Alien in the Playground*, a film about Asperger's Sydrome from the second series, the animation illustrates Joshua's struggle with interpersonal communication at school, and the subsequent bullying he was subjected to as a result of being different.[3] When he talks about his confusion over decoding facial expressions and body language in the playground, things that are as 'obscure as hieroglyphs', the image shows an animated version of Joshua surrounded by faces and pairs of figures interacting. As the facial expressions and body movements change, 'Joshua's' face is drawn in a frown, to illustrate his confusion. Similarly, later in the film he explains how he constructs an 'equation' of someone's personality to create a mask that he can then communicate through. As he says this, the camera pulls out on densely written equations to reveal them as the surface of a simple mask, against which the Joshua figure appears as the words 'hello' come out of the mask's mouth. This type of direct animated illustration of what we hear is common throughout the films and aids in our comprehension of the experiences being described by giving a visual equivalent to what is being said.

The *Animated Minds* interviewees often use metaphors in attempts to better explain their subjective experience, metaphors that are accompanied by an animated visualisation. In *Becoming Invisible*, Nicole describes the feelings that accompanied her progression towards severe anorexia as a strong feeling of something being wrong with her, as if she was in black and white while the rest of the world was in colour. This spoken metaphor is made overt in a classroom scene that animates the figure representing Nicole in monochrome tones, while those who surround her as well as the setting in which they are all placed are drawn in colour. In *Fish on a Hook*, agoraphobic Mike equates the panic attacks he experiences in association with his condition, and how his behaviour may be incomprehensible to an outsider, to the wriggling of a fish when caught on a hook. This metaphor is animated and a silhouette image of a fish on a hook morphs into a silhouetted human figure jerking around, recognisable as the representation of Mike from earlier in the film. As Mike says that such metaphorical physical behaviour makes no sense until you know what causes it, the camera pans out to reveal the source of the silhouette – an animated figure thrashing around with a fishhook stuck in its mouth. In both examples, the animation reiterates and gives image to the spoken metaphor.

While much of the animation in the *Animated Minds* series directly mirrors the words spoken on the soundtrack, there are instances when the films require more effort on the part of the audience's imagination as the imagery offers illustrations that are not made explicit in the spoken accounts. In *The Light Bulb Thing*, Hannah describes how her increasingly erratic behaviour brought about by manic depression led people to slowly 'withdraw their trust'. Hannah does not give specifics, but the animation visualises this experience in a way that makes it easier to imagine. A female figure sits on a couch, initially with two other people who are then erased from the frame one by one. First the person sitting next to the female figure disappears and then the other, who is sitting at the opposite end of the sofa from the woman, as if attempting to get as far away from her as possible, also leaves the frame. The subsequent metamorphosis of couch to hospital bed conveys a sudden, yet seamless transition, one that Hannah sums up as 'then you're on your own and then...you're in hospital.' Her experience of feeling lost and ungrounded after coming down from the manic phase of her illness is evoked in the final scene where a solitary female figure can be seen sitting on a chair in a vast empty space (see Figure 4.2). The limited style of animation – the lack of outline with space instead being demarcated by solitary objects – and the pallid hues of the colour palette, illustrate Hannah's sense of loss and isolation. This is further emphasised in comparison to earlier portions of the film, where Hannah describes the euphoria of the manic phase, which is visualised with a frame that is much more full and more colourful.

The films in the *Animated Minds* series are successful because they manage to effectively combine the subjectivity of the oral accounts with the more general, non-mimetic animation that facilitates empathy and identification on the part of the viewer at the same time as encouraging our imagination of what it is like to live in someone else's shoes. In *Fish on a Hook*, the prison cell-like safe confines of Mike's apartment, a small space with clearly demarcated walls drawn in perspective to make the area seem smaller, is contrasted to the terrifyingly vast boundlessness of the outside world. At one point, Mike describes himself as a 'prisoner who's moved out into a very hostile area' and he is drawn as a lone, white, faceless figure tiptoeing through a huge mesh-like box against a dark blue background. The agoraphobic's fear of open spaces is effectively evoked through this imagery, without the interviewee needing

Figure 4.2 Evocative emptiness as a metaphor for manic depression in *The Light Bulb Thing* (dir. Andy Glynne, animation dir. Paul Rains, Mosaic Films, 2003)

to overtly explain the pathology of his condition. Instead, Mike speaks about the specifics of his daily life – the lack of food in his refrigerator forcing him to leave his house, the fact that the local supermarket may as well be 'hell'. Similarly, the metaphor of a vast, looming staircase up which Mike, a tiny figure compared to the height of each step, must drag his shopping, clearly indicates the difficulty of a task that is simple and uneventful for most of us. It is the specificity of Mike's account combined with the broadly emblematic animation that allow viewers to imagine what it is like to suffer from agoraphobia. The animated figure that stands in for Mike, which lacks distinct facial and other features, is sufficiently non-realistic for anyone to be able to project themselves into the frame, in a similar way to how Scott McCloud theorises readers identify with symbolic, non-realistic faces in comic books. Yet, the design of this figure, with its large lumbering body and disproportionately small head, encourages us to image ourselves in a certain way, as having an uncomfortable physical form that awkwardly occupies space.

The predominantly direct relationship between spoken word and animation in *Animated Minds* gives insight into, and allows viewers to 'penetrate' subjective, conscious experiences unfamiliar to the majority. However, as Paul Wells (1998: 122) notes, penetrative animation can also 'characterise a condition or principle in itself, *without recourse to exaggeration or comparison*' (emphasis added). *An Eyeful of Sound* (Samantha Moore, 2009) and *Little Deaths* (Ruth Lingford, 2010) use animation to aid the imagination of, and empathy with, experiences and feelings that are hard to put into words and cannot be seen. In both cases, the animation is not directly representing an experience or even offering a tangible this-feels-like-something-else comparison. Instead, it works in a more subtle way to evoke the experiences being discussed by their interviewees.

An Eyeful of Sound evokes, rather than represents, the experience of synaesthesia, a neurological condition that causes someone to experience normally separated sensations together (for example, sight stimulated by sound, or taste stimulated by seeing colours). In the film, Moore focuses on people who have audio-visual synaesthesia, or who see sounds. Like most animated documentary, the film combines animated visuals with a soundtrack on which interviewees speak of their first-hand experience. At the beginning of the film, it appears as if the abstract animation has little connection to the words being spoken. That is, until it becomes clear later in the film that Moore's animated images are responding to the film's musical score in the way a synaesthetic person's brain will trigger images in response to sounds.

The film ostensibly follows the narrative of a return train journey to visit psychologist Dr Jamie Ward, an expert in synaesthesia, a journey that is shown through animated point-of-view shots. However, neither Ward nor any of the interviewees are represented in the film. Instead, the synaesthetic experience is evoked through abstract animation superimposed on the animated image, for example of the view out of the train window, in order to demonstrate how the synaesthetic perception of the world differs from the non-synaesthetic one. So, as the train pulls into the terminus in London, a beeping sound is heard – perhaps the sound of the warning signal given when train doors open – and as this happens a messy mesh of black squiggles is superimposed over the image of the station. As the film progresses it becomes increasingly clear that the abstract animation relates to the synaesthetic experience, something that occurs in part through repetition. As one interviewee says that she sees things in the road that are not actually there, a dog barks on the soundtrack and a bright pink asterisk is animated over the street scene that occupies the animated frame. The first hearing/viewing of this may go unnoticed, but the pink asterisk is then repeated several times throughout the film whenever a dog bark is heard, and this repetition enables us to make a connection between this sound and that colourful image. While the images in *An Eyeful of Sound* do not directly visualise the words spoken on the soundtrack in the way seen in *Animated Minds,* there is still an immediate relationship between sound and image when one realises that the abstract, superimposed animation occurs in response to ambient, abstract sounds and the music heard in the background.

The inadequacy of language to describe the synaesthetic experience is demonstrated in the pre-title sequence. Here several different voices can be heard saying things like 'it's sort of like ...', 'no, I can't think of the right word' and 'almost, only it's much thicker than that ...'. These words are written on the screen as they are spoken and this sequence indicates the difficulty of translating a sensorial experience into language. Instead of relying just on interviews, Moore worked very closely with her participants to try to evoke synaesthesia in an accurate way and she describes the film as a collaboration between herself, the interviewees and Dr Jamie Ward (Moore, 2011). This included giving the participants a Munsell colour chart and drawing, painting and other art materials to respond to the sounds they heard. Once Moore had turned these responses into still digital images, they were confirmed as accurate by the synaesthetic collaborator before being converted into animation (Moore, 2011). This becomes apparent in the second half of the film, when the nature of the abstract images is clarified as matching, as closely as possible, what the interviewees perceive when they hear the sounds on the audio track. So when someone describes a sound as 'oh! Green!' green circles are seen moving across the screen from left to right. However, the film does not slavishly follow the descriptions spoken, and taken holistically it is a kind of audio-visual melange that helps us to imagine synaesthesia. Its success in this regard is reported by Moore (2011) who states that the synaesthetic people with whom she collaborated felt *An Eyeful of Sound* 'represented not just their individual synaesthetic reactions but gave a more rounded view of the condition'. That it is more effective in doing this than language is implied by one participant's comment that after seeing the film her husband, who was not synaesthetic and to whom she had previously tried to describe her way of experiencing the world, had a better understanding of her condition.

Moore suggests that 'visual metaphor could have no place in the treatment of [synaesthesia] since the synaesthetic reactions themselves are entirely abstract to the non-synaesthetic eye; they only represent themselves' (Moore, 2011). A similar assessment could be made of the subject of Ruth Lingford's *Little Deaths*, which explores individuals' experience of orgasm and continues a trend in Lingford's work of 'celebrat[ing] key aspects of our experience that are often supressed' (Pummell, 2012: 76). The feeling of sexual climax cannot be directly compared to something else via visual metaphor and, like synaesthesia, 'cannot possibly be captured photorealistically' (Moore, 2011). Instead, Lingford uses an experimental animation approach that combines the abstract and the abstractly figurative to evoke the elusive physical and emotional experience of orgasm. There are moments in *Little Deaths* where Lingford gives a direct representation of something an interviewee says. For example, when several speakers talk about yellow and bright white colours in response to the question 'what do you see', the frame is taken up with an amorphous, abstract mandala-like shape that modulates to an increasingly bright yellow until the screen is almost entirely white, bordered to the right and left with thick wavy yellow lines. Earlier in the film, someone describes the feeling of orgasm as being like a roller coaster and the feeling of rising and falling. As this is said, the image moves along the feint, sketchy outline of a roller-coaster track, which soon metamorphoses into the vertebrae of a spine. Both the roller coaster and the spine remain relatively abstract and de-contextualised against a black background.

Overall, however, *Little Deaths* mostly avoids direct visualisation of the spoken. Animated images morph into each other and no one object, abstract or figurative, remains on the screen for long. Frequently, and especially with the more abstract images, the animation seems not to bear any direct relationship to the words being heard. Instead, it works to evoke the fleeting and indefinable experience of intense sexual pleasure. This occurs in part through the combination of abstract animation and animation that is figurative but non-realist. In addition, the moving, morphing outline of shapes and figures has a capacity to evoke in the sense suggested by Germaine Dulac in an essay first published in 1927. Here she petitioned for the importance of movement, as opposed to narrative, in the early development of cinema and claims that 'the shifting of a line, or of a volume in a changing cadence creates emotion without any crystallization of ideas' (Dulac, 1982 [1927]: 8). In *Little Deaths*, ideas summoned by the visual seem to evaporate as quickly as they appear, and the film has a sort of languid rhythm of melding movement and transformation. This, along with its visual non-specificity, evokes the personal, subjective experience of not only the sexual climaxes experienced and described by the interviewees, but orgasm in general.

Hybrids of reality

Ruth Lingford's film demonstrates the importance of animation style and materiality for evoking subjective conscious experience. Ruth Hayes (2012: 209) ascribes this potential as being in part due to how drawn animation's 'distinctive line quality emphasises the animation's constructed nature, and puts viewers on notice that the image is unstable. It might metamorphose at any moment.' Another way to emphasise the constructedness of animation is through hybridising expressive animation with either live-action or photorealistic imagery. Adopting this representational strategy in animated documentaries about subjective, conscious experiences encourages insight into the subjectivity of the documentary subjects (or in some cases collaborators and filmmakers) by contrasting insider and outsider perspectives on, and ways of interacting with, the world.

A Is for Autism (1992) differs from the films discussed so far in this chapter in that it uses drawings made by those whose subjectivity the film is investigating. The drawings are animated and combined with live-action images and a soundtrack in which autistic people talk about their experiences of living with the developmental disability. Autism manifests primarily in difficulty in social communication and interaction, and the contributors to the film represent the ten per cent of those with autism who are able to communicate and reflect on their condition. Because autism is a spectrum disorder, which can vary from mild to severe and impact on social communication, interaction and imagination, it will often affect people in different ways (The National Autistic Society, 2012). The film conveys the spectrum of the disability by picking out common traits of autism, such as love of routines, sensory sensitivity and intense special interests. While the film discourages broad generalisation through the first-person specificity of the voiceover interviews, and even though the understanding generated by the film is facilitated by autistic people who are at the more able end of the spectrum, their contribution can still 'provide a glimpse into the experience of the vast majority who are not able to communicate or express themselves in this way' (Arnall, 1992).

Producer Dick Arnall (1992) points out that 'animation was a tool used to present the subject, not an artistic medium in its own right.' However, I would contend that it is not only the contributors' drawings, but also the way these drawings are brought into motion and combined with live-action imagery that encourages an understanding of autism. Paul Wells (1998: 124–5) has suggested that the drawings in *A Is for Autism*, through:

> prominent colours, distortions and omissions in representative forms, over-elaborated or scarcely detailed figures and objects, or the mere spontaneity of the line, all reveal aspects of a condition which few can understand or engage with.

These traits, however, are less immediately identifiable as indicative of autism to the untutored eye seeing the images fleetingly on the screen. For example, it is not clear how the drawings of trains seen early on in the film relate to the topic of autism in general or how they might aid our understanding this condition. To an unaware viewer, they may look like any drawings from a child's hand. It is when these images crop up repeatedly and trains are frequently seen chugging through the frame, that they begin to gain a significance, one confirmed by hearing collaborator Daniel Sellers talk about how much he likes to draw these objects. His discussion reveals his intense interest in this topic, to the point of being able to draw from memory different types of locomotive in great detail. Daniel's drawings of the trains and their repeated appearance in the film become a metaphor for this common trait of autism, without the audience being overtly told that obsessive fixation on special interests is a characteristic of the condition. Trains, and even

Daniel's individual drawings of them, do not directly convey autism; it is only when these images are animated and included throughout the film that they begin to gain meaning.

Repetition of visual and aural elements in *A Is for Autism* becomes a key way of communicating the experience of the condition. Many of the contributors talk of their need to repeat tasks and the comfort that comes through this, yet they also talk of the frustration it creates for those around them. This is evoked particularly effectively in the final images of the film, which show the live-action image of a hand ripping strips from a sheet of paper on which a hand-drawn animated stick figure walks up a flight of stairs. As the child's hand rips at the sheet, the animated figure gets stuck in a loop at the top of the stairs. Like a needle jumping on a record, the figure reaches the top only to jump back down several steps before attempting once again to reach the top, ultimately failing to reach its goal before the child's hand rips off and crumples the final strip of paper. This sequence conveys both the necessity and futility of repeated action, and the frustration that arises for both the autistic person and his or her caregiver.

Throughout the film, the combination of live action and animation helps communicate the contrast between the autistic and non-autistic perspective on the world. This strategy is employed to convey the difficulties often associated with autism surrounding intimacy and personal interaction. In a sequence using a combination of pixilation and drawn animation,[4] a mother (played by an actress) sits cradling a 2-D drawing representing a little girl (see Figure 4.3). As the voice of an autistic woman describes how her difficulty with being touched conflicted with her craving for tenderness, the animated hand-drawn figure of the little girl shrinks in her mother's arms, getting smaller frame by frame until it finally disappears leaving the mother empty handed. This scene uses animation in two key ways to indicate how autistic people can feel isolated from society and family – by distinguishing between the live-action reality of the 'normal' mother and the animated embodiment of the autistic little girl, and by using stop-motion animation to gradually disappear the girl from the shot.

Two films from the first *Animated Minds* series also use a combination of live action and animation to evoke the contrast between how the interview subjects perceive reality and how the majority of society experiences it. In *Dimensions*, Chas talks about his experience of psychosis, or paranoid schizophrenia; in *Obsessively Compulsive*, Steve reveals the struggle of battling his obsessive–compulsive tendencies. To Chas, the world becomes increasingly disordered and confusing as

Figure 4.3 Animation and live action in *A Is for Autism* (dir. Tim Webb, prod. Dick Arnall, Channel 4, 1992)

he slips further into psychosis and is bombarded by frightening messages and voices that layer into a jumble of visual and oral static. This is evoked through live action that is manipulated, treated and overlaid with animated images. The use of mixed media, and in particular the layering of multiple live-action images which are then overlaid with animation, helps conjure up the sense of Chas' experience of the world as disjointed and disturbing. This sense is emphasised by the regular, persistent flickering of the visual elements of the film, accompanied by sounds of static on the audio track, as if reality is like a radio or television that constantly goes out of tune. Chas initially experiences a benign alternative reality with delusions of grandeur, but we get the sense of an increasingly threatening world through progressively disturbed and disturbing images. Chas' feelings of persecution and paranoia, for example, are conveyed with typescript messages encouraging self-harm that flash up on the screen in quick alternation with point-of-view shots of daily London life, such as the interior of an underground train, all taken from a canted angle.

Whereas Chas' psychosis involves an alteration of his perception of the outside world, something he describes as 'living outside consensus reality', Steve's obsessive–compulsive disorder manifests through intrusive thoughts about Saddam Hussein and Steve's conviction that a failure to banish these thoughts will result in an escalation in the Gulf conflict. In *Dimensions*, the audience is given a voyeuristic view of the world, always watching from a distance, removed from the images onscreen as if to mirror Chas' disconnection from reality. In *Obsessively Compulsive* the live-action images physically invade Steve's body, reflecting the intrusion of his obsessive thoughts. *Obsessively Compulsive* uses an actor, whose movements are superimposed on an animated backdrop using stop motion. These movements are then repeatedly looped to convey the behaviour of repetitive action that Steve feels he has to complete in order to clear his mind. The thoughts are visualised through the further superimposition of live-action images onto Steve's body and the objects of his daily life. Images of the Gulf Conflict play inside Steve's head, and later onto a cup of coffee, as he says that everyday tasks had to be completed in the absence of an intrusive thought. A stop-motion animated hand repeatedly picks up and puts down the coffee cup and the image of Saddam persistently appears on the surface of the dark liquid. The obsession with ridding his body and mind of intrusive thoughts is conveyed through further sequences such as when Steve repeatedly peels off the skin from the back of his hand, which is superimposed with images of the Gulf War that stubbornly refuse to disappear, no matter how many layers of epidermis are removed.

In *Obsessively Compulsive* the invasion of Steve's body and mind with thoughts about Saddam Hussein and the war is effectively evoked through the relationship between animation and live action. The superimposition of images onto the human body, and the manipulation of the body through stop motion, is a metaphor for the obsession and psychological distress that Steve describes, much as the voyeuristic nature of the live-action material evokes Chas' psychosis in *Dimensions*. While both films use a combination of live action and animation, the differences in style and approach work to evoke differently the two psychological disorders.

In his Oscar-winning short film *Ryan* (2004) Chris Landreth uses 3-D computer-generated animation in a combination of realist and expressionistic styles to convey both his own subjectivity and that of his subject, animator Ryan Larkin. The soundtrack edits together an interview between Landreth and Ryan with interviews with two other people from Ryan's past, along with Landreth's intermittent first-person voiceover narration. This accompanies a constructed visual world in which Landreth and Ryan talk in a cafeteria, based on the one in the mission house in Montreal, Canada, where Ryan lives. The film is an intriguing combination of photo-realism and fantastical animation and it is this contrast that gives insight into what goes on in both Landreth's and Ryan's heads.

In the opening moments of the film, Landreth establishes the premise of what he calls 'psycho-realism' (Singer, 2004). We see Landreth leaning on a hand basin in front of a mirror in a grimy public bathroom – his form is realised in a photorealistic way, and he clearly resembles the real Chris Landreth. That is, apart from the bright slashes of colour bisecting his cheek like scars, and the yellow nebula on the side of his head. Landreth introduces himself and, pointing to the 'scars' and 'nebula' says, these are 'from October 1989, when my unbridled romantic worldview was permanently shattered', and 'from September 1992 when I underwent a catastrophic failure to manage my finances in any meaningful way'. Immediately, Landreth establishes the relationship between the physical and the psychological, and the photo-realistic and the expressionistic, by showing us how mental scars are rendered visible. Unlike many of the films discussed in this chapter, *Ryan* bears a much closer resemblance to the physical world, and how it is represented in live-action imagery. It is, however, through the embellishment of expressionistic animated interpretations of subjectivity onto realistic animated images that this film works to evoke the internal world of its subjects.

Landreth's application of computer technology within a documentary to portray the internal, rather than to explain observable facts about the external world by mimicking the look of reality,[5] demonstrates a unique attitude to the possibilities of this technology. According to Landreth (Singer, 2004), this attitude comes from:

> a belief I have in using advanced tools and CG. Unlike the way they're generally used, to doggedly recreate photorealism or to tell superficially imaginative stories, what I think they can be used for is to show, in a very detailed and realistic way, something that is not necessarily realistic – which, in this case, is the psychological makeup of people and characters; often ordinary characters who nonetheless have very complex psychologies and personalities and behavioral dysfunctions.

The use of computer animation allows us to see the world through the 'looking glass', as Landreth (2005) describes it, of psycho-realism in which characters wear the internal as physical wounds, visibly betraying their personal issues and psychological baggage.

Ryan's existence as a panhandler on the streets of Montreal belies his background as the once rising star of the National Film Board of Canada's animation unit where, under the mentorship of Norman McLaren, he made the Oscar-nominated short film *Walking* (1969) at the age of twenty-five. Larkin, unable to deal with the pressure of his early success and his subsequent creative block, succumbed to alcohol and cocaine addiction in the 1970s, and by the time Landreth interviews him he is living in poverty. Ryan is animated as a decimated figure, battered by years of substance abuse and still bearing the scars of his artistic failure. His head is notable as much for what is absent as what is there. Most of his skull is missing and only the key distinctive features of a pair of round glasses and a forelock of grey hair are used to represent his face (see Figure 4.4).

Various computer effects are used to further convey the psychology of Ryan and Landreth, beyond the seemingly permanent scars they carry from their respective pasts. In the opening of the film, as Landreth talks of his fear of personal failure, his head is smothered by swathes of coloured threads that wrap around him like bandages. This motif is used later in the film to convey Ryan's loss of creativity. Derek Lamb,

Figure 4.4 'Psycho-realism' in *Ryan* (dir. Chris Landreth, Copperheart Entertainment and the National Film Board of Canada, 2004)

with whom Ryan worked at the Film Board, describes the flush of ideas that came with Ryan's early cocaine abuse and the subsequent cessation of that flow as Ryan's consumption of narcotics increased in a desperate bid to recapture those first moments of altered perception and heightened productivity. As Lamb mentions the words 'every artist's worst fear', the coloured threads of artistic failure wrap around the body of a young Ryan, a figure previously seen joyously dancing, superimposed into Larkin's last film that was made in 1971. The animated bandages of creative strangulation convey Ryan's plight, and Landreth's fears for a similar fate, in a way that live-action or photo-realistic animation could not, and allow us to imagine this fear through a visual image that is far more evocative than Lamb's commentary alone.

In one notable scene, Landreth confronts Ryan over his alcoholism. Throughout the film Ryan is seen sipping from a thermos flask that repeatedly reaches out to him with small, waving hands demanding attention. When Landreth mentions Ryan's alcohol addiction, the first time the film makes the audience aware of this, the metaphor of these small but insisting hands becomes apparent as signifying the hold this substance has over Ryan. As Landreth broaches the issue, a halo of fluorescent flickering light appears above his head. This slightly precarious looking contraption is attached to Landreth via two metal rods and reveals his saintly, yet misguided, intentions. During the twenty seconds of silence that follows, the background becomes distorted and increasingly less defined, like paint sliding down a canvas, until Ryan eventually, and explosively, responds to Landreth's do-gooding. Ryan's head fragments into angry, spiky tendrils, Landreth's halo flickers and dies, and a poster in the background melts into a Dali-esque puddle that drips down the wall as the cosy intimacy between interviewer and interviewee collapses.

Ryan is an intriguing combination of insider and outsider perspectives of subjectivity. Landreth is representing himself, as well as Ryan, and he admits towards the end of the film that his concern for Ryan is as much to do with his own issues with his mother's death from alcoholism as it is about Ryan's addiction. Landreth clearly projects his own fears and baggage onto Ryan, as is indicated by the several sequences involving the strangling threads of artistic failure. There are also moments, however, when the film offers Ryan's interpretation through the animation of the sketches he draws of two other interviewees, Derek Lamb and Ryan's ex-partner Felicity Fanjoy. Ryan's sketches were used to create 3-D models that are incorporated into the world of the film, yet remain distinct from it through their visual style. These animated sketches reveal Ryan's affection for these two people who played such significant roles in his past. They also work to emphasise that Ryan and Landreth are the subjects of the film, as these are the only two characters whose subjectivity is revealed through the computer-generated 'psycho-realism'. No such insight is provided into the psyches of Felicity and Derek, whose likenesses remain sketchy. In contrast to this, our understanding of Ryan and Landreth is facilitated by the juxtaposition of the realistic and the metaphorical. The computer-generated manifestations of the characters' psychology becomes an animated excess that is painted onto a canvas of realism, through which we begin to understand the inner worlds of both Ryan Larkin and Chris Landreth.

Landreth is aware that his interpretation of Ryan's subjectivity is heavy with the baggage of his own worldview and experiences when he cites a favourite quote that 'we don't see things as *they* are, we see things as *we* are' (Landreth, 2005). This highlights the epistemological complexity of the films discussed in this chapter and is a reminder that while these films are about subjective, conscious experience they are most often not autobiographical or first-person accounts and in the majority of films explored here, the animation is created by someone other than those whose subjectivity is being conveyed.

A film that is a first-person account of mental life, and also uses a combination of live action and animation to convey this, is Jonathan Hodgson's *Feeling My Way* (1997). In this film, Hodgson prompts us to imagine an everyday and relatable state of mind – the mental meanderings and stream of consciousness that accompany a regular and uneventful routine. The film combines animation with live-action footage of Hodgson's daily walk to work through London and offers an insight into his train of thought as he treads his familiar route. The combination of live action and animation emphasises the evocative potential of the latter as access to Hodgson's mental state is encouraged by the addition of the superimposed hand-drawn images and words. The animation in *Feeling My Way* allows us to quite specifically know what Hodgson was thinking and feeling as he walked through London, thus the film is a documentary of his thought processes more than it is, say, a film about London.

Hodgson used an animation process called xerography to create *Feeling My Way*. He filmed the point-of-view footage of his walk on Hi8 video and then digitised this footage using an Amiga computer. After roughly editing the material together, the individual frames were printed out on paper, onto which Hodgson added his hand-drawn images and words. These sheets of paper were then shot frame by frame on 35mm to produce the final film. Hodgson's choice to digitise only every other frame of the footage helped 'marry the animated quality of the drawings with live action' and the grainy, hazy quality of the treated video footage adds to the atmosphere of the piece (Hodgson, 2006: 64–5).

Instead of the first-person voiceovers heard in the other films discussed in this chapter, Hodgson's drawn musings are accompanied by diegetic noises of the bustling city, and the sound of his regular paced footsteps pounding the pavement lends the film a rhythmic quality. Through the xerography process, Hodgson communicates what he was thinking on his morning walk without the need for narration. We quickly learn that it is morning time (from the text '8 24' drawn on the top of an image of a sidewalk soon after he walks out of his house and onto the street) and that he is on the way to a meeting (from the text 'meeting starts at 9am'). We also gather that Hodgson is not too bothered about this meeting from the 'so what?' inscribed on the screen as the camera tilts up to capture the dappled morning light filtering through the leaf-filled branches of a large oak tree. This text–image combination sets the tone of the film, which plays like snippets of a daydream that is both interrupted and inspired by urban life. At one point we walk past a ringing telephone and realise the sound must have acted as a reminder to Hodgson when the text 'ring ring' and then 'ring Simon' is superimposed on the live-action image of the phone box. Later, Eastern European folk music is heard and the script 'Budapest' scrawls across the screen from right to left. Not only does this allow us to know what Hodgson thought upon hearing these noises, it also evokes our own experiences of how sensorial stimulation can nudge a memory of forgotten tasks or once-visited places.

Hodgson's written embellishments range from the mundane to the profound. Double yellow lines painted in the gutter prompt the response 'no parking', a simple verbalisation of the meaning of these road markings. The work 'ESCAPE' written over a busy street thronging with pedestrians and an earlier moment marking a quiet park as a 'clear spot' indicate Hodgson's value of peace and quiet. There is also an existential tinge to the film. As he walks through Soho he ponders, 'is that all there is'. This linkage between perception and contemplation is illustrated in one sequence where Hodgson walks through Kings Cross train station. Just prior to entering the station, he passes a homeless man lying in the street, and across this image we see the words 'dead...or alive?' Subsequently, as he makes his way through the busy rail terminus, the figures of several commuters are picked out in a chalky white outline with either 'DEAD' or 'ALIVE' written on their body in white text. By the time Hodgson exits the station, the bodies of all those visible in the point-of-view shot are superimposed with roughly drawn outlines of the human skeleton, as if he is surrounded by the living dead. This is a whimsical and witty attitude that characterises the film. A cat sitting behind a window becomes 'the family prisoner', the face of a passer-by is scrawled with a moustache and glasses, and poles of scaffolding evoke a 'parallel universe'.

The insight offered by the animated writing in *Feeling My Way* seems to contradict my earlier claims regarding the superiority of images, especially animated images, over language, in evoking subjective experience. Indeed, if we think of the superimposed text in Hodgson's film as labels or captions, something William J. Mitchell (1992: 192) describes as being 'used like declarative sentences to make assertions which are either true or false', this seems to move the animation into the realm of overt statement, rather than the implicit evocative nature of much of the imagery discussed earlier. Roland Barthes has even gone so far as to describe the text of a photographic caption as 'parasitic' on the image, a reversal from the historic relationship between text and image where the latter would clarify and elucidate the former (Barthes, 1977b: 25). When appended to a photograph, the text's role is 'one of making explicit, of providing a stress', and, 'simply amplifying a set of connotations already given in the photograph' (Barthes, 1977b: 27).

Feeling My Way destabilises this traditional relationship between the photographic and its label. Whereas captions have conventionally been used to bolster a photograph's factual status and to identify its contents, in *Feeling My Way*, the 'captions' are labels of expression rather than declaration. Barthes hints at the potential for photographic captions to go beyond the 'parasitic' when he notes that sometimes the text 'produces (invents) an entirely new signified which is retroactively projected into the image' (Barthes, 1977: 27). Of vital significance for the captions in *Feeling My Way* is that they are both handwritten (by Hodgson) and animated. Laura U. Marks (2011: 307) describes 'calligraphic animation' as the process of animating the written word. While the words in *Feeling My Way* are not animated in the process of writing, they instead appear as fully formed words, they are still clearly animated. They are instable, and they vibrate in a way that betrays their inscription frame by frame on the image. As 'writing tends to twist free of its subservience to the word and exhibit its individuality' (Marks, 2011: 309), the text in *Feeling My Way* becomes, rather than a factual label, an 'index of the hand that made it' (Marks, 2011: 309).

As animated writing, the text in *Feeling My Way* is more than the written words of language, it is part of the animated fabric of consciousness with which Hodgson overlays the indexical live-action images. As well as the written snippets of text, Hodgson embellishes his point-of-view footage with varying amounts of animation. At some moments, the image is almost entirely animated, such as when he shows a hand-drawn map of his route at the beginning of the film. Sometimes the animation is used to pick out objects, for example by giving them an outline, and sometimes the animation is used to obscure parts of the image, so only a few items are shown in live action. At other times, drawn animated embellishments remain unexplained and beyond easy interpretation, such as when UFOs are seen flying around Soho Square or the brief glimpses of bouncing animated figures superimposed on the screen just before Hodgson reaches his destination. The animated text and image in *Feeling My Way* allow access to Hodgson's state of mind as he walked across London that morning. It is these that make this a documentary of the internal, rather than a documentary of the external. Just as the animation in the films discussed earlier is more than a simple illustration of what is heard on the soundtrack, it is the case that Hodgson could attempt to explain via voiceover that when he walked through Kings Cross train station, he imagined commuters as walking skeletons, labelled with their own mortal potential. But, animation can convey this more efficiently, and in a way that evokes, rather than shows, that which eludes verbal description or visual representation.

Animated awareness

That animation is effective in communicating a sense of subjective, conscious experience is demonstrated by its uptake as a tool to raise awareness, especially around mental and personal health issues. Many of the animated documentaries discussed here were commissioned or funded by organisations and institutions with a remit of spreading knowledge and understanding to the general public.[6] *A is for Autism* was commissioned by the United Kingdom's Channel 4 television as part of a season called 'Disabling Worlds'. The desire was for a piece that would 'give a general audience a small window into the condition of autism' (Arnall, 1992). The first *Animated Minds* series was also made for Channel 4, with the second one being instigated by an educational cable TV channel and The Wellcome Trust, a United Kingdom-based charitable foundation that funds medical and science research. The films were conceived to 'communicate the subjective experience of mental health problems to a wider audience' (*Animated Minds*, 2012b). Samantha Moore's film, *An Eyeful of Sound*, was the outcome of a Wellcome Trust arts award. These arts awards are intended to enhance knowledge and interest around these areas, and Moore's film was funded with the intention of increasing understanding of synaesthesia.

Ellie Land's *Centrefold* (2012) demonstrates that animation is being used to raise awareness for socio-cultural issues that go beyond the psychological and neurological. Also funded by the Wellcome Trust, the film sought to open up discussion around female genital cosmetic surgery, and the reasons women are motivated to undergo often painful and unsuccessful surgery in pursuit of 'perfect' labia. The film uses a simple style of animation, with a limited colour palette, to tell the stories of three women who underwent labiaplasty. Animation was chosen not only to protect the identity of the interviewees, but also because the filmmaker believed the chosen style would be 'able to communicate the thoughts and feelings of the women directly to the audience through simplicity' (Land, 2012a). Additionally, the colours, which are somewhat reminiscent of feminine hygiene products, 'were chosen to be appealing and fun as we are looking for teens to be interested in watching the film too' (Land, 2012c). The film has to date had 150,000 views online (via the online streaming video site Vimeo)[7] and has generated significant discussion surrounding the issue of labiaplasty, both online and at the multitude of screenings, festivals and educational events at which Land has presented the film (Land, 2012b).

There is evidence that the other films commissioned and funded by third-party organisations have been effective in their aim of increasing awareness and understanding. *A Is for Autism* is sold online by the charity the National Autistic Society, with an endorsement of the insight it offers into the condition (The National Autistic Society, 2011). The *Animated Minds* series has received praise from teachers, mental health care professionals and sufferers of the issues the films discuss (*Animated Minds*, 2012a). The two series are also the recipients of numerous awards, including in the categories of educational media and mental health media (Mosaic Films, 2012a). Samantha Moore's *Eyeful of Sound* has also been lauded by science film festivals and has seen particular interest from the science community.

The reception of, and accolades for, these animated documentaries give an indication of why this form is becoming an increasingly prevalent way to approach the realities of subjective, conscious experience that, because they do not look like anything and do not have any visual equivalent, are unrepresentable via live-action media. As Bill Nichols

(2010: 110) notes, documentaries 'offer an orientation to the experience of others, and by extension, to the social practices we share with them' because they 'help us understand how others experience situations and events'. Such understanding is aided by metaphorical representation. Animation, because it is completely constructed, malleable and can be realised through a multiplicity of media and forms, is particularly suited to visual metaphors. But, the animated documentaries discussed here are often more than simple metaphors where a visual image or style of animation stands in directly for something else. Because much of the subject matter of these films – feelings, experiences, perceptions – are unrepresentable they, somewhat contradictorily, 'resist presentation' while at the same time lending themselves to 'actual pictures' (Elkins, 1998: 253). Animation is used as 'neither presentation nor representation' (Tyler, 1986: 123) and as such it cannot be understood as simply symbolic. While a non-mimetic animated image might evoke one thought or feeling for one viewer, it may evoke something very different for another, and this openness is crucial in the films' effectiveness, because in order for me to imagine, for example, manic depression, I have to do so by making a connection, via my imagination, between my own perspective and experiences and feelings and those being conveyed in *The Light Bulb Thing*. It is through this inarticulable and individual process of evocation and imagination that the animated documentaries discussed here do their most interesting work to convey subjective experiences that are irreducible to language or image.

These animated documentaries do not, of course, transport us into the heads of their subjects or offer us telepathic knowledge of their experiences. In fact, many of the films above enact the complex philosophical manoeuvre of making films about subjective, conscious experience from a third-person perspective as few of the films of this type are made by the person whose experiences are being documented. Sam Moore is not synaesthetic, Andy Glynne does not have anorexia or obsessive–compulsive disorder, Sheila Sofian is not a refugee from the Bosnian war. Human existence is, and always will be, characterised by the epistemological asymmetry of what analytical philosophy calls the problem of other minds. This arises because we lack 'the capacity to observe those mental states [of another human] as mental states belonging to that other human being' (Hyslop, 2010). That is, we can never observe or experience another person's mental state in the same way as that person does, even if we had the telepathic ability to plug ourselves into that other person's mind, because we can never gain all the knowledge and experience in which that specific person experiences that mental state.

This means that even animated documentaries about subjective, conscious experience that are made from a first-person perspective, such as *Feeling My Way*, or those that rely heavily on collaboration to construct their imagery, such as *An Eyeful of Sound* and *A Is for Autism*,[8] are performing the same epistemological leap, just once less removed.

Analytical philosophy generally accepts that I can suppose that other people have mental states that are similar to the mental states I experience, and without this empathy much human interaction would be impossible. The animated documentaries here work on this premise and, while they do not propose a solution to the centuries-old quandary of how I can know what you feel or perceive, they encourage us to use our skills of empathy that are based on our certainty that 'other human beings are mostly very like ourselves.' Animated documentaries about subjective, mental states use animation to provoke this empathy or, in the cases of films about mental health or unusual neurological states, imagine what it is like to be different. And while those of us without autism, for example, may never fully understand what it is like to live with that condition, *A Is for Autism* and *An Alien in the Playground* can help us to understand far more than a conventional documentary that uses live action and talking heads.

5
Animated Memories

In *Everything's for You* (1989) filmmaker Abraham Ravett constructs a compilation of photographic-based media in his search to understand his deceased father. Fragments of images flit and flicker on the screen, which often splits to display multiple versions of the same image. Items from the Ravetts' personal archive are shown along with those from the official archive of public history and family photographs, some of them recently discovered, appear juxtaposed with footage from the Lodz ghetto, where Ravett's father was interned with his previous wife and children before being sent to Auschwitz. We see observational documentary film of Ravett interacting with his young son, as well as footage of interviews with his father made before his death over a decade earlier. (See Ravett, 2011 for more detail on the production techniques and processes of this film.) All of these image sources attest to the significance of the relationship between photographic media and memory as a way of accessing the past.

There are, however, several moments in *Everything's for You* where Ravett represents remembered events not with found or newly made photographs or film, but through animation.[1] These animated sections stand out against the collage of photographic-based, indexical, archive media. With the accepted correspondence between photography and the past, what place does animation have in a film of personal history? The three events from Ravett's childhood, which he describes as 'unforgettable and, at times, volatile interactions with my father' (Ravett, 2011: 326) that are conveyed through the simple, line-drawn animation, are ones that took on great significance as he grew up. His father's behaviour on these three occasions has, for Ravett, become synecdochial of him as a person and the events haunt Ravett, their memory becoming manifestations of the emotional distance he felt from his father while he was alive. The animated sections in the film are fragments of his own past that he cannot understand, moments when his father's behaviour made no sense. Accordingly, these moments stand out, aesthetically, from the rest of the film. This is a film of fragments. A fragmented history of events half-remembered, the significance of which Ravett is still struggling to comprehend in order that he might better know himself. With his repeated mantra, 'Pop, I was looking for you', Ravett is searching to understand his father, and thus himself, through a complex interweave of images and sounds.

Marita Sturken (1997: 11) has observed that 'photographs are often perceived to embody memory.' Similarly, Esther Leslie notes (2003: 181), after Walter Benjamin, that photography is understood to be both mimetic and mnemic. Photographic media seems to provide direct access to the past because of the indexical relationship between image and the pro-filmic. Indeed, this is the foundational assumption of Roland Barthes' final work, *Camera Lucida*, in which he searches through old photographs for the essence, or *noeme*, of his deceased mother (Barthes, 1981: 77). The link between photography and the past has been much theorised, and Benjamin's oft-quoted words about the accessibility of history indicate a connection between photography and an otherwise elusive past when he says 'the true image of the past flits by. The past can be seized only as an image that flashes up at the moment of its recognizability, and is never seen again' (Benjamin, 2003: 390). Photography, through images that capture the flash of an instant flitting by, provides a record of a moment that would otherwise pass by, never to be seen or experienced again.

Photography's ability to freeze the ephemeral moment, and the absence inherent in all indexical media as pointed out by Mary Ann Doane (2007a: 2), means that this medium is often connected with the existential obsession with our own mortality. Barthes sought death in every photograph of himself and in each case he claims, 'death is the *eidos* of that photograph' (Barthes, 1981: 15). Eduardo Cadava, (Cadava, 1997: 10) in his analysis of Benjamin's work on photography and history, notes 'there can be no [photographic image] that is not also an image of death.' For Cadava, as for Barthes, the photograph is always already haunted by death, even if its subject is still alive. 'In photographing someone, we know that the photograph will survive him – it begins, even during his life, to circulate without him, figuring and anticipating his death each time it is looked at' (Cadava, 1997: 13). In creating a snapshot of time, photographs provide permanent visible evidence of a moment that is instantly past. Likewise, film and video enable us to play back a finite period in time that is, as soon as it is filmed, historical. Both moving and still images have a capacity, in their ability to replay the past, to revive and reanimate the temporal instant and physical bodies that have long since been lost. In their capacity to play with time, these media remind us of the ephemerality of our own existence.

The fragmented presentation of images of the past in *Everything's for You* begins to suggest that history, be it personal or collective, can never be completely grasped or understood. As Janet Walker points out, the photographic evidence in the film attests 'contrarily, to all we do not know and/or to what we do know but cannot quite comprehend or accept' (Walker, 2005: 165). Indeed, the film turns our expectations of photographic media on its head and 'undermines any "Eureka!" experience that might be had' in relation to these images (Walker, 2005: 166). This echoes the underlying sentiments of Benjamin's claim that we can never recognise the past as it really was, but can only ever appropriate 'a memory as it flashes up in a moment of danger' (Benjamin, 2003: 391). Ravett's compilation tells us that the photographic, despite its mimetic, indexical nature, does not guarantee unfettered access to the past. The temporal nature of the index, after all, is finite and limited and this sign alone, while it may have a physical connection with a historical moment, cannot offer unconditional knowledge of the past.

This grappling with the (in)accessibility of history is emphasised and consolidated by the use of animation in *Everything's for You*. Particularly so because the animated sequences are of the incidents in Ravett's childhood that he still struggles to understand and to put into the context of his father's history and the events that took place before Ravett's birth. In choosing to animate these memories, Ravett is suggesting that no matter how much digging he does in personal and public archives and no matter how much traditional archival material he finds, he will never be able to fully understand or integrate these memories into his own personal history. This is, in itself, a kind of reconciliation with past events and the behaviour of his father. By acknowledging the incomprehensibility of the past, and the unknowability of past events, Ravett suggests a different kind of coming to terms with history. One that does not entail complete knowledge of the causes and effects of past events.

A similar acknowledgement is made in Laura Yilmaz's 2011 film, *Places Other People Have Lived*. In this short animated documentary, made while she was a student at the University of Southern California, Yilmaz explores, visually and emotionally, her childhood home. The house is soon to be sold, and Yilmaz's film ponders how spaces that have such poignant meaning for her and her family can become divested of their aura once the people to whom the memories belong are no longer present. The film is made up of visual and aural fragments – a soundtrack of snippets of interviews with Yilmaz's family and her own narration, and images that are animated via a variety of techniques including pixilation, stop motion, rotoscoping and hand-drawn animation.

Particularly arresting is the technique Yilmaz uses to establish the three key spaces in the film – the kitchen, the family room and the bedroom she shared with her sister. Here, a 360-degree pan of each room is created using a patchwork of still photographs taken from multiple angles and positions. The room is at once complete and fragmented, a metaphor for Yilmaz's memory. In other parts of the film, animation is layered over photographic media, creating a contrast between Yilmaz's subjective perspective, inflected by her personal memory, and things as they might be observed by anyone. The film opens with a pixilation tracking shot through Yilmaz's neighbourhood. Most of the image is obscured, however, by a hand-drawn black-and-white image of her house, clasped between her hands. As the camera comes to rest in front of her childhood home, hand-drawn and photographic image of the house merge into one. Later in the film, Yilmaz remembers how she and her siblings enjoyed viewing their father's photographic slides, many of which were images taken before they were born, and how they would re-imagine these memories, impossibly remembering events that pre-existed them. Here, hand-drawn animated figures are superimposed on the slides, as Yilmaz and her siblings insert themselves into their parents' past. Through such uses of animation, *Places Other People Have Lived* reconstructs a spatially and temporally fragmented personal memory, the ephemeral traces of which are superimposed on disjointed photographic media.

Animation functions in these types of autobiographical animated documentaries as an alternative way of 'accessing' the past. Through animating personal, collective and post-memories, this aesthetic approach becomes a way to comment on the ephemeral nature of both history and, importantly, memory.[2] Just as the discussion of the history of the hybridisation of animation and documentary in the Introduction to this book suggests the history of the animated documentary is not a clear genealogical line from single origin to sole teleological heir, this chapter looks at how the animated documentary can be a medium for the exploration of a fragmented past of forgotten, perplexing, yet often formative memories. In addition to the rising number of animated documentaries about the subjective, conscious experience of others (see Chapter 4), this format is increasingly seen as a means of exploring experience from a first-person perspective. These films are autobiographical, something Michael Renov (2004: xi) characterises as 'imbued with history', 'mainly retrospective' and 'in which the author, the narrator, and the protagonist are identical'. While Renov (2004: xvi), in his study of subjective, autobiographical documentary film and video is asking, 'what differences arise when the autobiographer chooses film, video or the Internet [rather than the written word] for her mode of production', I am primarily concerned with the differences that arise when the autobiographer chooses animation as a mode of self-inscription.

In the films discussed in this chapter, animation becomes an archaeological tool for exploring one's own past. In the animated interview documentaries explored in Chapter 3, the interviewees speak of their personal experience in the present moment of recording. Derrida draws attention to the temporal specificity of testimony when he says:

> One must oneself be present, raise one's hand, speak in the first person and in the present, and one must do this in order to testify to a present, to an indivisible moment, that is, at a certain point to a moment assembled at the tip of an instantaneousness which must resist division...Consequently for testimony there *must* be the instant (Blanchot & Derrida, 2000: 33, emphasis in original).

Yet, despite this, Derrida says that the instant is also destroyed by what makes it possible through the inherent temporality of making a statement. That testimony does not 'refer to anything other than its present moment' rings true of the interview documentaries in Chapter 3. They seem temporally isolated from any sense of historical context or progress. We know little, for example, of what happens to Ryan Power outside of Bob Sabiston's two Rotoshop animated interview documentaries. We know nothing of his family history, where he was born, or of the formative experiences in his life. What we do know of Ryan, and the subjects of the other interview documentaries, is of the world specific to them at the moment of the audio recording. The ephemerality of the instant is reinforced, in those films, by the ephemerality of the animated image and its ambiguous relationship with reality.

Unlike the interview animated documentaries explored in Chapter 3 that did not, for the most part, temporally situate the personal stories of the interviewees, the films here seek to firmly ensconce the personal in a historical context. The accounts given by the residents of the retirement community in *Backseat Bingo* and the interviewees in Aardman's claymations, for example, do not work to situate their documentary subjects in a specific, locatable time or place. The interviewees' testimonies do not engage with the broader social context in a way that allows an audience to definitively situate them in history. In contrast, the meaning of the stories being told in the films discussed in the present chapter is inextricably bound up with the events and cultures in which they took place. Animation, as well as revealing the subjectivity of the film's subjects, becomes a means to draw them into a broader social, political and cultural history.

Animated documentaries about personal memory and history can be thought of as engaging with two cultural and intellectual developments witnessed at the end of the twentieth and beginning of the twenty-first centuries – the turn towards the autobiographical in documentary filmmaking and the growth of memory studies as a distinct area of interdisciplinary study encompassing fields such as literary studies, history and cultural and media studies. Both developments occurred independently of each other, yet they can be understood as deeply connected conceptually. Susannah Radstone and Katherine Hodgkin (2003: 2) note that it is frequently accepted that 'memory makes us' and cite Fentress and Wickham's statement that 'a study of the way we remember is a study of the way we are.' They also note that, 'since early modern times, memory has been conceived of as a storage space *and* as an internal writing' (6). In suggesting that memory and the process of self-inscription are intrinsically linked and entailed by knowledge of personal identity, these observations are significant for the animated documentaries examined in this chapter.

These twin intellectual and cultural developments can also be seen as a reaction to hegemonic systems of power. In documentary production and distribution from the mid-1970s, '16mm film, consumer-grade video, and the Internet have provided unique and increasingly accessible platforms for self-expression while opening up new audience frontiers' (Renov, 2004: xii). The turn towards self-inscription in documentary was socially and historically determined, bound up as it was in the activist movements of the time that situated the political in the personal. By the 1990s, autobiographical, personal and subjective filmmaking had become a means to protest political and social injustice and inequality. While it took decades of technological development to open up filmmaking to non-privileged makers, animation production has always been more accessible. The nature of animation's production process, and the relative affordability of tools and materials, means that those working outside the mainstream have often adopted it as a means of expression. Antonia Lant (2006) observes, for example, that the practicalities of animation production are far more workable for women with families than is a career in the film industry. Similarly, Paul Wells (1998: 198) points out that women animators have been attracted to independent animation because its aesthetic potentially 'resists the inherently masculine language of the live-action arena, and the most dominant codes of orthodox hyper-realist animation [i.e. Disney and other major studio animation] which also use its vocabulary'. Filmmaking practices, and animation in particular, have the potential to offer ways of challenging hegemonic power relations, particularly those regarding gender, something that further lends it to explorations of personal memory.

Radstone and Hodgkin (2003: 10) note that the influence of post-structuralism and postmodernism on contemporary memory studies means that memory has been used to 'destabilize the authority of the "grand narratives" with which History has become associated'. Similarly, Michael Rossington and Anne Whitehead (2007: 10) have observed that 'memory is often opposed to the hegemony of history' and that it 'serves as a therapeutic alternative to historical discourse'. While, as Marita Sturken (1997: 4) points out, it is hard to generalise the practice of history-making, history can still be thought of 'as a narrative that has in some way been sanctioned or valorized by institutional frameworks or publishing enterprises'. Memory, precisely because it is personal and locally situated, has the contestational potential to counter official histories. As such, memory has gained the positive associations of subjectivity in contrast to the negative qualities of 'public' and 'objectivity' that have become associated with history (Radstone & Hodgkin, 2003: 10).

The contestational potential of memory is particularly apposite for groups and individuals that have traditionally been left out of official histories. These are often the same groups and individuals who sought to redress social and political imbalance through autobiographical and subjective filmmaking. Precisely because 'public media and official archives memorialize the experiences of the powerful [...] it has [...] been necessary to turn to alternative archives [...] to hear the voices of [...] disenfranchised groups' (Whitehead, 2009: 13). Autobiography can be seen as a means of intervening in official history by way of invoking personal memories and exploring and creating 'alternative archives'. By inserting the self into the social and the personal into the public, autobiographical filmmaking and animation are ways of refiguring the past from a locally situated perspective, one that tells history from the bottom up instead of receiving it from the top down. As such, autobiographical media has the potential to be a powerful tool for (re-/de-)constructing our picture of the social, historical world.

This chapter explores how animation in particular enables this refiguring. Animation can also, through its nature as a medium that can be realised in multiple formats, techniques and styles, convey questions regarding forgetting and remembering, knowing and not knowing, the past. Animation, by virtue of its construction and creation, can present a subjective intervention into the discourses of autobiography, memory and history. In this way, animation as strategy for the re-presentation of personal history is a tool by which self-identity can be explored and understood. *Learned by Heart* (*Sydämeen kätketty*, Rimminen and Takala, 2007) and *Irinka and Sandrinka* (Stoïanov, 2007) both animate the self in the context of a broader (national, familial) history. *Silence* (Bringas and Yadin, 1998) and *Waltz with Bashir* (2008) confront unspoken and traumatic pasts. All of these films use the formal and aesthetic excess of animation as a means of accessing the now absent past and as a way of understanding personal identity.

(Dis)continuities: the self in history

Nicola King (2000: 2) reports that 'it is commonly accepted that identity, or a sense of self, is constructed by and through narrative.' Memory plays an important part in this formation of personal identity, as influentially attested to by John Locke in his seventeenth-century treatise, *Essay Concerning Human Understanding*. For Locke, our identity is dictated by our consciousness, which in turn is formed by ideas prompted by sensation and experience. Memory, importantly, allows us to recall earlier ideas and affords a continuity of consciousness and a coherent sense of personal identity. Marita Sturken (1997: 1) demonstrates the contemporary relevance of this Enlightenment understanding of the function of memory in her study of late-twentieth-century culture when she points out that 'memory establishes life's continuity; it gives meaning to the present, as each moment is constituted by the past. As the means by which we remember who we are, memory provides the very core of identity.' By telling stories of our past, and memorialising personal history, we can come to better understand and know ourselves.

Learned by Heart and *Irinka and Sandrinka* suggest that it is not only our own memories, but also collective memory and postmemory that constitutes personal identity. In *Learned by Heart*, filmmaker Marjut Rimminen explores her memories of growing up in post World War Two

Finland. French animator Sandrine Stoïanov's animated collage inspired by her elderly aunt's memories of a childhood lived during and after the collapse of the Russian monarchy is imbued with the filmmaker's own recollections of juvenile fantasies of a fairytale Russia. Both Rimminen and Stoïanov draw themselves within the context of a broader political and social history that is channelled through their own formative experiences and memories. Rimminen's identity is bound up with the role played by women in Finland during and after the war. For Stoïanov, the impact of 'History' is still being felt as she uncovers her family history. Both films point to the 'gendered and power-laden dynamics of remembering' (Chedgzoy, 2007: 217), and by offering a female perspective on significant historical events they present an alternative to the male-centric versions of the past that recount history through the exploits of 'great men'.

Maurice Halbwachs' writing on memory counters the late-nineteenth and early-twentieth-century philosophical, psychological and literary suggestion that memory is something that occurs solely within the mind of an individual.[3] In so doing, his work catalysed the 'recognition of memory as a social, rather than a purely psychological, phenomenon' (Waterson, 2007: 52). Halbwachs 'emphasizes the partial and incomplete nature of past recollections, and he attributes the ability to remember not to internal processes' (Whitehead, 2009: 126). Instead, memory for Halbwachs is 'socially produced' (Sturken, 1997: 4), and is constituted by belonging within social groups rather than being dependent on individual power of recollection of personal experiences. 'The group, in Halbwachs's understanding, provides the individual with a "framework" into which her remembrances are woven' (Whitehead, 2009: 126). This suggests that individual memories only come to have meaning when placed within a collective, social context.

As well as being distinguished from individual memory, collective memory is distinct from history. 'General history', as Halbwachs (2007: 139) terms it, arises precisely at the demise of collective memory because the failure of social memory necessitates the inscription and consolidation of facts and events. 'So long as a remembrance continues to exist, it is useless to set it down in writing or otherwise fix it in memory' (Halbwachs, 2007: 139). Such consolidation and fixing of the past in memory, for example in the history texts used in schools, leads to past events being 'combined, and evaluated in accord with necessities and rules not imposed on the groups that had through time guarded them as a living trust' (Halbwachs, 2007: 139). Halbwachs' contrast of official history and collective memory suggests that the former works to distance us from the experiential reality of the past. Collective memory is constituted by continuity, whereas official history is brought about by a break with the past.

Learned by Heart's thirty-minute duration is divided into five chapters that trace a trajectory of personal development within a national and gendered context. Rimminen's journey from infancy to adulthood is intertwined with the cultural and social changes that took place in Finland after the end of World War Two. The country emerged from the war 'in a schizophrenic state' (Rimminen, 2007), psychologically scarred and financially ruined by battles for independence from the Soviet Union. The film presents the liberating decade of the 1960s as a healing force where the young post-war baby boomers were freed from the authoritarian strictures of their parents' generation, one that still struggled to come to terms with the changes wrought by conflict and separation. The film is also an expression of Rimminen's memories of the changes in Finland since the 1950s. She ensconces this history in her own familial experiences and via extracts from her childhood journals. The film's chapters are also, importantly, structured around five old Lutheran hymns that 'recall memories of a time when [these songs] were an intimate element in everyday life' (Rimminen, 2007). The hymns are aural talismans for Rimminen, evoking the past and returning her to her childhood.

Visually, *Learned by Heart* is a collage of different types of images. Original filmed footage is combined with archive materials, including film and still images, which are presented alongside Rimminen's family photographs. These photographic-based images are often animated and computer manipulation software is used to bring still images to life and to layer images from different sources. The way in which the image is composited brings thematic resonance and meaning to the film. For example, layering stock footage of Hitler emphatically delivering a speech over the wedding portrait of a young couple (who are later revealed to be Rimminen's parents) articulates the idea that the war destroyed the happiness of Rimminen's parents' generation. Later, images of shells exploding on a battlefield are superimposed on the besuited torso of a male figure. The figure, seen from below, fills the frame and his domineering presence illustrates 'The Fear of the Lord' theme of the third chapter of the film in which it appears, as well as suggesting that the domestic violence experienced by Rimminen was a result of the war's impact on her father.[4]

Throughout the film, animation is layered on top of and embedded into the photographic material. This animation has a hand-drawn or painted aesthetic, despite its cut-out style of character movement being created through a computer programme.[5] This animation is one factor lending the film its air of nostalgia. Cut-out animation is one of the medium's oldest techniques and the earliest extant animated feature, Lotte Reiniger's *The Adventures of Prince Achmed* (Germany, 1926), was created using this method. This atmosphere of nostalgia is enhanced by the aesthetic qualities of the archival material – the sepia tones of the photographs and the grainy black-and-white film. Additionally, some of the new footage shot for the film is heavily desaturated, only using colour to accentuate particular elements such as the red-and-white checked cloth that covers the table in the reconstruction of Rimminen's childhood home. Aurally, the sounds of the traditional Finnish hymns lend the film a wistful air.

Mieke Bal (1999: xi) says that nostalgia:

> has often been criticized as unproductive, escapist and sentimental. It is considered regressive, romanticizing, the temporal equivalent of tourism and the search for the picturesque. It has also been conceived as longing for an idyllic past that never was.

Cultural geographer Yi-Fu Tuan (1977: 195) helps us understand nostalgia as a reaction to the feeling that 'changes are occurring too rapidly, spinning out of control.' Nostalgia is a kind of temporal digging-in of our cultural heels, slowing down the too-fast changes that threaten a loss of control, by looking back to a time that may or may not have existed. At these unsettling moments, the status quo often seems safer than the unknown offered by rapid change. Leo Spitzer (1999: 92) attempts to redeem the much-maligned concept of nostalgia and suggests it can be seen in a more positive light. He points out that 'nostalgic memory also plays a significant role in the reconstruction and continuity of individual and collective memory.' Nostalgia can, then, be thought of as a relevant element of collective memory, something Halbwachs understands as being constituted by continuity as opposed to official history, which is instead entailed by the fissures in collective remembering. The computer manipulation and animation of archival material, along with the superimposition of animated figures into found footage and photographs in *Learned by Heart* disrupts any simple understanding of its superficially nostalgic aesthetic as reactionary or sentimental. For example, in one sequence a girl in a red dress walks into a dancehall and takes her place among the young women waiting to be picked to dance. The girl is an animated figure, drawn in a scarlet dress on the black-and-white archive footage of the dancehall and this vibrant figure seems at odds with the sepia scene in which she is placed. She works both to connect the audience to the past in the present moment of viewing as well as to mark out its temporal distance. The scene, in which the red-dressed stand-in for Rimminen does not get picked to dance, also recalls the disappointments of teenage life. As such, the animation cuts through any easy, nostalgic or romantic reminiscence offered up by the old filmed footage.

Knitting, that traditional female pastime, forms a visual motif in *Learned by Heart*. The young Rimminen, played by a round-faced blonde actress, often sits knitting while observing the world around her. At the end of 'The Fear of the Lord' chapter, the father's empty suit is unravelled and the yarn balled up by aging female hands. This segues into the fourth chapter, 'Schools are out!' in which Rimminen's own sexual awakening mirrors Finland's emergence from years of austerity and hardship. Similarly, her discovery of the opposite sex and liberation from the overbearing dominance of her father reflects the wider liberation of social attitudes towards sex and gender roles. Even more broadly than this, the knitting motif is a metaphor for Rimminen knitting herself into the history of Finland as remembered from a specific, gendered position. This knitting-in is in part achieved visually by the insertion of the animated figure, representing Rimminen, into the compilation of photographic media. Animation is one tool that is used to construct continuity between Rimminen's personal memories and the collective memory of Finnish women since World War Two. These intertwined recollections also refigure the importance of Finland's female population in the country's postwar recovery, a recovery that the film suggests was more hindered than helped by the male figures of power that are traditionally honoured in the annals of history. The assemblage of the visual elements of the film echoes the words heard on the soundtrack from a speech given on Mothers' Day in 1947. 'Finnish women have never had it easy', the interlocutor says, reminding listeners that 'our mothers are tough' and that it is the strong women of Finland who have borne much of the responsibility for seeing the country through its hard times.

Marianne Hirsch coined the term 'postmemory' to 'describe the ways in which individuals can be haunted by a past that they have not experienced personally but which has somehow been "transferred" to them, often unconsciously, by family members' (Rossington & Whitehead, 2007: 7). This phenomenon is most often observed in the children of Holocaust survivors, and this is the focus of Hirsch's body of work within memory studies. There is, she argues, an important link between traumatic experience in one generation and the experience of postmemory in the next because trauma disrupts the continuity of collective memory. A frequent response of those who have lived through traumatic and catastrophic events is to not speak of the past, meaning the 'multiple ruptures and radical breaks introduced by trauma and catastrophe inflect intra-, and inter- and trans-generational inheritance' (Hirsch, 2008: 111). Children of trauma survivors experience the past as an overwhelming absence, in the form of silence, and overbearing excess, in the form of the weight of the unspoken past.

As a response to these ruptures and breaks 'postmemorial work [...] strives to *reactivate* and *reembody* more distant social/national and archival/cultural memorial structures by reinvesting them with resonant individual and familial forms of mediation and aesthetic expression' (Hirsch, 2008: 111, emphasis in original). In this way, the artistic and communicative works created by the second generation of survivors of traumatic events become a way of reconnecting with collective memory. The suffix 'post-', Hirsch (2008: 106) points out, 'signals more than a temporal delay and more than a location in an aftermath'. Like the other 'post-' intellectual movements and moments of the latter twentieth and twenty-first centuries, such as postmodernism and postcolonialism, postmemory 'reflects an uneasy oscillation between continuity and rupture' (Hirsch, 2008: 106). The existence of postmemory work in itself acknowledges a break with the past, albeit a past that continues to resonate with those who create the visual, literary and performative responses. While Hirsch specifically applies the concept of postmemory to the second generation of survivors of traumatic events such as genocide, in particular children of Holocaust survivors,[6] I think her theorisation of the appropriation of the affective force of ancestral memory and experience can be applied to other examples of inherited recollection. In particular, postmemory can shed light on situations in which familial or social collective memory has been disrupted by the geographical shifts of exile and emigration. In these situations, the ruptures with the past may be less 'radical' than with histories of trauma and devastation, but the separation of a younger generation from the homeland of their parents and grandparents causes a similar fissure in the continuity of memory and identity formation.

Sandrine Stoïanov's aunt Irene was raised in Russia during the fall of the monarchy. As Russian nobility, Irene and her mother, Stoïanov's grandmother, fled to Romania while Irene's father, whom she had not met, remained in exile in France. A childhood of fissures and separations was compounded by Irene's transplantation to France after her mother's death. In search of her own identity, Stoïanov created *Irinka and Sandrinka* based on taped interviews with the elderly aunt whom she barely knew. Stoïanov uses animation to weave together her aunt's memories and her own childhood fantasies of being a young Russian aristocrat. The short film can be thought of as a work of postmemory that seeks to connect Stoïanov to the collective memory of pre-revolutionary Russia, a past from which she has been cleaved by the political history of the Soviet Union and the enforced geographical separation experienced by the older generations of her family.

Hirsch (2008: 107) has suggested that photography, because of its indexical relationship with reality, is crucial to the conception of postmemory as it relates to the Holocaust. Irene's words at the beginning of *Irinka and Sandrinka* attest to the power of photography. In the opening moments of the film, a framed black-and-white photograph of a moustachioed man wearing a suit is seen as Irene is heard telling Stoïanov that 'for me, my father was a photograph', and that as a child she kissed this photo goodnight every evening after saying her prayers. For the young Irene, the photograph was her only connection with an absent father who was already living in France by the time she was born. Yet the film quickly dispels any presumption of family photographs providing a simple or direct access to the history from which Stoïanov feels so removed. Instead, the use of a collage style of animation that layers photographs with images from personal and official archives, along with drawings from children's books and Stoïanov's own illustrations, begins to suggest that

> Family life, even in its most intimate moments, is entrenched in a collective imagery shaped by public, generational structures of fantasy and projection and by a shared archive of stories and images that inflect the transmission of individual and familial remembrance (Hirsch, 2008: 114).

Through a brightly coloured animated canvas that resembles a child's pop-up book, Stoïanov creates a fantasy world that integrates her aunt's memories and her own childhood imaginings. This fantastical integration is conveyed by the superimposition of indexical and non-indexical imagery to create an affective whole. As such, the film illustrates Hirsch's (2008: 106) suggestion that 'postmemory's connection to the past is thus not actually mediated by recall but by imaginative investment, projection, and creation.'

Stoïanov's imaginative investment in the past takes the form of a fairytale of Russian culture and family history. By way of animation, Stoïanov inserts herself as a character – Sandrinka – in her aunt's memories. At one point, the young Sandrinka, a black-and-white drawn figure, throws open the doors of her ancestral home and explores the corridors, which are lined with photographs from Stoïanov's family archive (see Figure 5.1). The little girl's fascination with the portraits of her forebears that hang along the hallway mirrors Stoïanov's own discovery of her past through her aunt. When one gallant-looking Cossack springs from a photograph and waltzes Sandrinka down the hall, the merging of animation and photography within a mythical, fairytale world suggests a certain continuity with the past is being achieved through this work of postmemory. The melding of Stoïanov's fantasies and Irene's memories is demonstrated at the end of the film when Sandrinka meets Irinka, Stoïanov's animated projection of her aunt as a child. The two young girls connect and, through the encounter of these two animated characters, Stoïanov symbolises the fusion of herself with her family history as some of the gaps in her sense of personal identity are filled in. In *Irinka and Sandrinka* the past is being reimagined from Stoïanov's point of view. This animated work of (auto)biography is a way for Stoïanov to understand the implications of her family history for her own identity.

Figure 5.1 Stoïanov walks down the corridors of her ancestral past in *Irinka and Sandrinka* (dir. Sandrine Stoïanov, 2007)

As Hirsh (2008: 109) says, 'postmemory is not identical to memory, it is "post", but at the same time, it approximates memory in its affective force.' Stoïanov's interpretation of her aunt's memories, and her insertion of herself as a character in past events, is indicative of the affective power of these memories on her sense of self.

Irinka and Sandrinka and *Learned by Heart* both function to connect their creators to a broader, collective memory and it is via animation that the filmmakers weave themselves into a national or ancestral past. Through telling stories, not only about themselves, but also about their countries of origin and their families, Rimminen and Stoïanov's films are works of identity formation. By maintaining the continuity of collective memory, these films are avoiding the distancing effect of 'general History'. They suggest a specificity of collective memory that counters the often broad sweep of history, a discourse that frequently neglects the role played by women. As such, *Irinka and Sandrinka* and *Learned by Heart* go some way to redress the gender imbalance regarding memory observed by Kate Chedgzoy who notes that despite the traditional association of memory with femaleness imbued since the embodiment of memory in the female form of the Greek goddess Mnemosyne, 'women's contributions to cultural memory have scarcely been noted in the Twentieth Century's explosion of work in that subject' (Chedgzoy, 2007: 216). Rimminen and Stoïanov's films suggest the importance of gender-specific remembering for an understanding of cultural past and an understanding of the self.

Marita Sturken has distinguished a concept of cultural memory from both collective and individual memory as well as from history. For her, cultural memory is 'shared outside the avenues of formal historical discourse yet is entangled with cultural products and imbued with cultural meaning' (Sturken, 1997: 3). Cultural memory is distinct from collective memory because it is entailed by the production of the artefacts of culture, such as film and television images. Cultural memory is also 'bound up in complex political stakes and meanings' as a 'field of cultural negotiation through which different stories vie for a place in history' (Sturken, 1997: 1). Sturken's theorisation of cultural memory can help us understand how *Irinka and Sandrinka* and *Learned by Heart* engage in a 'cultural negotiation' regarding, respectively, the meaning of post-revolutionary Russian history and the relevance of women in postwar Finnish history for self-identity. By replaying and redrawing history from a first-person perspective, these two films interject into official 'History'. In so doing, they work to weave their creators into a collective recollection of the past and counter the absence of continuity.

They do this, in part, through the formal use of animation as an excess, something that goes beyond the mere indexical capacity of photographic images to recall past events and people. Rather than offering a simple 'umbilical cord' with the past (Barthes, 1981: 81), these films entwine their makers into the complex fabric of a subjective, familial and nationally specific recollection.

The unspoken and the forgotten: the trauma in/of history in *Silence* and *Waltz with Bashir*

Learned by Heart and *Irinka and Sandrinka* show how animation, in particular a collage of the animated and the photographic, can be used to articulate and overcome discontinuities in personal and collective history due to external forces. There are also other internal reasons for gaps in memory, such as responding to traumatic events by forgetting the past or hushing its events into silence. Orly Yadin and Sylvie Bringas' *Silence* (1998) is a short animated film that revisits Tana Ross' childhood in the Theresienstadt concentration camp and then in Sweden. Ari Folman's animated documentary feature, *Waltz with Bashir* (2008) is an exploration of the filmmaker's repressed memories of fighting in the 1982 Lebanon war.

Harald Weinrich's analysis of the etymology of the Greek word for truth, *alethia*, reveals the origins of the conflation of truth and memory when he says 'on the basis of the construction of the word *alethia* one can also conceive truth as the "unforgotten" or the "not-to-be-forgotten"' (Weinrich, 2004: 4). Accessing the truth of past events is conventionally aligned with remembering those events accurately. Such conflation is indicated by the dependence on the accuracy of witness testimony in legal trials, as well as the credibility of certain types of documentary resting on the credibility of interviewees' accounts of the past. Weinrich (2004: 4) points out, however, that we have more recently 'attempted to grant forgetting a certain truth as well'. This observation marks out an important area for the discussion of *Silence* and *Waltz with Bashir* – that it is not only what we remember, but what we forget or remember incorrectly that can come to take on great significance regarding the meaning of past events. Furthermore, I will suggest that animation can be seen as a means for overcoming the effacement of a past blocked by traumatic experience.

Traumatic events are often experienced as an absence – an absence of memory or an absence of feeling. Ernst van Alphen (1999: 25) has suggested that trauma is 'failed experience'. Following Teresa de Lauretis and Joan W. Scott, van Alphen theorises experience as discursive, rather than direct and unmediated. As such, trauma is an experience 'that has not come about and that shows negatively symptoms of the discursivity that defines "successful" experience' (26). As such, a traumatic event is often understood as an aporia in subjective experience and also for the possibilities of representation. Michael Renov (2004: 161) notes that 'the Holocaust offers itself as an aporia for aesthetic representation just as it does for historiography' and the unrepresentability of the Holocaust in particular has been frequently commented on since Theodore Adorno (1983 [1967]: 34) proclaimed in 1949 that there could be no poetry after Auschwitz. This aporetic impact of the Holocaust has often resulted, as Joshua Hirsch has observed, in artistic responses that reject conventional forms of narrative and representation. Regarding cinema in particular, Hirsch (2004: 3) notes that films about the Holocaust often resist 'classical realist forms of film narration traditionally used to provide a sense of mastery over the past [...] adopting instead modernist forms of narration'. Hirsch (5) goes on to claim:

> All historical representation is [...] limited in at least three ways: by signification (the ontological difference between the reality and the sign, including the memory sign), by documentation (limited documentation of the past), and by discourse (limited framing of documents by the conventions of discourse).

If modernist narration is a way of overcoming the limitations of historical representation by means of narrative structure and mode of delivery, then I suggest that animation is a means of overcoming these limitations by means of aesthetics. This echoes one of the central theses of Janet Walker's book *Trauma Cinema* (2005), in which she argues that non-realist aesthetic approaches are often the most appropriate style for films that engage with traumatic events.

Just as a 'modernist narrative' or an alternative style of filmmaking to classical or mainstream Hollywood lends itself to fictional films about the Holocaust, animation lends itself to documentaries about traumatic pasts. Orly Yadin reflects on the process of deciding what approach to take in re-telling Tana Ross's story of a childhood spent hiding from guards in a concentration camp, followed by an adolescence of hiding from her past in Sweden.

> A child's experience of being in a concentration camp as remembered 50 years later – how to convey it? Through archival footage

of children found by allies at the end of the war? Through symbolic effects of dark and light? By filming an interview with a 60-year-old woman and trying to imagine her as a little girl? Or...by creating a child's world view through animated images (Yadin, 2005: 169).

Here, Yadin implies the shortcomings of a conventional documentary approach to Ross's story. This is not only because Ross has no visual mementoes from her past beyond a few photographs and some letters and because there was no extant archival footage that could illustrate Ross's experience, only a Nazi propaganda film made of Theresienstadt, but also because live action could not convey her experience as effectively as animation. As a result, *Silence*'s aesthetic is as, if not more, revealing than any conventional documentary approach.

As a child in 1940s Berlin, Ross was separated from her mother and sent to Theresienstadt. Here, by miraculous coincidence, she found her grandmother who kept her hidden until the end of the war, safe from transportation to the death camps in the east. Later, when living with family in Sweden, Ross's voicelessness about the trauma she experienced in the camps was induced by her aunt's protestations for her to remain quiet about the past. 'Don't tell. Don't tell', her aunt urged her. 'We don't ever want to know. Ever.' This enforced silence mirrored the trauma of her early childhood, when her life depended on her ability to remain silent and disappear. Ross's life became a paradox of existence/ non-existence, the former depending on the latter, exacerbated by her aunt's frequent pleas for her to forget the past. Silence and denial became integral to Ross's identity. 'I didn't speak...I couldn't', she tells us.

Ross's first attempt to revisit her past was in a word-and-music piece co-written with composer Noa Ain.[7] The medium of this work, a kind of concerto-poem for cello and spoken voice, already points to the unrepresentability of Ross's memories. The past cannot, for Ross, be tackled head-on, a result of decades of doing just as she was taught as a child – forgetting and denying. Rather than a straight narrative re-telling of her experiences, Ross instead chose to express her past in a more interpretive and abstract way. Bringas and Yadin worked with the original text of Ross's poem, stripping that 'from sentiment and from words that could be better expressed through images' (Yadin, 2005: 171). The animated visuals are accompanied by a voiceover spoken by Ross, adapted from the original poem.

The animation in *Silence* is made in two distinct styles to reflect the two sections of the film, first Theresienstadt and then Stockholm. The former, animated by Ruth Lingford, is dark and foreboding in a black-and-white style that emulates the look of a woodcut. The film segues into this world from a short introductory section of stock footage of 1940s Germany, showing scenes of the persecution and ghettoization of the Jewish population. One of Ross's few photographs from her childhood, her mother holding her as a babe-in-arms, is superimposed on this footage. As Ross tells us that 'one day my mother left me', the baby Tana twists out of her mother's arms and morphs into a fragile white animated figure, curled in the foetal position and spinning on a black background. Once the film enters the camp, it leaves the potentiality of photographic images and their direct physical link with reality and from this point the image is subsumed into the darkness of the expressive, woodcut-style animation. The events that take place in Sweden are animated by Tim Webb in bright, strong colours. Immediately, the contrast in the two animation styles begins to convey Ross's experience of childhood. First there was darkness, a world filled with shadows. The woodcut-style animation renders everything but the demarcated objects and characters as a black void, a looming threat of emptiness. Only after liberation could life be lived in colour (see Figure 5.2). Upon arrival in Sweden the world is thrown into relief and begins to exist outside fear and horror. This is implied by the changes in colour palette and visual scope as the animated frame becomes fuller and more complete.

The few instances of archival material in the film stand in contrast to the animation. The black-and-white footage of 1940s Berlin and the ravaged streets of postwar central Europe seem general – images that have come to familiarly connote World War Two in Europe. They are used to provide a broader context for Ross's story, but seem removed and voyeuristic in comparison to the animation that, by contrast, functions to emphasise the specificity of the animation to this particular story. This contrast demonstrates Bill Nichols' observation that traumatic events, most especially the Holocaust, cannot easily be folded into a 'larger historical frame' (Nichols, 1994: 127). Animation is a way of resisting the generalisation of such a framework of understanding. Our understanding of Ross's story comes not from the animated characters' resemblance to Ross or the other people in the story, something that is unknowable anyway as the characters are only represented through animation. Neither does it come from accurately reconstructing scenes of the camps or postwar Sweden. The nature of the medium, its subjective mode of creation and the interpretive and metaphoric implications in the hand-created images, lends itself to carrying meaning

Figure 5.2 Life pre- and post-liberation in *Silence* (dir. & prod. Sylvie Bringas & Orly Yadin, 1998)

beyond its iconicity. When the image of the train carrying Ross and her grandmother to Sweden morphs from a bright colourful tableaux to the black-and-white oppressive style of the earlier Theresienstadt section it is clear, in that brief moment, the young Ross's dread of trains and all their implications of heading east to the death camps. The Swedish guard metamorphoses into a German officer and Ross' memory of the fear and trepidation of this journey is encapsulated in a few frames, without any support from an explanatory voiceover.

The choice to use animation, rather than conventional photographic-based images, to document Ross's childhood indicates the inadequacy of the latter in conveying the meaning and truth of decades of forgetting the past. Animation breaks Ross's silence in a way that also provides commentary on the act of silence itself. This is a past that must be excavated and re-drawn, frame by frame, not a history that can be easily accessed through a visual 'umbilical cord' (Barthes, 1981: 81). The enforcement of Ross's silence about her experiences in the camp is indicated at several moments during the Swedish section of the film. As her aunt tucks her up in bed and admonishes her not to tell of her past, the colour image of the young Ross safely lying under the bedclothes morphs into the black-and-white image of her being buried amongst the linens in the clothes basket in which her grandmother kept her hidden at Theresienstadt. The use of metamorphosis here, as at other moments in the film, 'destabilises the image' (Wells, 1998: 69) and reflects the uncertainty of self caused by Ross's traumatic past and her family's response to it. It also makes a visual connection between Ross's verbal silence and earlier physical invisibility and helps us understand her difficulty of speaking of the past. The lasting impact of her time in the camp is illustrated in a later sequence. The animated figure of Ross spins on a blue background, much as the foetal figure did earlier in the film against the black background. This time, Ross's figure grows to indicate the passing of years. 'I was twenty-years-old' Ross says on the soundtrack, 'yet I was still invisible, still the best at hiding.' As she speaks these words, the animated figure curls up into a suitcase, reminiscent of earlier scenes where Ross is packed away and hidden from the German guards.

Cathy Caruth (1995: 5) has suggested that 'the traumatized [...] carry an impossible history with them, or they become themselves the symptom of a history they cannot entirely possess.' One result of the impossibility of processing traumatic history is demonstrated in *Silence*. It takes Tana Ross fifty years to speak of her past, to verbalise her experience and gain some sort of possession of them, rather than them possessing her. The film also begs a broader question of how we come to terms with an unrepresentable past. Caruth (6) refers to Shoshana Feldman's concept of the 'crisis of truth' that is incited by trauma, which:

> extends beyond the question of individual cure and asks how we in this era can have access to our own historical experience, to a history

that is in its immediacy a crisis to whose truth there is no simple access.

The force of traumatic events, Caruth and Feldman suggest, dislocates us from them, making them hard to access and even harder to understand and assimilate into our sense of personal identity. The term 'disremembering' is coined by Janet Walker (2005: 17) to describe a certain tendency in our recollection of trauma. 'Disremembering [...] is remembering with a difference' and is a process characterised by 'conjuring mental images and sounds related to past events but altered in certain respects'. By this token, Walker stresses the importance of seemingly false memories for our reconciliation with past trauma. Particularly, she claims 'fantasy constructions in memory [...] are part and parcel of its character' (14). This chimes with Walker's assertion that non-realist modes of representation are most appropriate to 'trauma cinema'. She applies this suggestion equally to fiction and non-fiction film and suggests

> trauma documentaries warp the continuum by combining alternative strategies with those conventions that have established documentary as a nonfiction mode. They signal the abjection of supposedly objective forms of filmmaking in the process of disremembering history. (25)

If fantasy and disremembering play an important part in the recollection of trauma, it follows that a non-'objective' mode of documentary that embraces expressivity and metaphor, such as animation, can help explore a traumatic past.

Animation's potential to reconnect us to such a traumatic past is demonstrated in Ari Folman's *Waltz with Bashir*. The film is a vehicle for Folman to explore his suppressed memories of fighting in the Israeli Defense Forces (IDF) during the 1982 Lebanon War and it follows a trajectory of him coming to terms with his involvement in the massacre of Palestinian refugees at the Sabra and Shatila refugee camps in Beirut. The guilt Folman carries at being part of the IDF troops who lit illumination rounds to aid the Christian Phalangist militia's raid on the camp has blocked all his memories of the war. Hearing of a friend's recurring nightmare about the war triggers Folman's own flashback of the night of the massacre. While Folman's friend Boaz is haunted on a nightly basis by his memory of shooting dogs during the war, Folman can remember nothing of his time as a soldier and cannot determine whether this new flashback is a memory or fantasy. In order to determine its veracity, Folman goes on a quest to find other people who were with him in Beirut that night.[8] The film, which is entirely animated bar one short section at the end, comprises a series of interviews interspersed with visualisations of the experiences and memories described by the interviewees.

The animation style and its ability to seem simultaneously realistic and fantastical helps communicate the film's overall attitude to the reality and significance of memory and dreams. While it does not attempt photorealism in the manner of *Walking with Dinosaurs'* digital reconstructions, the animation in *Waltz with Bashir* seems to bear a close relationship to reality, so much so that the style is sometimes mistakenly attributed to Rotoscope techniques.[9] There was a concern for visual authenticity in the design of the animation – the characters were constructed using as a reference the video footage of the original, filmed interviews and Art Director David Polonsky used both still and moving archival images of Lebanon in the 1980s as a basis for his design of the backgrounds and layouts (Polonsky, 2008). The film is also devoid of the overt visual metaphor found in films discussed in previous chapters, such as *Animated Minds*. Characters and locations look realistic and we could recognise the 'real' person or place from their animated counterpart. The animation design, however, is still highly stylised, an effect gained in part through light-and-shadow techniques and the film's colour palette, which Garrett Stewart (2010: 58) has described as 'eerily acidic'.

The stylisation is most pronounced in the flashback to the night of the massacre that so perplexes Folman at the beginning of the film. Folman and two other young soldiers float on their backs in the Mediterranean Sea, staring up at an amber coloured night sky that is reflected on their naked bodies and turns the whole scene a tone of sepia. After Folman and his companions rise out of the sea, they dress and walk with dreamlike slowness into and through the city and into a crowd of women wearing hijab. The young Folman stands frozen as the throng of women passes around him. This sequence is accompanied by a haunting score, composed by Max Richter.

Other dreams, memories and hallucinations recounted by the interviewees are also inflected with a similar atmosphere of subtle surrealism, an effect achieved as much by the music and pacing of these scenes as from any intrinsic quality in the animation. Roni recalls swimming for miles down the coast after being separated from his tank battalion in an ambush. He breaststrokes in a dark sea under an inky night sky, the calmness of the ocean, which stretches to the edges of the frame, illustrating the conflicting emotions of peace and fear that Roni felt while swimming for his life that night. Carmi remembers the hallucination he had while passed out on the boat that was transporting him to war. In a misty, hazy, blue seascape Carmi is cradled in the arms of a giant female figure, at the same time sexual and maternal, accompanied by ethereal string music as she languidly backstrokes through the water. He watches impassively as the boat carrying his friends blows up in a dramatic fireball that turns the sky and ocean a vivid, burning shade of orange. At several times during the film, Folman consults his friend Ori, a psychologist. Ori points out that in our dreams, the sea functions as a manifestation of fear and feelings. For Folman, his fear and dread about his involvement in the massacre are projected onto a flashback involving the sea. Carmi's anxieties on his boat trip that took him to active service, and Roni's fears for his life while escaping an ambush, are similarly transferred onto memories involving the sea. The sea becomes a vessel that carries fear and feelings that are hard to come to terms with and painful to remember.

While the animation design in the more hallucinatory dream and flashback sequences takes on an air of stylisation, it is not markedly different, in terms of integral style, to the animation in the rest of the film (see Figure 5.3). Dream sequences, flashbacks and hallucinations are all presented in a style similar to the interviews. Elements of lighting and colouration may be more exaggerated or noticeable in the former, but the shape and likeness of characters and objects are equally as realistic (or non-realistic) throughout the film. The differences are subtle and ones of feel and atmosphere than look or style. This was a conscious choice by the filmmakers who did not want to prioritise the truth of one component of the film over another. Visually, little difference is made between what Landesman and Bendor (2011: 355) have labelled, after Heidegger, the factual ('that which lends itself to empirical validation') and the factical ('that which does not') elements of the film. Through the film's aesthetic consistency, dreams and memories are given equal epistemological weight to the present-day interviews. Hallucinations and, perhaps incorrect, recollections of the past are implied as significant as the delivery of verbal recollection. Both are evidence that can be used to unearth Folman's buried memories.

Folman's disremembering of the incident floating in the sea on the night of the Sabra and Shatila massacre becomes significant in several ways. Atmospherically, it is marked out as fantastical (or 'factical') because of its surreal colour and lighting. Conversely, its stylistic

Figure 5.3 *Waltz with Bashir* uses a consistent style of animation to represent interviews (top), actual memories (middle) and potentially false memories (bottom) (dir. & prod. Ari Folman, Bridgit Folman Film Gang, 2008)

similarity to the rest of the film knits it in as an important element in Folman's recovery of the past. The repetition of the flashback (we see it three times, although it feels like more) is an indication that Folman suffers from post-traumatic stress induced by the war and it fits Cathy Caruth's (1995: 4) description of post-traumatic stress disorder as:

> a response, sometimes delayed, to an overwhelming event or events, which takes the form of repeated, intrusive hallucinations, dreams, thoughts or behaviours stemming from the event, along with numbing that may have begun during or after the experience.

Traumatic events resist assimilation into a seamless narrative of autobiography, and the fragmented non-narrative playback of history in *Waltz with Bashir* has been described by Natasha Mansfield (1995: 4) as 'akin to a shower of sparks bursting intermittently from an exploding firework'. This resistance to narrative indicates the aporetic quality of traumatic events. They are experienced as an absence and this indicates, according to Dominick LaCapra (2007: 206), that they have not been 'viably worked through'. It is this 'compulsive repetition of the aporetic relation' that induces the repeated visions of the flashback. As Caruth (1995: 152–3) points out, 'the literal registration of an event – the capacity to continually, in the flashback, reproduce it in exact detail – appears to be connected, in traumatic experience, precisely with the way it *escapes* full consciousness as it occurs' (emphasis in original). The recurrence of the flashback demonstrates that at the beginning of the film, when Folman first has this dream, he experiences the war only as an absence – an absence of complete memory of the events and his role and an absence of understanding of the meaning and truth of this dreamt flashback. 'The flashback [...] conveys [...] both *the truth of the event*, and *the truth of its incomprehensibility*' (153, emphasis in original).

Not only is Folman's post-trauma experienced through the repetition of the flashbacks, but also in his dislocation from the memory. Visually, the flashback is presented almost entirely from a third-person point of view, but there are also two moments when we see things through Folman's eyes. We look down on Folman's face as he lies in the Mediterranean, staring up at the amber night sky. This perspective changes to Folman's point of view and we see the bombed-out high rises on the shore in the background and Folman's toes poking out of the water in the foreground before he uprights himself to walk out of the sea. Later, as he walks into the city, we see him in medium close-up, the 'camera' tracking backwards at the same pace as Folman and his companions walk through the streets. As he turns the corner into the crowd of women, we switch to a view from behind his head, maintaining the same distance of medium close-up. The 'camera' then pans around Folman and in tight on his face before cutting to the next scene. This sequence works to simultaneously envelop and distance us from the memory. There are moments that encourage the viewer to imagine they are experiencing events as Folman did that night – toes popping out of the sea, the ocean of women washing past. Other moments, however, contradict this suggestion and for the majority of the sequence Folman's position within the frame seems to imply a kind of out-of-body experience. The tension within this sequence in terms of spatial placement mirrors the 'fundamental dislocation implied by all traumatic experience' (Caruth, 1995: 9) and suggests Folman's own epistemological and emotional distance from these events. Just as the audience does not know if they are occupying the position of Folman or a third party, Folman himself does not know whether he was actually present at the events he is beginning to remember.

Here we can return to Caruth's claim that 'the traumatized [...] carry an impossible history within them, or they become themselves the symptom of a history that they cannot entirely possess' (5). Just as Tana Ross' years of silence prevent her owning her past in the concentration camps, so too Folman is a symptom of history. At one point during *Waltz with Bashir*, Folman's psychologist friend Ori suggest that his memories of the past are not only being impeded by his fears regarding the role he might have played in the Sabra and Shatila massacre, but that they are also blocked by the ever present postmemory of the Holocaust. Folman's parents were in Auschwitz and because of this, Ori tells him, 'the massacre has been with you since you were six' in the form of the 'other' massacre at the 'other' camps. Folman's discovery that he was part of a unit that fired the flares that lit the Phalangists' attack on the refugee camps explains his amnesia regarding the night of the massacre, and all of his actions in the Lebanon War. Folman feels guilt, Ori explains, at unwittingly taking on the role of the Nazi, regardless of whether he fired a gun, fired a flare, or just watched others do so. He did not stop the massacre, and in Folman's subconscious mind that negative action is as abhorrent as the Nazi guard who claims to only be following orders.

Just as *Silence* signifies Ross gaining ownership of her past, so too *Waltz with Bashir* is Folman's journey of coming to terms with, and claiming possession of, his past. The repetitious flashback functions as a working-through of the director's traumatic experience and fears regarding his culpability in the events of the massacre. Towards the end of the film, Folman regains his memory of the night of the massacre and remembers being on a rooftop close to the refugee camps. In this sequence, the colour palette of the flashback sequence suddenly makes sense as the exploding flares light the sky a rich shade of amber. At this moment, the style of the flashback sequence, which previously seemed surreal, is put in perspective. In fact, we realise, Folman was remembering accurately the way the city looked that night under the flares' light. The seemingly fantastical yellow skies of the dream, flashback and hallucination sequences have in fact been deeply connecting Folman's disremembering to the truth of the past.

Folman's integration into the past is, however, far from seamless, and *Waltz with Bashir* continues up to its final moments to complicate the relationship between memory, the past and truth. The film's final animated sequence, which is an illustration of a war reporter's memories of the aftermath of the massacre, ends with the 'camera' dollying through a crowd of Palestinian women walking out of the refugee camp. The 'camera' continues through the women and pushes towards two soldiers in the distance, one of whom, as the camera gets closer, is revealed to be the young Folman. The camera ends up in a medium close-up of Folman, the same shot that ended the three flashback sequences. This sequence works to make sense of the final section of the flashback in which Folman is silently enveloped by the wave of women, only this time their ululations of mourning can be heard on the soundtrack. One could further argue that what happens next also confirms that Folman has filled in the gaps in his memory. After we hold on the medium close-up of the young Folman, his breath visibly heaving in his chest as if he is trying to calm rising panic, the image cuts to the 'reverse shot' of live-action footage of mourning women emerging from the camps. The next, and last, few minutes of the film continue with live-action footage. Women cry with grief and rail at the television news cameras and then images are shown panning across scene after scene of dead bodies lying in the dusty rubble.

Concluding the film with live-action archive footage suggests narrative resolution. Folman has remembered his past and the journey of the film to find out what role he played in the massacres and to identify his flashback as true or false reaches its end. The question remains, however, as to whether the inclusion of live-action material undermines the potential of the animation that came before. If the film was attempting to suggest, as David Polonsky claims, an epistemological parity between present-day interviews and the recollections of the past by adopting a consistent animation style throughout, what does the addition of live-action documentary footage at the moment of narrative resolution say? Dave Saunders (2010: 184) has suggested it acts as 'an afterthought designed to wrench the viewer back into an empathetic engagement with mimetic reality'. We could read the switch as proclaiming the epistemological superiority of live-action material over animation. It is, after all, the former that is chosen to indicate that Folman has accessed his past, and it is this also that is chosen for the film's sober conclusion, suggesting it has more potential impact than the stylised animation. The inclusion of the live-action footage is more, however, than a simple resolution and there is, as Stewart (2010: 62) says, 'no formal recapitulation to routine verité'. This footage only makes sense in the context of the ninety minutes of animation that precedes it. Traumatic recollection, Caruth (1995: 151) reminds us, is not a simple memory. The television news images may reveal the truth of the event of the massacre, but the truth of the experience is, for Folman, as much about its incomprehensibility and his amnesia as about what actually happened. If forgetting has a truth, as Weinrich claims, then Folman's forgetting marks the severity of his traumatic memory and postmemory. It is through the animated journey that we learn the true meaning of the war for Folman. Memory, the film suggests, is as ephemeral as the past itself. Memory, as Ori tells Folman, 'is dynamic, it's alive'.

Waltz with Bashir, *Silence*, *Irinka and Sandrinka* and *Learned by Heart* use animation as a way of linking with a past from which the protagonists have become disconnected and dislocated. Unlike photographic media, which seem to highlight the distance of the past as an instant that cannot be recaptured, animation is a way to weave oneself into history and to bring oneself into proximity with that which is temporally distal. The specific and constructed nature of animation makes it particularly appropriate for telling personal stories that do not fit into the more general History that favours hegemonic power relations. Through animation, this History can be contested and filmmakers can instead connect themselves to a collective history that is identity specific.

It may seem counter-intuitive that non-indexical media may be the most apposite way of remembering the past. But, the absence of indexical evidence of the past combines with the rich tapestry of animation's visual excesses, which go beyond merely re-presenting the past, to convey the meaning of both personal history and the act of remembering it. The absence of indexical images speaks to the absences in knowledge and memory that several of these filmmakers have in relation to their pasts. The process of making the films is, in a way, a performative act of becoming that reconnects them to history. Stoïanov learns of her ancestral stories, Rimminen reconciles her childhood with the social evolution of Finland, Ross is given voice to talk of her youth, Folman realises the significance of his forgetting the Lebanon War. In each case, the aesthetic properties of the films' animation style speak to the specificity of the autobiographers' pasts. This specificity comes not through photographic media that can be linked to a certain time and place, but through the expressivity of animation that can be interpreted as speaking directly to the experience of those whose stories are being told. It is precisely because these images are not indexical, but at one and the same time something more and something less, that we come to understand how the past is (or is not) remembered. In the films discussed in this chapter, the evocative potential of animation allows the audience insight into subjective reality within the context of personal and collective history.

Afterword

'How are you going to supply a photograph of Jesus? Not an etching, engraving, or a painting [...] an actual photograph of Jesus.' So we hear a baffled archivist contemplate in Laurie Hill's 2008 award-winning short documentary *Photograph of Jesus*. The increasingly incredulous ruminations of the archivist to the many bizarre requests received by the Hulton Archive in London are accompanied by imagery in which photographs that cannot possibly exist are brought to life via animation that uses digital manipulation techniques to combine existing photos from the archive. Thus, Hilary Clinton is clutched in a passionate embrace with a Second World War soldier and Hitler springs over the hurdles at the 1948 Olympic games in London. What Hill's film illustrates, apart from the lack of common sense of many people who make requests of archives, is our desire to transcend the limits of photographic media. While *Photograph of Jesus* demonstrates the absurdity of granting unrealistic photographic wishes, it also shows animation's potential to respond to the shortcomings of the photographic.

Whether it be displaying prehistoric life in spectacular photorealism, or evoking subjective, conscious states through hand-crafted abstract images, *Animated Documentary* has argued that animation expands the range and depth of what documentary can represent and how it can do it. Such expansion is facilitated by the ontological differences between live-action film and animation and the way that animation releases documentary from its visual 'indexical bind' (Nichols, 1991: 149) with reality. In the absence of this indexical visual imagery stands animation, which by the nature of its processes of production and aesthetic realisation is at one and the same time less and more than the photographic. This less and more, or absence and excess as I have termed it, is something with which the viewer must contend, be that real-but-not-real dinosaurs, or the present voices and absent bodies in interview documentaries, or the evocative metaphorical animation that encourages us to use our imagination to empathise with an unfamiliar brain state or mental health issue.

The convergence of animation and documentary into the cohesive form of animated documentary is a development that transcends constricted definitions and binary understandings of what, and how, documentary and animation can show us. It is also a demonstration of our increasingly sophisticated ability to interpret complex audiovisual texts and our growing demand for images that challenge our conception of representation. These demands on visual representation are fuelled, in part, by a greater awareness of the malleable nature of the image and the potential for deception. By the mid-1990s there was a growing anxiety, observed by Brian Winston (1995: 5), regarding the ease with which photographs could be invisibly altered using digital technologies. This concern applied equally to moving images, and Winston ponders the effect of digital editing software on the documentary film when he asks 'what can or will be left of the relationship between image and reality' (6)? Fears over the veracity of the documentary image occurred concurrently with the rise of reality television and 'factual entertainment' – small screen formats with a capacity to depict highly manipulated situations in the style of observational documentary that placed further stress on the position of documentary. Not only could the image be altered without our knowledge, but the profilmic could be as much of a fabrication as any fictional scenario. The boom of animated documentary production from the late 1990s onwards makes sense in this context. At a time of documentary uncertainty, animation became a particularly appropriate tool for non-fiction as there can be no mistaking the constructed nature of the animated image that, by wearing its ontology on its sleeve, circumvents any potential duping or trickery. The animated documentary takes the viewer beyond the point of distrusting the origin of the image or the profilmic by embracing its quality as a constructed form.

Animation as a representational strategy in and for documentary seems here to stay, more than a short-term novelty. Its ubiquity can be seen through its now almost commonplace use. The 2011 documentary *Khodorkovsky* (Cyril Tuschi) uses a hotchpotch of documentary techniques to question whether imprisoned businessman and one-time richest man in Russia Mikhail Khodorkovsky is a fraudulent tax evader or just someone who got on the wrong side of Vladamir

Putin. Filmmaker voiceover and Nick Broomfield-style reflexivity are thrown together with elegiac landscape shots, talking heads, archival material and sequences of animation. The fact that animation is included in this documentary pick-and-mix is perhaps an indication that it is just another accepted approach in the post-observational documentary style that we are familiar with from mainstream television and theatrical documentary. The popularity and success of *Waltz with Bashir* in 2008 has certainly helped animation attain this status and has in its own way become a benchmark for how animation can be used in documentary. The animation in *Khodorkovsky* nods to the style used by Ari Folman in *Waltz with Bashir*, as it does in *The Green Wave* (Ali Samadi Ahadi, 2010),[1] another recent documentary that uses animation as part of a combination of non-fictional representational strategies.

While *Waltz with Bashir* may have become something of a standard for the use of animation in feature-length films, the animated documentary continues to evolve as a form. For example, the National Film Board of Canada's documentary *The Next Day* (2011) uses animation in the relatively new form of an online interactive documentary. The film uses interviews with people who have survived near-fatal suicide attempts and their stories are heard in snippets organised by theme. Viewers can use their computer mouse to click on a theme word and the first-person voiceovers are accompanied by animations of a house and its surroundings drawn in a childlike fashion in black-and-white outline. The house becomes symbolic in conjunction with the stories heard on the soundtrack as the interviewees discuss the formative experiences that may have directly or indirectly led them to attempt to take their own life. By refusing to show us the interviewees, even in animated form, *The Next Day* places emphasis on their voices in a similar way to the interview documentaries discussed in Chapter 3, but the interactive nature of the film allows the viewer more agency over the narrative and greater freedom than a linear animated documentary in terms of making connections between the different accounts heard.

The Next Day demonstrates a different approach to the animated interview documentary from those examined in Chapter 3. Similarly there are, or most likely will be, other ways to use animation to substitute for missing live action, to evoke subjective, conscious experiences and to revisit forgotten or repressed memory. Likewise, animation has, and no doubt will, lend itself to representing other aspects of the world out there and the world in here of lived experience. Life is rich and complicated in ways that are not always available to observation, something that is and will hopefully continue to be reflected in the diversity of style and subject matter of contemporary animated documentaries and the lively and growing discourse that surrounds them.

Notes

Introduction

1. By 'conventional alternative,' I mean the types of photographically originated media familiar to documentary, such as observational filming, archival footage, reconstruction, interviews, photographs, and so on.
2. These are some of the most frequent assumptions I have heard expressed by students in undergraduate documentary courses.
3. For brevity, I will refer to the audiovisual texts under discussion in this book as 'films', even though many of them are produced on digital video and are not intended for projection on the big screen.
4. A process that took two years and required 25,000 individual drawings.
5. Here McCay called on his previous experience of depicting real-life events in drawing as an artist–reporter at the Cincinnati *Commercial Tribune* (Crafton, 1982: 90). The emulation was clearly effective as the film was included in the Universal Weekly newsreel shown in movie theatres (See: Crafton, 1982: 116).
6. Despite enthusiastic marketing and strong reviews, *The Sinking of the Lusitania*, which McCay funded personally, was not a financial success, earning only $80,000, or $3.20 per drawing (Canemaker, 1987: 152).
7. While it was not labelled as an animated documentary at the time of its production or initial reception, an argument can be made for it being understood as such, according to the criteria set out earlier.
8. The production of the Canadian shorts was prompted by the enthusiasm of John Grierson, then head of the National Film Board of Canada, who had become receptive to the documentary potential of animation after viewing a 1940 speculative training film made by Disney for the Lockheed Aircraft Corporation – *Four Methods of Flush Riveting* – at a conference held in 1941 to debate the potential application of animation in a non-entertainment capacity (Shale, 1982: 15).
9. *Tommy Tucker's Tooth* (1922) and *Clara Cleans Her Teeth* (1926), both for Dr Thomas B McCrum of the Deener Dental Institute in Kansas City, Missouri (See: Shale, 1982: 112).
10. These can be thought of as mainstream applications of data visualisation, a significant example of the application of animation to non-fiction representation.
11. One of the Hubleys daughters, Emily, became an animator and some of her work appears in Abraham Ravett's autobiographical documentary *Everything's for You* (1989), discussed in Chapter 5, and Judith Hefland and Daniel B. Gold's *Blue Vinyl* (2002).
12. For example, IDFA (International Documentary Festival Amsterdam) included a special programme on animated documentary in 2007 and the London International Animation Festival, which launched in 2004, regularly includes a line-up of animated documentaries.

13. That is, how reality is represented in photographic-based media such as film and video.

1   Representational Strategies

1. Nichols initially suggested four modes: the expository, the observational, the interactive and the reflexive. He later added the poetic and the performative and re-named the interactive as the participatory mode. See Nichols (1991, 1994 and 2001).

2   Digital Realities

1. Something that is amplified by mock-documentary becoming its own genre of comedy, on television and in film, thus further separating these documentary codes from the representation of reality.
2. This can be attested to by the debate that surrounds films that refuse, either textually or paratextually, to confirm their documentary status. For example, Banksy's *Exit Through the Gift Shop* (2010) generated debate as to the authenticity of both the images and the profilmic.
3. And, more recently, a successful stage show.
4. A fact acknowledged by series producer Nigel Paterson in the *After Walking with Dinosaurs* clip. Available on the *Planet Dinosaur* website, http://www.bbc.co.uk/programmes/p00kf34s (accessed Aug 22, 2012).
5. For example, the giant herbivore sauropod class of dinosaurs had once been thought to be able to bend their long necks to graze from treetops, an impression bolstered by how these dinosaurs were represented in *Jurassic Park*. However, this inaccuracy is corrected in episode two of *Walking with Dinosaurs* (*A Time of Titans*), which shows that the immobile stiff neck of the Diplodocus would have meant it foraged exclusively from the foliage on forest floors.
6. By the time of *Planet Dinosaur*, palaeontologists had developed greater ability to discern these things from fossils, as demonstrated in episode two's explication of the deduction of the length and colour of the feathers of the sinornithosaurus. However, a voiceover in the *Building a Dinosaur* clip acknowledges that dinosaur 'colours and [skin] patterns are for the most part educated guesses.' Available at http://www.bbc.co.uk/programmes/p00kf34s (accessed Aug 22, 2012).
7. Heads-up display is a means of visually relaying information, such as health, lives remaining, and time remaining, to a player of a video game. The HUD is usually displayed on screen throughout the game, although sometimes can be called up at the player's demand. The use of HUD-like displays has been applied to documentary by Errol Morris in *Standard Operating Procedure* (2008).
8. The persistence of *Jurassic Park* as a reference is demonstrated in episode two of *Planet Dinosaur*, when the microraptor is identified as a member of the raptor family through a visual comparison with the velociraptor, the infamously fearsome dinosaur in Spielberg's film.
9. Karen D. Scott and Anne M. White have suggested that this visual referencing is, at times, even more specific and that *Walking with Dinosaurs* makes

several overt nods to BBC nature and wildlife documentaries through the replication of iconic images from earlier Attenborough documentaries. For example, they note the sequence early on in episode three where the sea-dwelling liopleurodon rises out of the ocean and snatches an unsuspecting dinosaur from the shore is reminiscent of the famous moment in Attenborough's 1990 series *The Trials of Life* in which a killer whale emerges from the water to prey on a basking seal (Scott & White, 2003: 329, n.7).

10. It is interesting to consider the connotations of such a sound effect, and Errol Morris uses a nearly identical one to accompany the appearance of HUD-like displays in *Standard Operating Procedure*.
11. This gendering of the voice of authority is something that is, in itself, problematic.
12. An act that further substantiates the claim, at least in Stella Bruzzi's eyes, that Branagh sees himself as the 'new Laurence Olivier' (Bruzzi, 2006: 254 n.2) – that earlier heavyweight British thespian having famously narrated the 1973–4 British documentary series *The World at War*.
13. At 18.91 million viewers, the first episode of *Walking with Dinosaurs* was also the most watched programme of any type in the United Kingdom the week it premiered, knocking off the top slots *Eastenders* and *Coronation Street* (United Kingdom's two longest-running primetime soap operas). See Broadcaster's Audience Research Board website for week Oct 04–Oct 10, 1999 http://www.barb.co.uk/report/weeklyTopProgrammesOverview/? (accessed Aug 18, 2012).
14. *The Independent* was the only UK national newspaper to review the series (Sutcliffe, 2011) and audience figures for only two of the six episodes register in the top 30 BBC1 programmes for their respective week's viewing – see http://www.barb.co.uk/report/weeklyTopProgrammesOverview/? for weeks Sept 12–Oct 23, 2011.
15. Although the defendants in the trial were initially referred to as the 'Chicago 8', and after Bobby Seale was dismissed, the 'Chicago 7', Morgen concurred with Yippie Jerry Rubin's suggestion that they should have been called the 'Chicago 10', to include the two defence lawyers who were also charged with contempt of court (Roadside Attractions, 2007: 12).
16. The style of Rotoshop may be familiar from its use in Richard Linklater's animated films, *Waking Life* (2001) and *A Scanner Darkly* (2006). US readers may also be aware of Sabiston's animation style through his production company's recent work on the Charles Schwab television commercials.
17. As the audience is informed by a title card at the beginning of the film.
18. Available at: http://www.flatblackfilms.com/Flat_Black_Films/Films/Pages/Project_Incognito.html (accessed Feb 13, 2009).
19. Available at: http://www.flatblackfilms.com/Flat_Black_Films/Films/Pages/Grasshopper.html (accessed Feb 14, 2009).
20. Interestingly, Branagh's tone of voice is far less authoritative and imposing in the *Making of* episode, and much more conversational and light, compared to his vocal delivery of the narration for the main series. This only adds to the sense that we are being given a special, 'insider' insight into the scientific validity of the series.

21. Available at http://www.bbc.co.uk/programmes/p00kf292 (accessed Aug 22, 2012).
22. *After Walking with Dinosaurs* clip. Available at http://www.bbc.co.uk/programmes/p00kf34s (accessed Aug 22, 2012).
23. It's questionable whether *Chicago 10*'s animation was visually appealing for viewers. Along with the film's lack of historical context, the quality of the animation is one of its most criticised aspects. For example, having a 'slapdash, lurching feel' (Scott, 2008) and 'the jelly-faced cartoon figures look like rotoscoped androids who just stepped out of the sequel you never wanted to see to *Waking Life*' (Glieberman, 2008), Morgen himself later acknowledged that the animation was not all he had hoped for (Luciano-Adams, 2008).

3 Animated Interviews

1. Claymation is a form of stop-motion animation using malleable puppets, usually made out of Plasticine and formed around a wire frame or armature.
2. The five films are *On Probation, Sales Pitch, Palmy Days, Early Bird* and *Late Edition* (all 1983).
3. And also led to many commissions for television commercials (See: Aardman Animations Ltd, 2010). The other films in this series are *Going Equipped, War Story, Next!* and *Ident*.
4. However, as Sabiston (2012: 82) notes, Rotoshop doesn't necessitate tracing and it is possible to use the software to create 'true' animation that is not based on pre-existing video footage.
5. Sabiston (2012: 78) has expressed dissatisfaction with this move towards photorealism, citing the conflicting desires of wishing to return to a more abstract style and the pleasure in achieving the detail of photorealism.
6. See Chapter 2 for a discussion of photorealism in Rotoshop.
7. The concept of the uncanny valley was first suggested by Japanese roboticist Masahiro Mori in 1970 (see Mori, 2012).
8. It is for this reason that much was made of the failure of the motion capture film *The Polar Express* (Robert Zemeckis, 2004) being due to the lifelessness of human characters, particularly their eyes, which made them seem 'creepy' (see, for example: Dargis, 2004; Park, 2004; Rooney, 2004).
9. Interestingly, Sabiston cites Aardman Animation's stop-motion claymation films, in particular *Creature Comforts* (1989), as an influence on his rotoshopped documentary shorts. He was inspired by 'the idea that you could easily run out and quickly capture anything, then use this animated lens to reinterpret it, amplify it and comment upon it' (Sabiston, 2012: 80).
10. Many continued to work with Sabiston on later films and one of whom, Jennifer Deutrom (née Drummond), used Rotoshop independently of Sabiston to make the short film *The F.E.D.S* (2003/4), a light-hearted short film of interviews with grocery store workers who hand out free food samples to customers (a.k.a 'food education demo experts').

11. Although the work of each individual animator is not labelled and thus not necessarily identifiable – we can just tell that it looks different.
12. It should be noted that Gaines theorises the power of the relationship between documentary and the world as deriving from mimesis rather than indexicality (see Gaines, 1999: 92–3).
13. Other than, it would seem, to take his own life. According to the film's postscript, this is what Giancarlo attempted several months after the filmmakers interviewed him. He and his family were subsequently granted permission to stay in Sweden.
14. Blazer informed me that once the subjects had seen the film they consented to their photographs being added as a postscript.
15. Indeed, as noted earlier, Tupicoff describes the film as a 'mother's song'.
16. Chion (1999: 29) gives the example of the Wizard in *The Wizard of Oz*, whose omniscience and omnipotence disappears as soon as Toto draws back the curtain, revealing a little old man operating the machinery behind the Wizard's façade.
17. However, the fact that Kathy is played by an actress does not become clear until the closing credits.
18. Tupicoff filmed at a house in Melbourne, rather than Brisbane, albeit one 'chosen and dressed with the Brisbane suburb and milieu in mind' (Tupicoff, 2009).

4 The World in Here

1. See Chapter 1 for a more detailed exploration of how, and how not, animated documentaries fit into Nichols' modes.
2. Full details of her work can be found on her website at http://www.sheilasofian.com/.
3. It should be noted that even though *Animated Minds* is described by the filmmakers as being about mental health issues, Asperger's is in fact a brain condition. *An Alien in the Playground* fits in with the series because it is about Joshua's experience of alienation and being bullied because of his condition, rather than the condition itself.
4. Pixilation is the frame-by-frame manipulation and movement of people and objects to create movement, which often then appears jerky or fragmented in the final film.
5. See Chapter 2 for a discussion of films that use computer animation in this way.
6. There are many other animated documentaries that are made with similar remits. For example, the *Autism Portraits* Project made by Art and Graft for the autism charity Spectrum (viewable at http://vimeopro.com/user4829604/spectrum-portraits-project) and *Why I Had an FGC*, a film commissioned by Camden council social services (London, UK) to promote the use of its family group counselling services.
7. The film can be viewed at http://vimeo.com/46035152.
8. Another animator who is notable for her collaborative working process is Canada-based Shira Avni. Avni has done much work with the Down's Syndrome community and *Tying Your Own Shoes* (2009) is an animated documentary that combines live-action footage with animation created by collaborators with Down's Syndrome.

Notes 179

5 Animated Memories

1. The cels for the animation were created by Emily Hubley, daughter of John and Faith Hubley, whose work is mentioned in the Introduction.
2. Post-memory, discussed later in this chapter, is a term coined by Marianne Hirsch (1997) to describe memories not experienced directly, but 'inherited' from a previous generation.
3. Halbwachs' two works on memory are *Les cadres sociaux de la mémoire*, 1925; and *La Mémoire collective*, published posthumously in 1950.
4. A super-title at the beginning of this chapter informs viewers that 'Lord' in Finnish translates as 'Sir' and 'man'.
5. Cut-out animation creates the illusion of movement through the frame-by-frame manipulation of objects, or limbs, that are cut out, traditionally of card or stiff fabric, and moved incrementally between shots.
6. Hirsch (2008) references Art Spiegelman's graphic novel *Maus*, in which Spiegelman explores his father's experiences as an Auschwitz survivor, as a key example of postmemory work. There are other examples of the interrelationship between animated documentary and graphic novels, for example Marjane Satrapi's *Persepolis*, her autobiographical account of growing up in Iran, which appeared first as a graphic novel (2000) and was later adapted to a feature-length film (2007), and this topic deserves further attention.
7. Commissioned by the municipality of Stockholm in 1995.
8. Some of the interviewees are friends of Folman's, or people he served alongside during the war. Other participants were found via an online appeal for people to tell stories of their experiences fighting during the Lebanon War. Interviews with Ron Ben Yisahi, a television journalist who played a prominent role in reporting the war, and Professor Zahava Solomon, a Post Trauma Stress expert, are also included in the film.
9. See, for example, Anderson (2009). This attribution is perhaps understandable due to *Waltz with Bashir*'s passing stylistic similarities to Bob Sabiston's film achieved via the Rotoshop software (see Chapters 2 and 3). David Polonsky (2008), Art Director of *Waltz with Bashir*, is keen to point out, however, that the animation in this film was painstakingly produced through a computer-based cut-out technique.

Afterword

1. At a screening of *The Green Wave* at the Edinburgh Film Festival in 2011 Ahadi commented that the French–German broadcaster ARTE, who put up funding for his film and who also invested in *Waltz with Bashir*, pushed him towards a *Waltz*-like style of animation.

Bibliography

Aardman Animations Ltd (2010) About Us/ History. Available from: http://www.aardman.com/about-us/history/ (accessed 22 October 2012).

Adorno TW (1983 [1967]) Cultural Criticisms and Society. In: *Prisms*. Cambridge: MA: MIT Press.

van Alphen E (1999) Symptoms of Discursivity: Experience, Memory, and Trauma. In: Bal M, Crewe JV, and Spitzer L (eds), *Acts of Memory: Cultural Recall in the Present*. Hanover, NH: University Press of New England, pp. 24–39.

Altman R (1980) Moving Lips: Cinema as Ventriloquism. *Yale French Studies*, 60, pp. 67–79.

Anderson J (2009) "Waltz with Bashir" Brings a Dark Memory into Light. *The Washington Post*, 23 January. Available from: http://www.washingtonpost.com/wp-dyn/content/article/2009/01/22/AR2009012203855.html (accessed 10 October 2012).

Andrew D (2005) Foreword to the 2004 Edition. In: Bazin A, *What Is Cinema? Vol.1*, trans. H. Gray. Berkeley: University of California Press, pp. ix–xxiv.

Animated Minds (2012a) Press and Feedback. Available from: http://animatedminds.com/press_and_feedback/ (accessed 5 October 2012).

Animated Minds (2012b) The Concept. Available from: http://animatedminds.com/the_concept/ (accessed 1 October 2012).

Aristotle (1986) *De Anima (On the Soul)*, trans. H. Lawson-Tancred. London: Penguin.

Arnall D (1992) *A Is for Autism* DVD sleeve notes. London: BFI.

Aronowitsch D (2010) Being an Animated Character. Available from: http://www.labkultur.tv/en/blog/being-animated-character (accessed 9 September 2012).

Austin T (2008) "... To Leave the Confinements of His Humanness": Authorial Voice, Death and Constructions of Nature in Werner Herzog's Grizzly Man. In: Austin T and de Jong W (eds), *Rethinking Documentary: New Perspectives, New Practices*. Maidenhead, UK: Open University Press, pp. 51–66.

Bal M (1999) Introduction. In: Bal M, Crewe JV, and Spitzer L (eds), *Acts of Memory: Cultural Recall in the Present*. Hanover, NH: University Press of New England, pp. vii–xvii.

Banks-Smith N (1999) Roar of Approval: Last Night's TV. *Guardian*, London, 5th October, Available from: http://www.guardian.co.uk/media/1999/oct/05/tvandradio.television2 (accessed 22 August 2012).

Barnouw E (1993) *Documentary: A History of the Non-Fiction Film*. 2nd rev. ed. Oxford and New York: Oxford University Press.

Barry AMS (1997) *Visual Intelligence: Perception, Image and Manipulation in Visual Communication*. Albany, NY: State University of New York Press.

Barthes R (1977a) The Grain of the Voice. In: *Image, Music, Text*, trans. S. Heath. London: Fontana Paperbacks, pp. 179–189.

Barthes R (1977b) The Photographic Message. In: *Image, Music, Text*, trans. S. Heath. London: Fontana Paperbacks, pp. 15–31.

Barthes R (1981) *Camera Lucida: Reflections on Photography*, trans. R. Howard. New York: Hill and Wang.
Bazin A (2005 [1967]) *What Is cinema? Vol.1*, trans. H. Gray. Berkeley, University of California Press.
BBC (n.d.) Walking with Dinosaurs. Available from: http://www.bbc.co.uk/sn/ prehistoric_life/tv_radio/wwdinosaurs/ (accessed 19 October 2012).
BBC (2012) Planet Dinosaur. Available from: http://www.bbc.co.uk/programmes/ b014r8bx (accessed 17 August 2012).
BBC Worldwide (2004) *Walking with Dinosaurs* (DVD Booklet). BBC Worldwide.
Beattie K (2008) *Documentary Display: Re-Viewing Nonfiction Film and Video*. London: Wallflower.
Beattie Z (2011) Wonderland: The Trouble with Love and Sex. Available from: http://www.bbc.co.uk/blogs/tv/2011/05/wonderland-trouble-with-love-and-sex.shtml (accessed 9 September 2012).
Beckman K (2011) Animation on Trial. *Animation: An Interdisciplinary Journal*, 6 (3), pp. 259–275.
Benjamin W (2003) On the Concept of History. In: Eiland H and Jennings MW (eds), *Selected Writings: v. 4, 1938–1940*, trans. E. Jephcott et al. Cambridge, MA: Harvard University Press, pp. 389–400.
Berger J (1972) *Ways of Seeing*. London: BBC/ Penguin.
Bioscope (1919) Review of *The Sinking of the Lusitania*. Bioscope, 41(650), p. 74.
Blanchot M and Derrida J (2000) *The Instant of My Death: Demure: Fiction and Testimony*, trans. E. Rottenberg. Stanford, CA: Stanford University Press.
Blazer L (2009) Research Questions on Backseat Bingo. Email message to author, 17 February.
Bolter JD and Grusin R (2000) *Remediation: Understanding New Media*. Cambridge MA: MIT Press.
Bouldin J (2004) Cadaver of the Real: Animation, Rotoscoping and the Politics of the Body. *Animation Journal*, 12, pp. 7–31.
Bruzzi S (2006) *New Documentary*. 2nd ed. London and New York: Routledge.
Bukatman S (2000) Taking Shape: Morphing and the Performance of Self. In: Sobchack V (ed), *Meta-Morphing: Visual Transformation and the Culture of Quick-Change*. Minneapolis: University of Minnesota Press, pp. 225–249.
Cadava E (1997) *Words of Light: Theses on the Photography of History*. Princeton, NJ: Princeton University Press.
Canemaker J (1987) *Winsor Mccay, His Life and Art*. New York: Abbeville Press.
Capino JB (2004) Filthy Funnies: Notes on the Body in Animated Pornography. *Animation Journal*, 12, pp. 53–71.
Carroll N (1996) Nonfiction Film and Postmodern Skepticism. In: Carroll N and Bordwell D (eds), *Post-Theory: Reconstructing Film Studies*, Madison: University of Wisconsin Press, pp. 283–306.
Caruth C (ed.) (1995) *Trauma: Explorations in Memory*. Baltimore: The Johns Hopkins University Press.
Chanan M (2007) *The Politics of Documentary*. London: British Film Institute.
Chapman J (2009) *Issues in Contemporary Documentary*. Cambridge, UK: Polity.
Chedgzoy K (2007) Introduction. In: Rossington M and Whitehead A (eds), *Theories of Memory: A Reader*. Edinburgh: Edinburgh University Press, pp. 216–218.
Chion M (1994) *Audio-Vision*, trans. C. Gorbman. New York: Columbia University Press.

Bibliography

Chion M (1999) *The Voice in Cinema*, trans. C. Gorbman. New York: Columbia University Press.

Cholodenko A (2007) Speculations on the Animatic Automaton. In: Cholodenko A (ed), *The Illusion of Life II: More Essays on Animation*. Sydney, Aus: Power Publications, pp. 486–528.

Connor S (2000) *Dumbstruck – A Cultural History of Ventriloquism*. Oxford: Oxford University Press.

Cowie E (2011) *Recording Reality, Desiring the Real*. Minneapolis: University of Minnesota Press.

Crafton D (1982) *Before Mickey: The Animated Film, 1898–1928*. Cambridge, MA: MIT Press.

Dargis M (2004) Do You Hear Sleigh Bells? Nah, Just Tom Hanks and Some Train. *The New York Times*, 10 November. Available from: http://www.nytimes.com/2004/11/10/movies/10pola.html (accessed 9 September 2012).

Darley A (2000) *Visual Digital Culture: Surface Play and Spectacle in New Media Genres*. London and New York: Routledge.

Darley A (2003) Simulating Natural History: Walking with Dinosaurs as Hyper-Real Edutainment. *Science as Culture*, 12 (2), pp. 227–256.

DelGaudio S (1997) If Truth Be Told, Can 'toons Tell It? Documentary and Animation. *Film History*, 9 (2), pp. 189–199.

Dickinson M (ed.) (1999) *Rogue Reels: Oppositional Film in Britain, 1945–90*. London: British Film Institute.

van Dijck J (2006) Picturizing Science: The Science Documentary as Multimedia Spectacle. *International Journal of Cultural Studies*, 9 (1), pp. 5–24.

Doane MA (2007a) Indexicality: Trace and Sign: Introduction. *differences*, 18 (1), pp. 1–6.

Doane MA (2007b) The Indexical and the Concept of Medium Specificity. *differences*, 18 (1), pp. 128–152.

Doane MA (2009) The Voice in the Cinema: The Articulation of Body and Space. In: Braudy L and Cohen M (eds), *Film Theory and Criticism*, 7th ed. Oxford; New York: Oxford University Press, pp. 318–330.

Documentary Australia Foundation (n.d.) *It's Like That*. Available from: http://www.documentaryaustralia.com.au/case_studies/details/53/its-like-that (accessed 9 September 2012).

Dolar M (2006) *A Voice and Nothing More*. Cambridge, MA: MIT Press.

Dulac G (1982 [1927]) The Aesthetics, The Obstacles. Integral Cinegraphie, trans. S. Liebman. *Framework: A Film Journal*, (19), pp. 6–9.

Eisenstein S (1988) *Eisenstein on Disney*, ed. J. Leyda, trans. A. Upchurch. London: Methuen.

Elkins J (1998) *On Pictures and the Words That Fail Them*. Cambridge and New York: Cambridge University Press.

Elkins J (1999) *The Domain of Images*. London: Cornell University Press.

Ellis J (1982) *Visible Fictions: Cinema, Television, Radio*. London: Routledge.

Ellis JC and McLane BA (2005) *A New History of Documentary Film*. New York: Continuum.

Elsaesser T (2006) Early Film History and Multi-Media. In: Keenan T and Chun WHK (eds), *New Media Old Media*. London and New York: Routledge, pp. 13–25.

Flat Black Films (n.d.) Rotoshop. Available from: http://flatblackfilms.com/Flat_Black_Films/Rotoshop.html. (accessed 24 August 2012).

Fleischer R (2005) *Out of the Inkwell: Max Fleischer and the Animation Revolution*. Lexington: University Press of Kentucky.
Forceville C (2008) Metaphor in Pictures and Multimodal Representations. In: Gibbs RW (ed.), *The Cambridge Handbook of Metaphor and Thought*. Cambridge and New York: Cambridge University Press, pp. 462–482.
Foucault M (2008 [1969]) *The History of Sexuality, vol 1: The Will to Knowledge*, trans.A.M. Sheridan Smith. London: Routledge.
Freud S (2003 [1919]) *The Uncanny*. London: Penguin.
Furniss M (1998) *Art in Motion: Animation Aesthetics*. London: John Libbey.
Gaines J (1999) Political Mimesis. In: Gaines J and Renov M (eds), *Collecting Visible Evidence*. Minneapolis: University of Minnesota Press, pp. 84–102.
Galt R (2008) It's So Cold in Alaska': Evoking Exploration Between Bazin and The Forbidden Quest. *Discourse*, 28 (1), pp. 53–71.
Garwood I (2012) Roto-Synchresis: Relationships between Body and Voice in Rotoshop Animation. *Animation: An Interdisciplinary Journal*, 7 (1), pp. 39–57.
Glieberman O (2008) Movie Review: Chicago 10. *Entertainment Weekly*. Available from: http://www.ew.com/ew/article/0,,20180593,00.html (accessed 25 August 2012).
Goss J (2011) Drawing Voices. *Animation: An Interdisciplinary Journal*, 6 (3), pp. 247–258.
Grierson J (1933) The Documentary Producer. *Cinema Quarterly*, 2 (1), pp. 7–9.
Gunning T (1990) The Cinema of Attractions: Early Film, Its Spectator and the Avant-Garde. In: Elsaesser T (ed.), *Early Cinema: Space, Frame, Narration*. London: British Film Institute, pp. 56–62.
Gunning T (2004) What's the Point of an Index? Or, Faking Photographs. *Nordicom Review*, 1–2, pp. 39–49.
Gunning T (2007) Moving Away from the Index: Cinema and the Impression of Reality. *differences*, 18 (1), pp. 29–52.
Halbwachs M (2007) From *The Collective Memory*. In: Rossington M and Whitehead A (eds), *Theories of Memory: A Reader*, Edinburgh, Edinburgh University Press, pp. 139–149.
Hanks R (1999) Television Review. *The Independent*, London, 5th October.
Hayes R (2012) The Animated Body and Its Material Nature. In: Pilling J (ed.), *Animating the Unconscious: Desire, Sexuality and Animation*, London and New York: Wallflower Press, pp. 208–218.
Hight C (2008) Primetime Digital Documentary Animation: The Photographic and Graphic Within Play. *Studies in Documentary Film*, 2 (1), pp. 9–31.
Hirsch J (2004) *Afterimage: Film, Trauma, and the Holocaust*. Philadelphia: Temple University Press.
Hirsch M (1997) *Family Frames: Photography, Narrative and Postmemory*. Cambridge, MA: Harvard University Press.
Hirsch M (2008) The Generation of Postmemory. *Poetics Today*, 29 (1), pp. 103–128.
Hodgson J (2006) Jonathan Hodgson. In: Cook B and Thomas G (eds), *The Animate! Book: Rethinking Animation*, London: LUX, pp. 62–68.
Holmlund C and Fuchs C (eds) (1997) *Between the Sheets, In the Streets: Queer, Lesbian, Gay Documentary*. Minneapolis: University of Minnesota Press.
Honess Roe A (2009) Animating Documentary. PhD Dissertation, Los Angeles, CA, University of Southern California.

Honess Roe B (2011) The Canadian Shorts: Establishing Disney's Wartime Style. In: Van Riper AB (ed.), *Learning from Mickey, Donald and Walt: Essays of Disney's Edutainment Films*. Jefferson, NC and London: McFarland & Co., pp. 15–26.
Hosea B (2010) Drawing Animation. *Animation: An Interdisciplinary Journal*, 5 (3), pp. 353–367.
Hyslop A (2010) Other Minds. In: Zalta EN (ed.), *The Stanford Encyclopedia of Philosophy*. Available from: http://plato.stanford.edu/archives/fall2010/entries/other-minds/ (accessed 5 October 2012).
IDFA (2007) IDFA Programme Guide 2007.
Jellyfish Pictures (2012) Planet Dinosaur. Available from: http://www.jellyfishpictures.co.uk/job/planet-dinosaur (accessed 22 August 2012).
King N (2000) *Memory, Narrative, Identity: Remembering the Self*. Edinburgh: Edinburgh University Press.
Klein NM (2000) Animation and Animorphs: A Brief Disappearing Act. In: Sobchack V (ed.), *Meta-Morphing: Visual Transformation and the Culture of Quick-Change*, Minneapolis: University of Minnesota Press, pp. 21–40.
LaCapra D (2007) From *History in Transit: Experience, Identity, Critical Theory*. In: Rossington M and Whitehead A (eds), *Theories of Memory: A Reader*. Edinburgh: Edinburgh University Press, pp. 206–211.
Land E (2012a) FAQs. Available from: http://www.thecentrefoldproject.org/ (accessed 5 October 2012).
Land E (2012b) Impact. Email message to author, 12 October.
Land E (2012c) Unique Animated Documentary – Launch in London. Email message to author, 18 July.
Landesman O and Bendor R (2011) Animated Recollection and Spectatorial Experience in *Waltz with Bashir*. *Animation: An Interdisciplinary Journal*, 6 (3), pp. 353–370.
Landreth C (2005) *Ryan*: Director's commentary track. Burbank, CA: Rhino Home Video.
Lant A (2006) Women's Independent Cinema: The Case of Leeds Animation Workshop. In: Friedman LD (ed.), *Fires Were Started: British Cinema and Thatcherism*. London and New York: Wallflower Press, pp. 159–181.
Leslie E (2003) Absent-Minded Professors: Etch-a-Sketching Academic Forgetting. In: Radstone S and Hodgkin K (eds), *Regimes of Memory*. London and New York: Routledge, pp. 172–185.
Low R (1949) *The History of the British Film: 1906–1914*. London: Allen and Unwin.
Luciano-Adams B (2008) When Docs Get Graphic: Animation Meets Actuality. *International Documentary Association website*. Available from: http://www.documentary.org/content/when-docs-get-graphic-animation-meets-actuality (accessed 24 August 2012).
Manovich L (2002) *The Language of New Media*. Cambridge, MA: MIT Press.
Mansfield N (2010) Loss and Mourning Cinema's 'Language' of Trauma in Waltz with Bashir. *Wide Screen*, 1 (2), pp. 1–14.
Marks LU (2011) Calligraphic Animation: Documenting the Invisible. *Animation: An Interdisciplinary Journal*, 6(3), pp. 307–323.
McCloud S (1994) *Understanding Comics: The Invisible Art*. New York: Harper.
McKie R (1999) Who Put the Pee in the Postosuchus? *The Observer*, London, 10 October. Available from: http://www.guardian.co.uk/uk/1999/oct/10/robin-mckie.theobserver (accessed 22 August 2012).

Menache A (2000) *Understanding Motion Capture for Computer Animation and Video Games*. San Diego: Morgan Kaufman.

Metz AM (2008) A Fantasy Made Real. The Evolution of the Subjunctive Documentary on U.S. Cable Science Channels. *Television & New Media*, 9 (4), pp. 333–348.

Mitchell WJ (1992) *The Reconfigured Eye: Visual Truth in the Post-Photographic Era*. Cambridge, MA: MIT Press.

Moore S (2011) Animating Unique Brain States. *Animation Studies Online Journal*, 6. Available from: http://journal.animationstudies.org/category/volume-6/samantha-moore-animating-unique-brain-states/ (accessed 2 October 2012).

Moran JM (1999) A Bone of Contention: Documenting the Prehistoric Subject. In: Gaines J and Renov M (eds), *Collecting Visible Evidence*. Minneapolis: University of Minnesota Press, pp. 255–273.

Morgan D (2006) Rethinking Bazin: Ontology and Realist Aesthetics. *Critical Inquiry*, 32 (3), pp. 443–481.

Morgen B (2008) Political History Gets Animated in *Chicago 10*. Radio Interview with T Gross. *Fresh Air*, WHYY, 28 February. Available from: http://www.npr.org/templates/story/story.php?storyId=37759288 (accessed 26 October 2012)

Mori M (2012) The Uncanny Valley. *IEEE Spectrum*. Available from: http://spectrum.ieee.org/automaton/robotics/humanoids/the-uncanny-valley (accessed 6 September 2012).

Mosaic Films (n.d.) Animated Minds – Series 2 (Teachers TV/ Wellcome Trust, 2009). Available from: http://mosaicfilms.com/2009/11/animated-minds-series-2.php (accessed 5 October 2012a).

Mosaic Films (n.d.) Animated Minds (Channel 4, 2003). Available from: http://mosaicfilms.com/2007/11/animated-minds-channel-4-2003.php (accessed 1 October 2012b).

Mulvey L (2006) *Death 24x a Second: Stillness and the Moving Image*. London: Reaktion Books.

Mulvey L (2009) Visual Pleasure and Narrative Cinema. In: Braudy L and Cohen M (eds), *Film Theory and Criticism*, 7th ed. New York and Oxford: Oxford University Press, pp. 711–722.

Nichols B (1991) *Representing Reality: Issues and Concepts in Documentary*. Bloomington: Indiana University Press.

Nichols B (1993) "Getting to Know You …": Knowledge, Power, and the Body. In: Renov M (ed.), *Theorizing Documentary*. London and New York: Routledge, pp. 174–191.

Nichols B (1994) *Blurred Boundaries: Questions of Meaning in Contemporary Culture*. Bloomington: Indiana University Press.

Nichols B (2001) *Introduction to Documentary*. Bloomington: Indiana University Press.

Nichols B (2010) *Introduction to Documentary*. 2nd ed. Bloomington: Indiana University Press.

North D (2008) *Performing Illusions: Cinema, Special Effects and the Virtual Actor*. London and New York: Wallflower Press.

O'Pray M (1998) The Animated Film. In: Hill J and Gibson PC (eds), *The Oxford Guide to Film Studies*. Oxford and New York: Oxford University Press, pp. 434–439.

Park E (2004) Strangers on a Train: Wobbly Cartoon Spectacle Lacks Human Element. *The Village Voice*. Available from: http://www.villagevoice.com/2004-11-02/film/strangers-on-a-train-wobbly-cartoon-spectacle-lacks-human-element/ (accessed 9 September 2012).

Patrick E (2004) Representing Reality: Structural/Conceptual Design in Non-Fiction Animation. *Animac Magazine*, 3, pp. 36–47.

Peirce CS (1991) *Peirce on Signs*, ed. J Hoopes. Chapel Hill, NC: University of North Carolina Press.

Pilling J (2012) Introduction. In: *Animating the Unconscious: Desire, Sexuality and Animation*. New York: Columbia University Press, pp. 1–16.

Polonsky D (2008) How Real Can It Get? Animated Documentary – Life, Politics and Audiences. Panel discussion as part of the 2008 UK Jewish Film Festival. ICA: London.

Power P (2008) Character Animation and the Embodied Mind–Brain. *Animation: An Interdisciplinary Journal*, 3 (1), pp. 25–48.

Pummell S (2012) Truth Under Oppression: The Films of Ruth Lingford. In: Pilling J (ed.), *Animating the Unconscious: Desire, Sexuality and Animation*. London and New York: Wallflower Press, pp. 70–76.

Radstone S and Hodgkin K (2003) Introduction. In: Radstone S and Hodgkin K (eds), *Memory Cultures: Memory, Subjectivity and Recognition*. New Brunswick: Transaction, pp. 1–22.

Ravett A (2011) *Everything's for You*: Reflections on Animating a 'Fierce and Inexorable Bond'. *Animation: An Interdisciplinary Journal*, 6 (3), pp. 325–334.

Renov M (2002) Animation: Documentary's Imaginary Signifier. Paper presented at Visible Evidence Conference X, Marseilles, France, December.

Renov M (2004) *The Subject of Documentary*. Minneapolis: University of Minnesota Press.

Rimminen M (2007) Sydämeen kätketty (*Learned by Heart*). Available from: http://www.marjutrimminen.com/ (accessed 7 October 2012).

Roadside Attractions (2007) *Chicago 10* Press Notes. Available from: http://www.participantmedia.com/pm-films/chicago-10/ (accessed 21 August 2012).

Rodowick DN (2007) *The Virtual Life of Film*. Cambridge, MA: Harvard University Press.

Rooney D (2004) The Polar Express. *Variety*. Available from: http://www.variety.com/review/VE1117925345?refcatid=31 (accessed 9 September 2012).

Roscoe J and Hight C (2001) *Faking It: Mock-Documentary and the Subversion of Factuality*. Manchester: Manchester University Press.

Rosen P (2001) *Change Mummified: Cinema, Historicity, Theory*. Minneapolis: University of Minnesota Press.

Rossington M and Whitehead A (eds) (2007) *Theories of Memory: A Reader*. Edinburgh: Edinburgh University Press.

Ruddell C (2012) 'Don't Box Me In': Blurred Lines in *Waking Life* and *A Scanner Darkly*. *Animation: An Interdisciplinary Journal*, 7 (1), pp. 7–23.

Sabiston B (2012) Bob Sabiston in Conversation with Paul Ward. *Animation: An Interdisciplinary Journal*, 7 (1), pp. 73–82.

Satrapi M (2000) *Persepolis*. Paris: L'Association.

Saunders D (2010) *Documentary*. London and New York: Routledge.

Schwartz V (1999) *Spectacular Realities*. Berkeley: University of California Press.

Scott AO (2008) Movie Review: *Chicago 10*. New York Times, 29 February. Available from: http://movies.nytimes.com/2008/02/29/movies/29chic.html (accessed 24 August 2012).
Scott KD (2003) Popularizing Science and Nature Programming: The Role of 'Spectacle' in Contemporary Wildlife Documentary. *Journal of Popular Film and Television*, 31 (1), pp. 29–35.
Scott KD and White AM (2003) Unnatural History? Deconstructing the *Walking with Dinosaurs* Phenomenon. *Media, Culture & Society*, 25 (3), pp. 315–332.
Shale R (1982) *Donald Duck Joins Up: The Walt Disney Studio During World War II*. Ann Arbor: UMI Research Press.
Singer G (2004) Landreth on Ryan. *VFX World Magazine*. Available from: http://www.awn.com/articles/profiles/landreth-iryani (accessed 3 October 2012).
Snyder J (1980) Picturing Vision. *Critical Inquiry*, 6 (3), pp. 499–526.
Snyder J and Allen NW (1975) Photography, Vision, and Representation. *Critical Inquiry*, 2 (1), pp. 143–169.
Sobchack V (2000) Introduction. In: Sobchack V (ed.), *Meta-Morphing: Visual Transformation and the Culture of Quick-Change*. Minneapolis: University of Minnesota Press, pp. xi–xxiii.
Sobchack V (2006) Final Fantasies: Computer Graphic Animation and the [Dis]illusion of Life. In: Buchan S (ed.), *Animated Worlds*. Eastleigh, UK: John Libbey, pp. 171–182.
Sofian S (2004) Documentary Animation: The Evolution of a Hybrid Medium. Talk given at the China International Cartoon and Digital Arts Festival, Changzou, China, 28 September–5 October.
Sofian S (2009) More Questions! Email message to author, 19 March.
Sontag S (1997) *On Photography*. New York: Picador.
Spitzer L (1999) Back Through the Future: Nostalgic Memory and Critical Memory in a Refuge from Nazism. In: Bal M, Crewe JV, and Spitzer L (eds), *Acts of Memory: Cultural Recall in the Present*. Hanover, NH: University Press of New England, pp. 87–104.
Sproxton D (2008) Email message to author, 1 October.
Stewart G (2010) Screen Memory in *Waltz with Bashir*. *Film Quarterly*, 63 (3), pp. 58–62.
Strøm G (2003) The Animated Documentary. *Animation Journal*, 11, pp. 46–63.
Sturken M (1997) *Tangled Memories: The Vietnam War, the Aids Epidemic, and the Politics of Remembering*. Berkeley: University of California Press.
Sutcliffe T (2011) Last Night's TV: Planet Dinosaur/BBC1 Live Rugby World Cup/ITV1. *The Independent*, London, 15 September. Available from: http://www.independent.co.uk/arts-entertainment/tv/reviews/last-nights-tv-planet-dinosaurbbc1br-live-rugby-world-cupitv1-2354849.html (accessed 15 August 2012).
The National Autistic Society (2012) Autism and Asperger Syndrome: An Introduction. Available from: http://www.autism.org.uk/ (accessed 3 October 2012).
The National Autistic Society (2011) Our Online Shop: A Is for Autism. Available from: http://www.autism.org.uk/products/dvd-media-or-software/a-is-for-autism.aspx (accessed 4 October 2012).
Thomas N (2002) Imagination. *Imagination, Mental Imagery, Consciousness, and Cognition: Scientific, Philosophical and Historical Approaches*. Available from: http://www.imagery-imagination.com (accessed 30 September 2012).

Tuan Y-F (1977) *Space and Place: The Perspective of Experience*. Minneapolis: University of Minnesota Press.

Tupicoff D (2009) Questions. Email message to author, 15 February.

Tupicoff D (2003) Radio with Pictures (Thousands of Them). Talk given at the Art of Documentary Conference, Canberra, Australia, 26–30 November.

Tyler SA (1986) Post-modern ethnography: From Document of the Occult to Occult Document. In: Clifford J and Marcus GE (eds), *Writing Culture: The Poetics and Politics of Ethnography*. Berkeley: University of California Press, pp. 122–140.

Walker J (2005) *Trauma Cinema: Documenting Incest and the Holocaust*. Berkeley: University of California Press.

Ward P (2000) Defining 'Animation': The Animated Film and the Emergence of the Film Bill. *Scope*, December. Available from: http://www.scope.nottingham.ac.uk/article.php?issue=dec2000&id=289&section=article (accessed 20 September 2012).

Ward P (2004) Rotoshop in Context: Computer Rotoscoping and Animation Aesthetics. *Animation Journal*, 12, pp. 32–52.

Ward P (2005a) *Documentary: The Margins of Reality*. London: Wallflower.

Ward P (2005b) 'I was dreaming I was awake and then I woke up and found myself asleep': Dreaming, Spectacle and Reality in *Waking Life*. In: *The Spectacle of the Real: From Hollywood to Reality TV and Beyond*. Bristol: Intellect, pp. 161–171.

Ward P (2006a) Animated Interactions: Animation Aesthetics and the World of the 'Interactive' Documentary. In: Buchan S (ed.), *Animated Worlds*. Eastleigh, UK: John Libbey, pp. 113–129.

Ward P (2006b) Some Thoughts on Theory–Practice Relationships in Animation Studies. *Animation: An Interdisciplinary Journal*, 1 (2), pp. 229–245.

Ward P (2008) Animated Realities: The Animated Film, Documentary, Realism. *Reconstruction: Studies in Contemporary Culture*, 8 (2). Available from: http://reconstruction.eserver.org/082/ward.shtml (accessed 24 August 2012).

Waterson R (2007) Trajectories of Memory: Documentary Film and the Transmission of Testimony. *History and Anthropology*, 18 (1), pp. 51–73.

Webb C (2003) Birds of a Different Feather. *The Age*, Melbourne, Australia, 17 November. Available from: http://www.theage.com.au/articles/2003/11/14/1068674377213.html (accessed 9 September 2012).

Weinrich H (2004) *Lethe: The Art and Critique of Forgetting*. Ithaca, NY: Cornell University Press.

Wells P (1997) The Beautiful Village and the True Village: A Consideration of Animation and the Documentary Aesthetic. In: Wells P (ed), *Art and Animation*. London: Academy Editions, pp. 40–45.

Wells P (1998) *Understanding Animation*. London and New York: Routledge.

Whitehead A (2009) *Memory*. London and New York: Routledge.

Winston B (1995) *Claiming the Real: The Griersonian Documentary and Its Legitimations*. London: British Film Institute.

Winston B and Tsang H (2009) The Subject and the Indexicality of the Photograph. *Semiotica*, 173, pp. 453–469.

Wollen P (1998 [1969]) *Signs and Meaning in the Cinema*. 4th ed. London: British Film Institute.

Yadin O (2005) But Is It Documentary? In: Haggith T and Newman J (eds), *Holocaust and the Moving Image: Representations in Film and Television Since 1933*. London: Wallflower Press, pp. 168–172.

Index

A is for Autism (Tim Webb, 1992), 13, 124–6, 135, 136, 138
Aardman Animations, 11, 12, 76–8
absence, 28, 117, 155, 165
absence/excess, 14, 39, 80, 84, 96, 170
 of a body, 15, 84, 88–90, 94–7, 102
 of filmed material, 7, 24, 27, 168
 abstract animation, *see* animation, abstract
Abuelas (Afarin Eghbal, 2011), 4–5
Adventures of Prince Achmed, The (Lotte Reiniger, 1926), 149
Age of Stupid, The (Franny Armstrong, 2009), 10, 11, 34–5
Alien in the Playground, An (*Animated Minds*, 2009), 118–19, 138, 178n3
All Men Are Created Equal (*Blind Justice*, Monique Renault, 1987), 13
American Homes (Bernard Friedman, 2011), 35
analogy, 29–30, 32, 39
Animated Conversations, see *Confessions of a Foyer Girl* and *Down and Out*
animated documentary
 classification of, 18–21
 definition, 4, 27
 functions, 17, 22–6
 history of, 1, 5–6, 12–13
 materiality, 27, 112
 representational strategies, 37–8
 see also ontology of animated documentary
animated interviews, *see* interview, animated
Animated Minds (Andy Glynne, 2003, 2009), 11, 15, 25, 26, 117–21, 126, 135–6, 178n3
animated writing, *see* captions
animation
 abstract, 25, 112–14, 121–4
 as compared to live-action film, 2, 6, 23, 27, 37, 72, 168

definition, 4
epistemological-phenomenological dichotomy, 82, 84, 97–8
expressive capabilities, 15, 34, 87, 96, 113, 117, 124
as representational strategy, *see* evocation; mimetic substitution; non-mimetic substitution
 styles/techniques, 4, 37
 tool for illustration/clarification, 8
 and the unrepresentable, 108, 136–7
 visual appeal, 68–70
animatronics, 45, 46, 50
anonymity, 24, 79–80, 89, 93–4, 113–14
archival images, 41–2, 58, 59, 70, 139, 141, 148–50, 158, 162, 170
Aronowitsch, David, 89, 94, 105
Attenborough, David, 45, 175–6n9
audio recordings, *see* sound
authentication, 42, 44, 49–50, 63–7
autobiography, 132, 142–6, 165
 see also first-person perspective
Azaria, Hank, 60

Backseat Bingo (Liz Blazer, 2003), 24, 92–6, 100, 178n14
Barthes, Roland, 32–3, 100, 134, 140
Battle 360 (The History Channel, 2008), 41–2, 45
Bazin, Andre, 29, 32–3, 42
Becoming Invisible (*Animated Minds*, 2009), 119
Blind Justice (Orly Yadin, 1987), 13
Blue Vinyl (Judith Helfand and Daniel B. Gold, 2002), 10, 174n11
Bowling for Columbine (Michael Moore, 2002), 1, 10
Branagh, Kenneth, 28, 50–4, 65–6, 176n20
Bray, Randolph, 9

captions, 134

189

causality, 29–32, 37
cel animation, 4, 37, 61, 81
Centrefold (Ellie Land, 2012), 136
Chicago 10 (Brett Morgen, 2007), 1, 23–4, 26, 55–61, 68–70, 80, 106, 177n23
Clara Cleans Her Teeth (Walt Disney, 1926), 174n9
claymation, 4, 12, 76
Cockaboody (John and Faith Hubley, 1973), 11
collage style of animation, 148, 152
computer animation, 4, 14, 23–4, 37, 71, 90, 128, 130–2
 see also digital animation
computer generated images (CGI), 9, 43–4, 45, 46, 51, 54–5, 66–7, 83–4
confession, 91–2
Confessions of a Foyer Girl (Aardman, 1978), 12, 77
Conversation with Haris, A (Sheila Sofian, 2001), 112–13, 115–16
Conversations Pieces (Aardman, 1983), 12, 78, 105
Creature Comforts (Aardman, 1989), 12, 61, 76–9
cut-out animation, 93, 149, 179n5

DelGaudio, Sybil, 17–18
digital animation, 4, 9, 14, 34, 41–2, 45–9, 55, 70–1, 115, 170–1
 see also motion capture; rotoscope; Rotoshop
Dimensions (*Animated Minds*, 2003), 126–8
Direct Cinema, 3, 43
Disney, Walt, 8, 9, 80
Down and Out (Aardman, 1978), 12, 77
Drawn People (Harrie Geelen, 1985), 13, 79

Edison, Thomas, 9
Einstein's Theory of Relativity (Fleischer Brothers, 1923), 9
embodiment, 15, 28, 58, 77–8, 88, 97, 102
 embodied/disembodied knowledge, 76, 95–6
 embodied/disembodied voice, 53, 98–9, 101, 103–5
ephemerality, 102, 115, 142–3
Even More Fun Trip, The (Bob Sabiston, 2007), 61–4, 81–2, 87
Everything's for You (Abraham Ravett, 1989), 139–41, 174n11
evidence, 28–30, 36
evocation, 23, 25–6, 107, 109, 137
excess, 72, 103, 146, 155
 absence/excess, 14, 39, 80, 84, 96, 170
 visual excess, 27, 28, 44, 168
Exit Through the Gift Shop (Banksy, 2010), 175n2
expressive animation, 87, 96, 117, 124
Eyeful of Sound, An (Samantha Moore, 2009), 15, 25, 26, 121–3, 136, 138

F.E.D.S., The (Jennifer Deutrom, 2003/4), 177n10
Feeling My Way (Jonathan Hodgson, 1997), 15, 25, 26, 132–5, 138
Fight for the Dardanelles (Percy Smith, 1915), 8
first-person perspective, 132, 138, 142–3, 154
 see also autobiography
Fish on a Hook (*Animated Minds*, 2003), 119–21
flashback, 161–7
Fleischer, Max, 8, 56, 80
Folman, Ari, 11, 155, 161–3, 165–9
Foucault, Michel, 6, 91
Four Methods of Flush Riveting (Disney, 1940), 174n8

Grasshopper (Bob Sabiston, 2003), 61–2, 63, 81–2, 84–5, 87
Green Wave, The (Ali Samadi Ahadi, 2010), 172, 179n1
Grierson, John/Griersonian documentary, 3, 50, 74, 174n8
Gunning, Tom, 30, 33, 69

Haines, Tim, 46, 47
hand-drawn animation, 13, 37, 61, 80, 85, 90, 112, 115, 124–6, 132–5, 142, 148–9

Heads-up Display (HUD), 47, 49–50, 55, 66–7, 175n7
Heilborn, Hanna, 89, 93–4
Hidden (David Aronowitsch and Hanna Heilborn, 2002), 15, 24, 89–92, 93–6, 100, 105
His Mother's Voice (Dennis Tupicoff, 1997), 13, 15, 28, 97, 98–101, 103–5
history, 149, 154, 168
  of animated documentary, 1, 5–6, 12–13
  family history, 147–8, 152–3
  history documentary, 42; *see also* natural history documentary
  (in)accessibility of, 141
  personal history, 139–41, 144–7, 168
  traumatic history, 160, 166
Hodgson, Jonathan, 10, 34–5, 132–5
Hoffman, Abbie, 55–6, 57–8, 60
Holocaust, the, 152, 156–8, 166
Housing Problems (Arthur Elton and Edgar Antsy, 1935), 74
How Spiders Fly (Percy Smith, 1909), 9
Hubley, Emily, 10, 174n11
Hubley, John and Faith, 11–12
Hurt, John, 50, 52–4

iconicity, 31, 38, 42
identity
  hidden, 89, 94–5
  identity formation, 152–4
  identity politics, 88–9, 93–4, 136
  Locke, John, 146
  self-identity, 116–17, 146–7
  see also anonymity; memory
illustration, 1, 8, 9, 12, 20–1, 112–13, 118–19
imagination, 25, 50, 107, 110–11, 121
indexicality
  of animation, 37–9
  aural indexicality, 27–8, 59–60, 64–5, 110
  authentication, 44
  double index, 87
  faked indexicality, 42, 48–9, 55
  indexical affect, 42
  indexical sign, 29–31, 32–3, 87

Peircian semiotics, 29–31, 36
  and photography, 28–33
  relationship between image and reality, 3, 29–31, 36, 72, 82, 140–1
  see also resemblance
interactive documentary, 18–19, 172
interjections, animated, 10–11
internal, 26, 106–7, 129, 135
interviews
  animated, 12–13, 15, 24–5, 61–5, 68, 84–9, 128–9, 143–4
  anonymity, 78–9, 89–90, 94
  the body/embodied knowledge, 76, 80–4, 88, 95–7
  as confession, 91–2
  credibility, 75–6
  and "iconic authentication," 27
  and identity, 90–3
  interactive documentary, 172
  legal origins, 75
  paratextual, 44–5
  talking-head, 74–5
  and visual metaphor, 112–14, 119–21
  the voice, 77–80, 97–101, 104–5
Irinka and Sandrinka (Sandrine Stoïanov, 2007), 16, 146, 152–5, 168
It's Like That (Southern Ladies Animation Group, 2003), 15, 24, 26, 90–6, 100

Jellyfish Pictures, 66–7
Johansson, Mats, 89
Jurassic Park (Steven Spielberg, 1993), 46, 47, 175n8

Khodorkovsky (Cyril Tuschi, 2011), 171–2

Landreth, Chris, 128–32
Larkin, Ryan, 128–32
Learned by Heart (Marjut Rimminen and Päivi Takala, 2007), 15–16, 146–7, 148–50, 154–5
Light Bulb Thing, The (*Animated Minds*, 2003), 38, 119–20
line-drawn animation, 10, 35, 139

Lingford, Ruth, 123, 157–8
Lip Synch (Aardman, 1989), see *Creature Comforts*
lip-synching, 57, 61, 64
Little Deaths (Ruth Lingford, 2010), 15, 121, 123–4
live-action
 animation in live-action documentary, 10–11
 as contrasted with animation, 2, 6, 23, 27, 37, 72, 168
 limitations of, 106–7, 115
Lord, Peter, 12
Lye, Len, 37

Making of Walking with Dinosaurs (BBC, 1999), 65–7, 70
maps, animated, 8–9
McCay, Winsor, 6–8, 174n6
McLaren, Norman, 4, 37, 130
Mechanics of the Human Brain, The (Vsevolod Pudovkin, 1926), 9
memory, 133
 collective, 34, 142, 146–52, 154
 contestational potential, 145
 cultural memory, 154
 false, 161
 and identity/self-inscription, 144, 146, 154
 memory studies, 144, 145
 personal, 15–16, 26, 34, 139–45
 post-memory, 142, 146, 150–4, 166, 168, 179n2, 179n6
 relationship with photographic media, 139–40
 repressed/absent, 155, 157, 165, 166–7
mental health issues, 15, 106–7, 117–18, 135–6
metamorphosis, 15, 39, 115–17, 160
metaphor, 15, 39–40, 96, 158–9, 161
 and emotional resonance, 92
 linguistic metaphor, 113
 and metamorphosis, 115–17
 as mode of address, 90, 114
 visual metaphor, 111–12, 118, 119–21, 123, 137
microcinematography, 9
mimesis, 72, 109

mimetic substitution, 23–4, 26, 38, 43–4, 70, 72
mock-documentary, 43, 65
Moonbird (John and Faith Hubley, 1959), 11
motion capture, 23, 38, 56, 71, 80, 177n8
Murders Most Foul (*Blind Justice*, Gillian Lacey, 1987), 13

Naked (Mischa Kamp, 2006), 79
National Film Board of Canada, 8, 130, 172
natural history documentary, 9, 11, 45–6, 47–9, 55
Next Day, The (National Film Board of Canada, 2011), 172
Nichols, Bill, 3, 76, 95–6, 99
 modes of documentary, 18–19, 109, 175n1
No Lies (Mitchell Block, 1973), 75
non-mimetic substitution, 24, 26, 76–7, 108–9, 111, 120, 137
nostalgia, 149–50

observational documentary, 48, 64, 171
 see also Direct Cinema
Obsessively Compulsive (*Animated Minds*, 2003), 126, 128
ontology
 of animated documentary, 27, 41–2, 44, 63, 71
 of animation, 34–8, 41, 44
 of film and photography, 29–37, 42

painting-on-glass animation, 37, 115
Pallotta, Tommy, 84
paratext, 14, 44–5, 70, 176n20
 paratextual authentication, 65–7, 72
Park, Nick, 77
Paterson, Nigel, 67
Patrick, Eric, 18, 19, 20–1
Peircian semiotics, *see* indexicality
performative documentary, 18–19, 109
Photograph of Jesus (Laurie Hill, 2008), 170

photography
  link between photography and the past, 33–4, 36, 41–2, 139–42, 152–3, 168–9
  and reality, 28–33, 59, 170
  see also captions; time-lapse photography
photorealism, see realism
pixilation, 5, 126, 142, 178n4
Places Other People Have Lived (Laura Yilmaz, 2011), 141–2
Planet Dinosaur (BBC, 2011), 23, 46–50, 52–5, 65–8, 70–1, 175n6
Polar Express, The (Robert Zemeckis, 2004), 38, 84
political mimesis, 88
Polonsky, David, 162
postmodernism
  crisis of, 21–2
  postmodern mode, 20
Prayers for Peace (Dustin Grella, 2009), 101–3
Project Incognito (Bob Sabiston, 1997), 61, 62, 80–1, 84, 85
puppet animation, 4, 12, 24, 83, 90

Ravett, Abraham, 139–41
realism, 3, 37, 42–5, 62–3, 72–3
  photorealism, 37–8, 57–8, 129, 177n5
  psychorealism, 129–30, 132
reality television, 49, 171
re-enactment, 3, 23, 30, 57–60, 75, 104
remembering, 147, 149, 154–5, 168–9
  disremembering, 161
  see also memory
repetition, 122, 126, 165–6
resemblance, 31–4, 36, 42
Richter, Max, 162
Rimminen, Marjut, 146–7, 148–9, 150, 169
Roadhead (Bob Sabiston, 1998), 61, 62, 63, 81, 85–6
rotoscope, 56, 80–1, 84
  and body politics, 82
  epistemological-phenomenological dichotomy, 97–8
  rotoscoping, 55–6, 80, 97, 142
  and uncanniness, 83, 97–8, 103

Rotoshop, 56, 61, 63, 64, 71, 80–1, 84–7, 176n16, 177n4
Ryan (Chris Landreth, 2004), 128–32

Sabiston, Bob, 55–6, 61–5, 68, 71, 80–1, 84–5
Scanner Darkly, A (Richard Linklater, 2006), 108, 176n16
self-inscription, see autobiography
semiotics, see indexicality
She's a Boy I Knew (Gwen Haworth, 2007), 10
Shoah (Claude Lanzmann, 1985), 76
Silence (Sylvie Bringas and Orly Yadin, 1998), 16, 26, 34, 146, 155–60, 168
Sinking of the Lusitania, The (Winsor McCay, 1918), 6–8, 10, 23, 174n6
Smith, Percy, 8, 9
Snack and Drink (Bob Sabiston, 1999), 13, 61, 62, 64, 81, 84–7, 100
Snow White (Disney, 1937), 80
Some Protection (*Blind Justice*, Marjut Rimminen, 1987), 13
Someone Must Be Trusted (*Blind Justice*, Christine Roche, 1987), 13
sound/soundtrack
  audio recordings, 27–8, 89–90, 102–3
  importance in animated documentary, 2, 14–15, 27–8, 79, 105
  indexicality, 64, 109–10
  non-linguistic vocal expression, 78
  oral/aural link with reality, 27, 60, 77–8, 110
  reconstructed, 59–60
  visualized sound, 103–4, 121–3
  see also interview, voice, voiceover
Southern Ladies Animation Group (SLAG), 90
spectacle, 68–72
Sproxton, David, 12, 77, 83
Stoïanov, Sandrine, 147, 151–4
stop-motion animation, 9, 12, 38, 77, 80, 90, 126, 128, 142, 177n1
Stranger Comes to Town (Jacqueline Goss, 2007), 79

subjectivity/subjective experience, 2, 25, 26, 106–11, 119–21, 124, 128–9, 132, 135–8
  see also autobiography; first-person perspective
substitution, *see* mimetic substitution; non-mimetic substitution
Survivors (Sheila Sofian, 1997), 13, 112–17

television documentary, 45, 47–8
testimony, 74–6, 90–2, 97, 143
Thin Blue Line, The (Errol Morris, 1985), 75
This is Spinal Tap (Rob Reiner, 1984), 75
time-lapse photography, 9
Tommy Tucker's Tooth (Walt Disney, 1922), 174n9
trauma/traumatic experience, 16, 150–1, 155–61, 165–8
  disremembering, 161, 163
Trouble with Love and Sex, The (Jonathan Hodgson, 2012), 79
Troubled Minds, see *Animated Minds*
Tupicoff, Dennis, 99, 100, 104, 105
Tying Your Own Shoes (Shira Avni, 2009), 178n8

uncanny, 83–4, 87
  Freud, 83
United Productions of America (UPA), 11

visibility, 87–8, 91–2, 94, 160
visual metaphor, *see* metaphor
vocalic bodies, 15, 78, 80, 86, 96, 100, 105
voice, human
  acousmêtre/acousmatic, 101–3
  animated interpretations, 77–9
  as bearer of truth, 28
  disembodied, 53, 98–9, 101, 103–5
  "grain," 99–100
  offscreen commentary, 101
  and the self, 103
  vocal re-enactments, 60–1
  voicelessness, 157
  see also vocalic bodies
voice-of-God/voiceover narration, 14, 44, 50–4, 99, 101

Waking Life (Richard Linklater, 2001), 68, 108, 176n16
Walking (Ryan Larkin, 1969), 130
*Walking with...*franchise, 45
Walking with Dinosaurs (BBC, 1999), 11, 23–4, 26, 34, 45–55, 65–8, 70–1, 72, 176n13
Wallace and Gromit in The Curse of the Were-Rabbit (Steve Box and Nick Park, 2005), 38
Walt Disney Studios, *see* Disney, Walt
Waltz with Bashir (Ari Folman, 2008), 1, 11, 15, 26, 34, 146, 155, 161–8, 172, 179n8
Ward, Paul, 18–19
Webb, Tim, 158
Wellcome Trust, the, 117, 135, 136
Wells, Paul, 17, 19–22, 107, 115–16
Why We Fight (Frank Capra, 1942–5), 1, 8–9, 11
Windy Day (John and Faith Hubley, 1967), 11
Wollen, Peter, 29, 31
Wonders of the Solar System (BBC, 2010), 9
Workshop Movement, 87

Xerography, 132–3

Yilmaz, Laura, 141–2

Druck: KN Digital Printforce GmbH · Schockenriedstraße 37 · 70565 Stuttgart